radical position than most contemporary theologians. His purpose is to make a contribution toward the revitalization and unification of the Church: "The mission of the Church is to achieve community, a oneness through the Christ-event, so that every man may affirm with freedom his authentic *being* with God and with his fellow man."

Charles B. Ketcham is the author of *The Search for Meaningful Existence, Faith and Freedom,* and *Federico Fellini: The Search for a New Mythology.* He is the Bishop James M. Thoburn Professor of Religion at Allegheny College.

A Theology of Encounter

A Theology of Encounter

The Ontological Ground for a New Christology

Charles B. Ketcham

The Pennsylvania State University Press
University Park and London

Library of Congress Cataloging in Publication Data
Ketcham, Charles B
  A theology of encounter.
  Includes bibliographical references and index.
  1. Jesus Christ—Person and offices. I. Title.
BT202.K38   232   77-21905
ISBN 0-271-00520-3

To my Mother and Father

whose faith was ever responsive and
whose exploration never ceased

Contents

Preface

We have witnessed nearly a century of intense theological excitement. Many scholars have predicted, however, that as death silences the early twentieth-century giants—theologians such as Barth, Brunner, Donald Baillie, Bonhoeffer, Bultmann, the Niebuhrs, Tillich—the creative period will be over, and the theological task remaining will be one of evaluation, consolidation, reassessment, perhaps even retrenchment. Indeed, there has been some response to theological future shock: the emergence of the conservative, Neo-Calvinist movement in Protestantism; and in Roman Catholicism, following the dramatic, new developments of Vatican II, the reassertion of a conservative traditionalism by Pope Paul.

But the ferment has not ended. For many of us it proceeds unabated. The recent work in New Testament criticism and biblical theology, process theology, hope theology, liberation theology, and the new hermeneutic attest to the continuing creativity and productivity of our times.

One of these areas of continuing excitement is that of the "new" ontology which is indebted to contributions of the phenomenologist Edmund Husserl, the existential ontologist Martin Heidegger, and the existential theist Martin Buber. Karl Rahner, Rudolf Bultmann, and John Macquarrie all stand in this tradition. Yet, despite the monumental contributions of these men, there have been few consistent and thorough attempts to employ the methodologies of existentialism and phenomenology to the perennial problems of Christian theological claims. To that end this book is an attempt to establish a new groundwork for Christology within this new ontological context. It begins the theological quest with an analysis of human experience, of self-awareness understood in the corporate terms of Martin Buber's *I-Thou*. Therefore, it is necessary to give a new description of what it means *to be* and, consequently, to give new definitions for "time," "history," "thought," "reason," and "revelation." Only then can one speak of the contours of a new Christology, the person and place of the Christ in man's faithful response to God.

It is my hope that such a study, by avoiding the difficulties of classical Greek metaphysics (which have precluded any real contribution by natural theology), will provide a new basis for those who seek to understand better the Lordship of Jesus, the Christ.

1

The Radical Context

Christian theology is in disarray. The great systematic theologies of Thomism, Calvinism, and Anglicanism, which once demanded reverential obedience and tolerated loyal reform, are now being challenged by radical, innovative ecumenical thought. In most urban areas dominated by Western culture, it is possible to find many Christians who no longer recognize such traditional, historical affirmations as binding and final, but rather accept, as a basis of convenience more than anything else, such loose theological descriptive categories as "liberals," "fundamentalists," "conservatives," "neo-orthodox," "existentialists," "neo-liberals," and "neo-traditionalists." As a matter of fact, these labels are so loose and often so misleading, that Christians seldom apply such to themselves, only to others. Of course, not all of these movements are radically new or innovative—obviously those which employ the prefix *neo-* are not—yet the fact that they must share the Christian claim, even compete for allegiance, indicates a tacit if not explicit recognition of the dramatic changes which are taking place. For some, such changes are very threatening to their sense of total religious commitment. To claim absolute Truth for oneself (as many religions have traditionally done in practice, liturgy, and doctrine) and yet seriously to admit the possibility of another's Truth (as many religions are now doing) is simply, in the eyes of many Christians, to give way to chaos. For most theologians, the result of such claims and counterclaims is a climate of theological restlessness and a search as diverse, exciting, and occasionally acrimonious as any time since the struggles within the Church during the sixteenth century, perhaps since the disputes which led to the great ecumenical councils of the fourth and fifth centuries.

This current theological agitation is not new, a happening of the sixties and seventies. New theology, like many of its "new" counterparts in the humanities, e.g., art, music, literature, and philosophy, has its beginnings in the second half of the nineteenth century. The nineteenth century seems now to be the end of one era and the beginning of another. Although it is not within the scope or the intent of this book to provide an exhaustive, scholarly study of this period of radical transition, the comprehensive nature of the transition should be acknowledged to provide a context for the theological development.[1] The changes taking place in the thinking and expression of the nineteenth and early twentieth centuries are not matters of styles or vogues or even epistemologies. These changes have to do with our understanding of the very nature of reality—its form, content, and self-disclosure—in short, with metaphysics. Consequently, no aspect or expression of life is left unaffected.

In the developing expression of Christian thought, such changes are most clearly evident in relation to the central focus of the Church on the person and work of Jesus the Christ. Throughout its history, the Church has consistently claimed that God was in Christ reconciling the world to Himself. Because this claim involves both transcendent and human expression, any metaphysical shift of the magnitude implied previously will affect both the understanding and theological description of that event. It is the purpose of this book, in terms of what has been labeled the "new ontology," to provide an alternative to the traditional doctrine of the Incarnation, an alternative which will do justice to the witness of Scripture, to the history of faith, and to the insights of a phenomenological ontology.[2]

The new ontology, as an expression of this contemporary shift, implies more than a juggling of terms or a mere change in traditional emphasis. It signals, according to the Protestant theologian Paul Tillich, even more than the end of an "age," such as Rationalism or Romanticism.[3] These ages do represent distinguishable movements of thought, but they are variations on one theme—that there is such a fixed thing or state or condition, in some way perceptible or knowable by man, which can be called *The* Truth or *The* Reality. The variations merely concern the nature of our appropriation or comprehension of such Truth. Alfred North Whitehead observed this by suggesting that all Western philosophers, from Aristotle to the twentieth century, have offered us only footnotes to Plato's claims about the basic metaphysical structure of appearance and reality—that temporal, physical life is only apparent Reality, only transient life in-formed by the Reality of eternal, unchanging Forms. However, the end of the era marked by the end of the nineteenth century means that the basic presupposition of these variations and footnotes is being called into question. The traditional, well-ordered universe with its absolute laws, absolute values, and its absolute God or gods no longer provides an adequate ground for man's existential understanding of himself or his world. There are gaps, inconsistencies, ambiguities, paradoxes, anxieties—none of which can be satisfactorily reconciled to such an ordered, complete, and idealistic scheme of things. Likewise, there are limitations on and within man himself which would seem to preclude possible recognition of any such absolute Truth even should it "exist" or be. The "absolute" claim cannot admit any limitations other than the nature of its own self-expression.

Any total picture of the radical changes taking place would necessitate a far more intricate and complex development than such a short account indicates. However, our immediate concern in this study is what has happened and is happening to theology, specifically in the development of an acceptable Christology. The sketch which I have provided simply establishes the background against which the radical theological debate may be more clearly seen. The development of theological thought is just as dramatic as it is in all other human expressions of our times; that is, it is not just a reform, it genuinely is a radical break, a revolt. It is not, for example, the kind of historical debate we ordinarily associate with traditional Christian thought: What are the limits of Jesus' human particularity? Does creation or redemption take doctrinal priority? Is reason superior to faith or faith to reason? Is our salvation achieved by God's legal, gracious, or victorious act? What is the Trinity really like? The list is almost endless, as anyone versed in Christian theology knows. But these are not the questions posed by the more revolutionary thinking of what has come to be known as "radical theology." Or, if some of the previous questions do seem to be posed, they are done so within such a different context that their meaning is fundamentally altered.

Background for radical theology must include more than the nineteenth century. Although a scholar invites debate the minute he declares a particular point of initiation, most will agree that David Hume, the eighteenth-century Scottish philosopher, has had a profound effect on the current theological debate. Hume, suspicious of any thinking (save logic) which could not be empirically verified, believed that any *necessary* connection between cause and effect simply could not be known. Thus the stage was set for the dismissal of any proof of the existence of God, proofs which St. Thomas and Aristotelian logic made so appealing—God as First Cause, Prime Mover, Cosmic Designer, etc. Only poetry, not logic, could permit one to look at a newborn infant and say, "There must be a God." Hume's argument encouraged the German philosopher Immanuel Kant to look again at reason in an effort to save causality. Kant's two major *Critiques* on reason, however, suggest that man's reason functions in two distinct ways. Pure reason gives him true knowledge, but such knowledge is limited to intuition and the function of the structure or "categories" of the mind, e.g., time and space, mathematical relations, causality, logic. Consequently, we can never escape the limitations of the human mind to which the world of objects must adapt; we can never "know" something "in itself" but only in terms of the space-time-causal operations of our own minds. Neither can an individual "know" another person or (least of all) God "in Himself." What we call knowledge of others is phenomenality, i.e., our own awareness of the other. What we call knowledge of God is revelation, i.e., the self-disclosure of God in the moral imperative, our own awareness of duty which is in the scope of Kant's Second Critique.

Kant's second function of reason was "practical." Practical reason is the realm of morals, values, and faith. Because we live within the categorical imperative of duty—the world of moral obligations—morals, values, and faith are understood to be states which guide us to action but never things which we can "know." Although Kant had hoped to provide a new dignity for faith by delimiting reason, he very neatly divided the world into two mutually excluding spheres, something which the Christian tradition—particularly in light of the doctrine of creation—found it hard to accept. God, for the Kantians, soon became the guarantor of the moral law and the kingdom of ends. This virtually eliminated the more traditional understanding of the community of the Kingdom of God, personal encounter, and the communion of prayer.

Most Roman Catholic philosophers and many traditionalists among Protestant ones simply dismissed Kant as wrong. For them, the priority, whether metaphysical or epistemological, was with God. Such theological reaction gained support at the turn of the nineteenth century from the writings of G.W.F. Hegel. Hegel, too, thought Immanuel Kant was mistaken in so dividing the world and maintained that all of reality expresses itself as an absolute all-encompassing scheme which he termed the "Absolute Idea." This Absolute includes (and in its unity transcends) the whole of "logic" which describes and regulates the internal relationships of that unity. Consequently, Hegel could maintain that historical processes, such as the development of the Christian Church itself, can be understood as expressions of logical processes. For Hegel, Kant's pure reason and practical reason are simply distinctions within a greater rationality. Thus identity or knowledge of any given thing or event is theoretically possible because of the self-consistency of the Absolute. In accordance with Hegel's logic, all things are related dialectically, so that logically any one entity can be seen as related to another. It is, for example, this relationship that the poet Tennyson reminds us of with his flower in the crannied wall, which potentially can tell us "what God and man is." Hegel had produced a magnificent all-embracing system which claims to account for the continuously developing whole of Reality. The ideal is the real and the real is the ideal. With Hegel, metaphysical idealism is again the ground for system and knowledge, Reality's self-expression.

Hegel's nineteenth-century critics, men such as Schelling, Kierkegaard, Nietzsche, Marx, and Feuerbach, were quick to point out that such a "closed" scheme (which we might call an infrastructure), even if it includes movement, eliminates any genuine uniqueness, novelty, or creativity. In fact, the question arose whether life, i.e., existence, could ever be accounted for solely in terms of system. Certainly Kierkegaard and Nietzsche were vociferous in their denials of Hegel's claims. Writes Kierkegaard at his scathing best:

> I shall be as willing as the next man to fall down in worship before the System if only I can manage to set eyes on it. Hitherto I have had no success; and though I have young legs, I am almost weary from running back and forth between Herod and Pilate. Once or twice I have been on the verge of bending the knee. But at the last moment, when I already had my handkerchief spread on the ground, to avoid soiling my trousers, and I made a trusting appeal to one of the initiated who stood by: "Tell me now sincerely, is it entirely finished; for if so I will kneel down before it, even at the risk of ruining a pair of trousers . . ."—I always received the same answer: "No, it is not yet quite finished." And so there was another postponement—of the System and of my homage.[4]

At this point, historically, it would appear that Christian theology takes one of three major directions. There are those who, via St. Thomas or ecclesiastical tradition, remain with or return to the orthodox affirmation. A second group, influenced by the philosophical writings of Hume and Kant or Hegel, endeavors to reinterpret Christian theology in the light of these new philosophical insights. The third group represents two minor strains of theological rebels who are related more by the nature of their rejection of classical tradition than anything else. These rebels are inspired either by the writings of the Danish theologian Søren Kierkegaard or by the philosophical speculation of Karl Marx. It is out of the first of these two rebellious movements that this book comes, but before setting forth its particular thesis, a closer look at the other two groups would be instructive.

The first group, those who remain close to orthodox tradition, is comprised of church theologians who, as Neo-Thomists or Anglicans or catechetical Lutherans and Calvinists, believe that any major change in the Christian proclamation or articles of faith is heresy. They believe that Christian theology, rooted as it is in historical revelation, has little in substance to learn from new philosophical trends or cultural exchange. Jerusalem, as Tertullian reminded Christians centuries ago, has little to do with Athens. Methodology and language may change, but the Truth to which these witness does not. Although members of this group may argue among themselves about the efficacy or possibility of natural theology, all recognize the priority of the revelation of God, particularly in Jesus Christ, and most begin the theological task within the trinitarian *Word* of the Creed of Nicaea, ratified at Chalcedon in A.D. 451:

> And (we believe) in one Lord Jesus Christ, the Son of God, begotten from the Father, only-begotten, that is, of the essence of the Father, God from God, Light from Light, very God from very God, begotten not made (i.e. created), of one substance (*homoousios*) with the Father, ... and in The Holy Spirit ... that proceedeth from the Father.[5]

The most recent and notable of these traditionalists is the twentieth-century "neo-orthodox" scholar Karl Barth. Although he has been profoundly influenced by members of the two other schools previously discussed, his major premise is simply that "Jesus Christ is Lord." That is, all Christian truth and insight starts from the Christ-event, and apart from God's final and complete revelation in this event, nothing can be known about God or redemption. Man alone can have no knowledge of his salvation. There is, for Barth, an absolute qualitative distinction between God and man, a distinction which man cannot bridge. God is "Wholly Other." Consequently, there can be no natural theology for Barth; there can be no valid argument by means of unaided reason to the existence of God. There can be only the gracious acceptance of the gift of God's revelation of Himself in Jesus Christ. Barth believes that the mistake of many important nineteenth-century theologians, e.g., Schleiermacher, Ritschl, Hermann, and Troeltsch, is that of substituting the word of man for the Word of God, reason for revelation, argumentation for truth.

For Karl Barth, the paradox (or contradiction) of the Infinite God expressing Himself in the humanity of Jesus is not justified or rationally explained; it is simply accepted on the authority of the witnessing event (the Christ-event) itself.

> We cannot make them [God's absoluteness, exaltation, inviolableness, transcendence, divinity, "Wholly-Otherness"] the standard by which to measure what God can or cannot do, or the basis of the judgment that in doing this He brings Himself into self-contradiction. By doing this God proves to us that He can do it, that to do it is within His nature. And He shows Himself to be more great and rich and sovereign than we had ever imagined. And our ideas of His nature must be guided by this, and not vice-versa.[6]

To Barth, who remains loyal to Reformation thinking, final authority is with revelation and not with tradition, although tradition is an important witness to that authority. Christianity, he believes, does not need to justify itself to the world; the world needs to respond, rather, through

Christianity to God—to the declaration that the world has already been saved by the gracious act of God in Christ. To proclaim this is to be true to the insights of the Reformation and the early Church and to be faithful to the Christ who continues to reveal Himself to us.

That Barth's *Church Dogmatics* is a brilliant theological study is not the question. Its excellence is recognized, but its relevance to contemporary life and times is now being questioned. Barth's claims are the claims of reason grounded in faith and revelation as traditionally understood. Yet such an understanding is rooted in a Neo-Kantian idealism even though the terminology is Christian. There is an absolute Reality (the triune God) who has chosen to reveal Himself to us in the temporal, physical world. We are able to respond to this Eternal Reality through the gift of faith, though there is no way to verify objectively or rationally the truth of our responsiveness. The validity of faith, like that of Scripture, is self-authenticating; God is his own justification. However, for many contemporary theologians such claims in terms of the nature and exclusiveness of faith place an intolerable burden on the phenomenon of revelation. What Barth appears to do is to translate the intimate, personal, existential sense of God's presence, the Divine *Thou*, into the faithful response "Jesus Christ is Lord." Then, on the authority of this response, he reasserts it as a metaphysical claim. Barth can then exploit the descriptive claims of divinity (God's omnipotence, omniscience, omnipresence) as well as the descriptive claims of humanity (man's dependence, limitations, finitude) without fear of self-contradiction. The nature of Jesus Christ and, consequently, the nature of the Trinity itself are both analytically granted in the revelational event.

There is some reason to suspect, therefore, that the *analogia fidei* which Barth wishes to claim for his christological speculations covertly rests upon the more traditional *analogia entis*. The analogy of faith is informative because the revelational Word is, despite Barth's protestation, the universal Ground of Being. Further evidence of this may be seen in the *Dogmatics;* the classical idealist paradoxes remain: time and eternity, finite and infinite, relative and absolute, appearance and reality, man and God. If the presuppositions and the givens of Barth's thinking can be accepted, the resulting theological scheme has much to offer mankind: an unqualified forgiveness of sins, an accomplished salvation, a promise of eternal life, and a joy in faith. However, it is just such an acceptance of presuppositions and givens that the other two major groups are not willing to grant Barth.

The second major theological group of the nineteenth century was comprised of those who took seriously the critiques of the philosophers mentioned earlier. The resulting theological innovations led to the loose labeling of these men as the "liberals" of nineteenth-century theology.

This group includes, among others, Friedrich Schleiermacher, Albrecht Ritschl, Wilhelm Hermann, A. E. Biedermann, Ludwig Feuerbach, and Ernst Troeltsch. These men took seriously the Kantian injunction about our limited knowledge of God, about metaphysical speculation. Finite minds are limited to their human categories of thought. Such strictures obviously had their effects on these theologians' understanding of the Christ-event, as we shall presently note. Nevertheless, these "liberal" theologies do not escape from the idealist reliance upon the "given" unity or totality of Reality. We shall look at four of these men who represent the major development of this movement.

Schleiermacher, for one, asserts with Kant that we can have no knowledge of God, but he does so for somewhat different reasons which reflect his fundamental dependence upon a Platonic type of idealism. For Schleiermacher, our knowledge can be only the result of thinking which is responsive to sense data, i.e., to being. But there are no sense data for God. Even if we should equate God with "The Universe" or the "World-All" in a Spinozistic way, as Schleiermacher does in the *Addresses on Religion,* both the totality per se of that universe and its infinity of sensible data escape us in our finitude; we have no possible way of an adequate interpretation of the divine from our fragmented experience. Put in another way, Schleiermacher asserts that God cannot be known because He is not an *object* for knowledge; instead, God is the ground, the underlying unity, the *terminus a quo* which makes knowledge possible. Nor does Schleiermacher believe we can assume the existence of God because of what Kant called the categorical imperative of duty experience as "oughtness." Morality is the nature of my free and mature response to the world and the community of men. For Schleiermacher, volition, like knowledge, is grounded in God and is not an entree to knowledge of his Being.

Awareness of God, for Schleiermacher, is much more direct, almost deserving the descriptive term *existential.* Although his claims are ambiguous, he believes that man's awareness of God is a *feeling,* a "feeling of absolute dependence," a feeling, in fact, which each man acknowledges as pertinent to his own life. At times in *Addresses* this feeling seems to be no more than a private, immediate, emotional experience; in *The Christian Faith,* however, Schleiermacher contends that *feeling* means self-consciousness, an intuitive awareness of self in the presence of the Being of God, a sense of being "placed" in the world, of receiving one's existence from a "Whence." According to Schleiermacher's analysis, "the self encounters itself at its deepest level as limited, as finite and as posited. This 'Whence' that structures the immediate self-consciousness is not the product of any philosophical or theological speculation; rather as it issues in the feeling of absolute dependence, it constitutes the most original expression in self-consciousness of the 'immediate existence-relationship' in which self-hood or the person has its being. The word, God, Schleiermacher adds, has no other original meaning than this."[7] Consequently, an encounter with God is not a real confrontation with Him in the sense of mutual responsiveness, for there can be no personal response to me from a primordial "Whence." My awareness of God is my awareness of the universal causal reality which we call God, or the "Divine Will," or the "Divine Good-Pleasure." For Schleiermacher, therefore, despite his interest in individuality and self-hood, there can be no genuinely new, unique, or supernatural intervention by God in His creation. Everything, including the Christ-event, is *there*, immanent, from the beginning.

For Schleiermacher the Divine Will which created the world is the same Will which appointed Jesus as the inaugurator of the Kingdom of God, one and the same with no differentiation. Thus Schleiermacher can say "that Christ even as a human person was ever coming to be simultaneously with the world itself. He [Jesus] is the one in whom the God-consciousness enters the race as regnant and in whom the consciousness of kind becomes as broad as the race itself, enabling him to communicate to all the dwelling of God with man."[8]

In the development of a Christology, Schleiermacher rejects the "Two-Nature" doctrine of Chalcedon as untenable and asserts that Jesus can have only one nature. "Son of God" and "Son of man" do not describe two natures but rather two relation-contexts of one man. What is different about Jesus is the potent indwelling of God, which marks him as a new creation. He objectively exhibits what human nature ideally is; he is the second (i.e., last) Adam. "Jesus of Nazareth is the archetypal man. His ideality (*Urbildlichkeit*) expresses the special presence of the creative power of God in him. The creative power of God, however, does not merely manifest itself in Christ; it becomes productive in him and through him, ramifying outward from him through his communicating and imparting himself to others, in alliance with the Spirit."[9]

The problems of such a Christology are immediately evident. If Schleiermacher wishes to make the claim of uniqueness for Jesus, maintaining that Jesus does not stand on any continuum with the rest of humanity, then he must justify his claim that Jesus is the true exemplar of perfected human nature. To do this, Schleiermacher must resort to asserting that Jesus' ideality, his *Urbildlichkeit*, is the normative eidos, or form, of Platonic philosophy. Establishing this claim endangers Schleiermacher's previous acknowledgment of limited human knowledge on the one hand and risks losing Jesus' common identity with man and the historical reality of the event on the other. We can sympathize with Schleiermacher's christological claims but must reject his theological justification.

In Albrecht Ritschl's theology, there is another early attempt to save Christianity, first, from the sterility of Platonic metaphysics which dominates much of theological tradition and, second, from the subjectivism of mysticism—the specific trap into which he believed Schleiermacher had fallen. Ritschl is sensitive to Kant's criticism of metaphysical speculation and inference and wishes to avoid crediting man's knowledge with more information or awareness than it can rightfully have. Since we cannot have intimate information about the transcendent or the miraculous, Ritschl believes that talk of such doctrines and beliefs as the "Immaculate Conception," the "Two Natures of the Christ," the "Virgin Birth," the "Trinity," and the "Ascension" is meaningless. To talk in any real way about the person of the Christ is to talk about his work, about what is witnessed to in Scripture (particularly in the synoptic Gospels) and is historically preserved by the Church. For Ritschl, the revelation of God is *historically* evident in the Christ-event, which is the theological way of affirming a Kantian inspired principle that we can know God only through His effects upon us, His worth for us. It is our ethical assessment of Jesus' work which leads us to a religious evaluation. Ritschl thus believes that he has established in terms of history an objective verification of God. In the Kingdom of God on earth, which Jesus came to establish, the presence of God is made evident to the world. Philosophically speaking, the world of appearance has become the world of reality. Ritschl's work has awakened a lively theological interest in history and its role in Christian thought and practice. The work of the contemporary German scholar Wolfhart Pannenberg is evidence of this concentration and reliance on history.[10]

However, the escape from idealist metaphysics is only apparent itself, not real. The revelation of God in Christ, its verification and original affirmation, immediately suggests a suprahistorical stance. In fact, the assumption of the continuity and judgment of history is, in itself, a transcendent appeal; so, too, is history's claim to *be* revelation. Perhaps it is not too gratuitous to say that Ritschl's motivation to make Christianity historically verifiable is more praiseworthy than his philosophical assumptions.

The third theologian in this development of "liberal" tradition is Ernst Troeltsch. Troeltsch was a student of Ritschl and brings to his work an appreciation of Kant, Hegel, and Schleiermacher among others. Though Troeltsch is able to reject the metaphysics of Scholasticism, he cannot escape an indebtedness to metaphysical idealism, particularly as it is formulated by Hegel. Troeltsch believed that the intellectual principles which are evident in the sciences, humanities, and social sciences are one and the same with those of Christian thought. The basic principle is "the real is the rational, the universe a significant, because reason-pervaded, system of things."[11] Thus Christianity is an expression of dialectic in which the Divine Spirit self-evolves. In keeping with Kant, Troeltsch believes that man is able to perceive this self-evolution through a religious a priori with which he is endowed. It is this a priori which assures religion of its universal and necessary character. Consequently, revelation should be understood as the intuition of unseen reality imma-nent in man's own nature. Such claims as the Incarnation and Resurrec-tion should be understood as symbols, the poetry of religious spirit; the person of Jesus is to be understood within the context of the history of religion. Troeltsch's position results in a religious and historical rela-tivism which most traditionalists found unacceptable and heretical. The reaction of such "liberal" influence in America was the establishment of its polar extreme in the ultra-conservative "fundamentalist" movement.

Perhaps the most logically consistent of the liberals was Ludwig Feuerbach. For him, the philosophical critique meant one thing: metaphysical speculation about the nature of God was simply impossible. Therefore, any reference to or dependence upon such speculation was false. Religion, in fact, is the projection of our own minds, the symbolic objectification of our participation in the Infinite. Its nature is a matter of wish fulfillment or psychological compensation; thus we can easily understand why *God* becomes associated with love, mercy, and forgive-ness. Such personifications of desire may serve a useful psychological or social purpose; that is not denied. However, its Truth or validity is another question. Final maturity is to be beyond religion; theology is at last reduced to anthropology. Mackintosh summarizes Feuerbach's posi-tion this way: "Knowledge of 'God' is not false, if it be interpreted accu-rately, for it is genuine knowledge possessed by the Ego of its own being. . . . The transcendence of the individual's life which all religion implies is a transcendence that measures not vertically but horizon-tally—not above and beyond us, but around us on our own level."[12] Any Christology on the basis of this analysis must be nonexistent. Feuer-bach provides his own best summary in the twenty-first of his pub-lished lectures:

> I do not deny that Jesus lived, that he was an historical person to whom the Christian religion owes its origin; I do not deny that he suffered for his teachings. But I do deny that Jesus was a Christ, a God or son of God, a wonder-worker, born of a virgin, that he healed the sick by a mere word . . . in short, I deny that he was *as* the Bible represents him; for in the Bible Jesus is a subject not of straightforward historical narrative, but of religion . . . that is, a

creature transformed by the imagination. And any attempt to sift the historical truth from the additions, distortions, and exaggerations of the imagination is absurd, or at all events, fruitless.... The Christ who has come down to us in the Bible—and we know no other—is and remains a product of human imagination.[13]

Man has, for Feuerbach, become the measure of all things.

There seems to be some family resemblance between Feuerbach's position and that of the contemporary "Death-of-God" theology and the new hermeneutic, the critical study of religious language. While all reject the possibility of any "knowledge" of a transcendent God, all nevertheless depend upon the Platonic metaphysical structure of Reality as an implicit presupposition. Historically speaking, Liberalism replaced the idea of transcendence by that of immanence—the indwelling of God in man and the world. God could be found in, revealed Himself through, man and the evident continuity of all creation. The result of such Liberalism, as we have just seen, was a growing theological anthropology. Religious thought became increasingly identified with secular thought, and the concept of a transcendent God became increasingly irrelevant.

Nietzsche was perhaps the first to realize the true implications of such a development, for it was he who pointed out to the world that an irrelevant God is a dead God. The restrictions placed upon man's religious expression and knowledge are basically those Plato placed upon the world of appearance—transience and imperfection. Paul van Buren, one of the contemporary Death-of-God theologians, believes that Christianity, if it is about anything, is about man, not God. For van Buren, the word *God,* which has no empirical referent, has become meaningless. *Christian* is the descriptive word for those who find in Jesus the logical and historical center of faith. It is in Jesus' life, ethically and historically understood, that man becomes aware of his freedom and identity and achieves his understanding of reality. Van Buren maintains that the church fathers at Nicaea and Chalcedon were, in a highly symbolic way, saying the same thing; though the symbols were transcendent and mystical, the meanings were historical and existential. Theology is therefore left with the study of the cause, effect, and meaning of religious language and acts, and the clarification of what has traditionally been called the "faith-experience." For Thomas Altizer, a theologian of more mystical persuasion, God has become incarnate in the world with the Christ-event, annihilating Himself by becoming immanent as Spirit within creation. Now every man stands as the expression of *God,* an expression of meaningful, creative continuity.[14] Though different in origin and vocabulary, the effect is like Feuerbach: each man can now speak authoritatively for himself.

A third representative, William Hamilton, believes that God died some time in the nineteenth century and asserts that man has come of age and must now speak for himself. Hamilton's reason for calling himself "Christian" is that in Jesus—his words, life, sensitivity to others, and way of death—he sees in a paradigmatic way what it means to be "a man for others." Christ symbolizes the way to meaningful life.[15] All of these men have cut themselves off from anything that could be termed "Absolute Reality," "Absolute Truth," or "God" and are content to cope as meaningfully as possible with the world of appearance and phenomena or with the interpretation of religious language sets. This seems to be one final and extreme position of classical Platonic idealism whose metaphysical validity has been truncated leaving only the world of appearance and transience.

It would be theologically and historically improper at this point if no mention were made of the German theologian Dietrich Bonhoeffer, for his writings have provided much of the insight and inspiration for the radical theologians previously mentioned. Bonhoeffer questions much of the method, thought, form, and contribution of traditional Christianity and writes of a Christianity come of-age, even of "religionless Christianity."[16] But there is a puzzling ambiguity about Bonhoeffer's thought, for he also writes of the validity of the sacraments and the Church as the presence of Christ or "Christ existing as community." His tragic and early death in a Nazi prison does not permit us to do more than speculate about his theological position. His work and writing have been insightful to the whole spectrum of theology, not just to the Death-of-God theologians. In the long run, the ambiguity of his "Christian worldliness" or "Christian secularity" may prove more fruitful to the development of theological thought than his specific and tentative speculations in *The Cost of Discipleship* or *Ethics*.

To summarize the Liberal position, it seems clear that the critiques brought by Hume, Kant, and Hegel have just about destroyed the effectiveness of Hellenistic Idealism as a basis for Christian Christology. To accept the limitations of Kantian thought is to deny the possibility of religious knowledge and to hopelessly divide the world into areas of faith and reason, or to restrict such knowledge to the world of appearance. To accept the dialectical Idealism of Hegel is to relegate the historical Jesus to a developmental phase moving toward some final synthesis, or to consider Him to be merely symbolic of a philosophical, not theological truth. To combine Kant's and Hegel's thought, as Troeltsch has done, is to end up with an inconsequential historical relativism. No one of these possibilities gives adequate expression to the complex claims of traditional Christian experience and thought—the reality of a living God and the uniqueness of a mediating, historical Christ.

It is the third major group of theologians who provide alternative routes to this Liberal cul-de-sac. Perhaps what ends so blindly is not Christianity at all, but simply our traditional reliance upon Platonic Idealism. The problem is not that the critiques of Hume, Kant, and Hegel are too radical but not radical enough.

To say that the third group of theologians is "major" is perhaps misleading. In terms of numbers and general influence in the nineteenth century, existentialists such as Søren Kierkegaard certainly represented a minority movement. Some members of this third and more radical movement were not even theologians—men like Nietzsche, Dostoevski, Freud, Marx; but their revolt against classical Idealism and its structured, predictable world was a common theme. One of these secularists who revolted against such metaphysics in its Hegelian expression was Karl Marx. Marx did not disagree with Hegel's development of the dialectical process—a thesis countered by its antithesis resulting in a synthesis which, in turn, becomes the new thesis. What Marx objected to was enclosing such a process within the comprehension of the Absolute Ideal. Such a comprehensive system, Marx believed, excluded genuine novelty and freedom—excluded, in short, the reality of the historical process. Consequently, Marx substituted a dialectical materialism for Hegel's dialectical Idealism, a real contention of historical forces ("theses" and "antitheses") which would eventuate in a harmonious, classless society. The philosophical criticisms of Marx's position and the subsequent development of this philosophy in the political expression we now call "communism" are well known and are hardly germane to the development we are following, so I do no more than note their exclusion while noting the importance of Marx's revolt against Idealism in the name of a new historical reality.

In this philosophical tradition is the contemporary Neo-Marxian philosopher Ernst Bloch. Bloch wants to avoid the limitations of the incipient Idealism in the Marxist utopian society, but at the same time he believes that man and the universe are moving toward some yet unachieved essence. For Bloch, the logic of reality is the logic of change, for the historical reality of "now" is continuously passing into the "not-yet." My orientation in life is therefore toward the future, rather than the past, toward a creative expectation of fulfillment. The logic of change engenders hope; for in the continuously developing present, I participate in the shaping of the future, the fulfillment of my "utopian consciousness and utopian obligation."

> The not-yet-come-into-being is a thing which is pending in the world process—in physical, medical, judicial, and theological proceedings—and can neither be thwarted nor coerced; it always remains in suspense. The substratum of the real seethes on a

dialectical fire. The essence must still be brought forth into a world which knows not which way is up, and therefore is in need of man.[17]

Although Bloch is a secularist, a self-styled atheist, his influence on some of the younger theologians in Europe has been notable. Two of the most prominent of these theologians, the Roman Catholic Johannes Metz and the Protestant Jürgen Moltmann, disagree with Bloch's Marxist leanings, but their thought has been stimulated by Bloch's new arguments for "hope" and the future, an emphasis which theology has traditionally associated with eschatology. Bloch has succeeded, incidentally and unwittingly, of course, in revitalizing interest in the eschatological character of Scripture and the possible eschatological nature of theology itself. Traditional eschatology is a study of the "logic" of "end" or "final" issues—the consummation of reality. In the understanding of eschatology dominated by classical metaphysics, the reality consummated is the eternality of God, the appearance of the Kingdom of God with finality and power, a reality which was, is, and ever will be—i.e., eternal.

Consequently, time and history reveal nothing genuinely new, nor are they the context for the new; it is only the "already" as the "eternal" which is made increasingly evident in time and through history. In rejecting such traditional arguments, many of these younger theologians have made common cause with the Marxist Bloch, not because of his political leanings but because of the radical seriousness with which he views time and history. Moltmann writes: "Because Christians [of the classical, traditional persuasion previously described] believed in a 'God without future', those who willed the future of the earth had no option but to join forces with atheism to seek a 'future without God'. That is the schism of modern times in which many Christians and many atheists are suffering today."[18]

The result of this cross-fertilization of ideas and analysis for Christians is the emergence of the "theology of hope" which seeks to be this-worldly in its approach to life rather than subordinating such an interest to some other-worldly, ideal form. Theology should no longer be characterized by *reaction* to the world but rather by *action* within the world; theology should no longer be systems analysis but, rather, commitment. As Walter Capps points out, however, such a shift from "systems" to "action" which alters the *God*-world polarity to a *world*-God polarity pays a price in security for such a shift. Under the conditions of the primacy of action and commitment, the truth-support of systems is lost: "Systems of thought tend to be sensitive to the *essential* quality of a phenomenon: its underlying structure, or its fundamental form. Such systems are generally not disposed toward surprise. They are not geared for the once-in-a-lifetime. They are not suited for the perpetually spontaneous."[19]

The theology of commitment and action, the theology of hope, therefore shifts its emphasis away from the *logos*—the logicizing of religion into a system—to *mythos,* the acceptance of the mythopoeic as the only adequate form of religious expression. "The transition requested by hope-theology is not a movement from logos back to *mythos,* but a movement ahead to *mythos.* This, in turn, is in keeping with Ernst Bloch's suggestion that the future is present only in anticipations, in images and dreams."[20] The mythopoeic for Moltmann is the Resurrection of Jesus Christ in which the promise of salvation is already manifest. This is the ground of our hope within which we take responsibility for the present as determinative of the future. This is the new eschatology which de-Hellenizes the kerygma and acknowledges the reality of the spontaneous and changeable. This is the revelation which guides our "pilgrimage" toward the longed-for destination of being in the full presence of God. Thus Moltmann agrees with Ernst Käsemann's thesis that apocalypticism is the mother of all theology. The Resurrection of the Christ is the apocalyptic image of hope:

> By that [the Resurrection of the Christ] the earliest Christians did not mean a return of the dead Christ into moral life or a restoration of the fallen creation. They meant, rather, the entrance of something completely unexpected, the inbreaking of a qualitatively new future and the appearance of a life which is no longer "life toward death" but "life out of death." In the historical *novum Christi* they saw the anticipation and the already effective promise of the ultimately and universally new world.[21]

Thus for Moltmann the new eschatology means the doctrine of Christian hope "which embraces both the object hoped for and the hope inspired by it."[22]

However, it is just at this point that the claim of freedom and spontaneity, of orientation toward this-world and the future, breaks down. In Moltmann's frontal attack on the confinement of Hellenistic metaphysics and in his effort to free the future from the "melancholy of fulfillment,"[23] he has actually let these same metaphysics return through a Hegelian flank. Space and purpose do not permit the kind of detailed analysis required by such a charge, but several points will be examined to sustain the criticism.

First of all, the theology of hope claims to take time and history seriously as the context for the new, spontaneous, and responsible actions of men; yet Moltmann's statements about God and the Christ-event seem to contradict directly these claims in terms of a metaphysical Absolute:

> The original creation was created out of the will of God. But in its future God will dwell in it with his essence [sic]. This is to say that the new creation corresponds to the essence of God, being illuminated and transfigured by God's earthly presence.

> The all-embracing vision of God and of the new creation is for Christian hope anchored in the resurrection of the crucified Christ. In the resurrection of Christ we can know a new freedom in history which is not only liberation from the tyrannies within history but also a liberation from the tyranny and agony of history itself.[24]

These statements can hardly be compatible with the following assertion which stands in his *Theology of Hope* and definitely affirms our place in history: "The present of the coming parousia of God and of Christ in the promises of the gospel of the crucified does not translate us out of time, nor does it bring time to a standstill, but it opens the way for time and sets history in motion, for it does not tone down the pain caused us by the non-existent, but means the adoption and acceptance of the non-existent in memory and hope."[25]

A second argument concerning Moltmann's failure to avoid Platonic metaphysics may be found in his understanding of the revelation of God in the Christ. Moltmann wants to avoid the Barthian position of revealed Lordship and the more traditional claim of revealed knowledge, e.g., the Virgin Birth. To avoid these essential pitfalls, Moltmann argues from negation—only to fall victim, as did Paul Tillich before him, to an unacknowledged dependence on a variation of the ontological proof of the existence of God.[26] Moltmann writes: "What new has come into the world with Christ? The vision of God along with the vision of a new creation and the vision of the new man. But what actually was seen in Christ of this new future of God, of the world, and of man? At first only the negation of the negative and *index falsi*." Again, and more specifically Hegelian, "One might say that the anticipations and analogies of the future become manifest in present reality through the historical dialectic of the negation of the negative. The dialectic of thesis and antithesis is the presupposition by which one can recognize in the thesis the prefiguration of the future synthesis."[27] Only some form of Hellenistic metaphysical system could support such an argument.

A third and, theologically speaking, most telling argument against Moltmann's attempt to free himself from the stultifying effects of classical metaphysics is his acceptance of a *logos* of change. In his essay on the theology of hope, W.H. Capps states that this position has substituted *meta-chronics* for *meta-physics*. It has substituted a horizontal projection for a vertical one.[28] I do not believe that Capps meant this to be a criticism of

Moltmann's position, but it seems to be a most devastating one. In effect, Moltmann has not escaped idealist metaphysics; he has merely changed models, a linear dialectic for a vertical one, a change not unlike that which Marx effected with the Hegelian dialectic. Moltmann's *logos* of change is, perhaps, most evident in his account of revelation:

> The revelation in the appearances of the risen Christ has therefore to be described not only as "hidden," but also as "unfinished," and has to be related to a reality which is not yet here. It is still outstanding, has not yet come about, has not yet appeared, but is *promised* and *guaranteed* in his resurrection, and indeed is given along with his resurrection as a *necessary consequence:* the end of death, and a new creation in which amid the life and righteousness of all things God is all in all.

Promise "contradicts existing reality and discloses its own process concerning the future of Christ for man and the world."[29] These reservations, these allusions to eternal essences, truths, and necessities on the part of Moltmann rob the theology of hope of any radical departure from Hellenistic metaphysics. A change in emphasis and direction hardly constitutes a "new" eschatology.

The second strain of our third group of theologians is best understood by starting with the nineteenth-century theologian Søren Kierkegaard. As noted earlier, Kierkegaard believed that the neat, tidy, dialectical world of Hegelian Christianity had little or nothing to do with the "gut-level" living of one's life. For him, Christianity was not a philosophical description of life but was rather a way of life, that is, a way of living. Kierkegaard wished to get back to what he believed were the dynamic insights of the early Church, to get back *behind* the "monstrous illusion" called Christendom.[30] He did this by repudiating the institutional dominance of the State Church of Denmark and by rejecting the stultifying effects of Hegelianism on theological thinking. Kierkegaard did not wish to produce a rival theological system—in terms of his criticism *that* would be self-destructive. Rather, he set out to confront the life of Christendom with its own expression of faith. The discrepancy between the responsibility of a redeeming community and the lip service offered the world through allegiance to a liturgy was the constant target of Kierkegaard's ironic wit.

He believed that the reality of faith, and thus the reality of life, can be known and understood only when the individual, as a unique person, stands in awe and dread before God. Religion is not a matter of avowed creedal Absolutes but of an ultimate concern which involves my total life—public and private, mental and physical. To live existentially in faith is to be aware that I am, in the totality of my life, continuously being addressed by God powerfully and personally in the Christ. The God-

Man is not so much an ontological as an existential paradox. "'The God-Man is himself the existential.'" Kierkegaard's Christology, however, never escapes the Chalcedonian dilemma. The Christ-event involves a paradox of the most fundamental order: Almighty God and real humanity together despite their fundamental incommensurability. The Incarnation involves an intrinsic incognito which prevents any direct communication of God with man. "Kierkegaard approves Pascal's word that God is hid more deeply in the Incarnation than in creation."[31] In Kierkegaard, the search for a new ontology, a new understanding of *being*, begins. Though both philosophers disavow the "existentialist" label, it is upon the existential insight into *being* that both Martin Heidegger and Martin Buber build. Heidegger and Buber actually bring us into the twentieth century, but they are the direct heirs of the nineteenth-century revolt.

Martin Heidegger, as Kierkegaard before him, claims that our quest for an understanding of reality must be far more radical than reforms; it must be the expression of a whole new ontology, a completely new understanding of who I *am* rather than how I am *classified* or of what I am *composed*. This means for Heidegger that we must get behind the metaphysical categories of Platonic thought which have dominated Western philosophical and theological traditions for twenty-five hundred years. As a matter of fact, for Heidegger it means getting behind metaphysics altogether. The root of the problem has been that Western thought has consistently, thanks to Platonic traditions, misunderstood the word *being*. Western thought has taken a verb form, the participle of the verb *to be*, and used it as a noun in such a way that the force of its verb origin is completely excluded. *Being* as in the phrase *human being* is simply part of a static classification system. It in no way suggests a dynamic presence here-and-now. The word *Being* has, therefore, become identified with the determination of a thing's essence, its *what*ness, not with a thing's presence, its *is*ness. But reality, i.e., *living* itself, cannot exclude this latter implication of the word. *Being* restores to our understanding of self and the world the reality of time, change, and creativity which Plato dismissed when he relegated them to the world of appearances.

For Heidegger, *Being* is that dynamic context of *is*ness in which all things participate and meet and by which all things are animated by presence, i.e., by being here-and-now and by being self-revelatory. Thus when I meet another, I am not only aware of his physical presence, but also of the presence of *himself* as a *person*, an identity. It is, of course, true that we are not aware of total presence, physical and personal, on the occasion of every encounter. Each time, however, we are aware to some extent of both aspects of his *being*. The person whom I meet may choose to withhold himself from me in either or both aspects, but that withholding determination on his part is also an expression of what and who he is and, therefore, reflects the authenticity of that meeting. If another chooses not to be "open," i.e., to withhold who-he-is from me, then in such a case I say that he is "cold" or "withdrawn" rather than "warm" or "friendly." Under these conditions he is not authentically expressing his *being,* for he is not, as Heidegger puts it, letting the truth of his *living* reveal itself although the very act of withholding is an act of revelation itself, inhibiting as it is. This is descriptive of man in his "fallen" condition. Of course in a like manner, I may not choose to be open to such revelation were it there, but then I would be the one guilty of inauthenticity, a kind of arbitrarily enclosed expression of *Non-being.* Consequently, meaning is time-full, revelatory, and historical; not timeless and ideal; and so is what we call reality.

But, as may be already evident, our intimate awareness of *being* comes through the awareness of our own existence, which Heidegger terms *Dasein* ("being-there"). Man is *Dasein;* that is, man is self-conscious-existence who finds himself being-in-the-world-here-and-now. Because of his self-consciousness, man is aware of his expression of *being* which he neither creates nor determines. Because of his anticipated death, however, man is aware of his pending *Non-being,* i.e., Nothingness. My existence, therefore, is constituted by these two tensions which for Heidegger form an infrastructure. The result is a time-full existence characterized by my anxiety about death and my consequent free resolve to exist meaningfully in the always present possibility of death. Such existence Heidegger calls transcendence; it is my self-expression in terms of my historical context and in terms of my possibilities of which I am made aware by my relationship to *Being-Itself,* the ground of my *being, Is*ness.

So man learns from the world (from all that is) by surrendering or opening himself to the presence and mystery of everything about him, and in such a context, sustained by *being,* he is able to comprehend, and is free to pursue, the possibilities of his own existence. Such comprehension and pursuit are expressive of those time-full qualities of *being,* which Heidegger calls ontological, e.g., care, anxiety, and resolve, rather than ontic goals, e.g., success, power, wealth. These ontological qualities of *being* are constitutents which characterize *my* existence in time and are formative for my attitudes toward *being* and Nothingness, life and death. Because existence and not essence is central, man reveals his own humanism; he is not simply conforming to some predetermined form or ground or set of essential qualities. *Dasein,* incomplete and timefull as it is, is the ground for a New Humanism. If one is sensitive to the anxiety and mystery of the I-was-not, I-am, and I-will-not-be context within which we continuously live, then Heidegger has made his ontological point.

On the basis of this argument, it is possible to see why man can speak about a New Humanism in Heideggerian terms. Because of the ontological possibilities which constitute man's existence as *Dasein,* Western traditional thought—which argues from particular to universal and back—is "reversed." For Heidegger, possibility in *being* is prior to actuality. Man is constituted by possibilities whose actual expression in time produces the historical reality we call human existence. Thus authentic man expresses his own humanism in terms of care, anxiety, and resolve, rather than an embodiment of traditional humanism expressed in terms of immutable and Absolute laws, e.g., "Thou shalt not kill," or teleological goals, e.g., "liberty and justice for all." What Heidegger seems to have done is to provide contours for the continuously unique relationship engendered between man and man, or between man and the physical world, when time and history are considered with radical seriousness. For this New Humanism, classification and judgment of action are as meaningless as they are impossible in terms of standard sets of criteria. Time-full contingencies defy any absolute ethical calculus.

Meaningful human action is conditioned and informed by two things for Heidegger: the world-here-and-now into which I have been thrown and into which I now project myself; and my self-revelation in *being* through which I become aware of my possibilities. Such action does not imply a subject-object world which I can manipulate for my benefit or the benefit of all mankind; such action is rather the response of my openness to the truth of *being* in which both I and the world are expressive participants. Authenticity of any action thus depends upon the mutual openness of those involved.

The second twentieth-century prophet of this third movement of theological development is, like Heidegger, neither Protestant nor Roman Catholic; he is the Jewish scholar Martin Buber. It is Buber's descriptive ontological analysis of the *I-Thou* relationship which has revolutionized theological anthropology and has prepared the way for the New Humanism and a new theological interpretation. As diverse thinkers as Gerhard Ebeling, Paul Tillich, Rudolf Bultmann, Karl Heim, H. Richard Niebuhr, Donald Baillie, Emil Brunner, Paul Lehmann, Karl Barth, Carl Michalson, Charles Hartshorne, and Henry N. Wiemann acknowledge a profound indebtedness to this aspect of Martin Buber's thought.

It is noteworthy that this brilliant scholar should emerge out of the Jewish religion and that his influence is more profoundly felt in Christendom than in Judaism. I believe the first observation to be true, because Christendom recognizes in Buber the authentic prophetic voice in response to which both early Judaism and Christianity have developed. It takes Christians behind the Greek influence of the early councils to their Hebraic origins. This point introduces the second observation which I made. Buber's thought has had greater impact on Christian thought than on Jewish thought because the Greek heritage for Christians has necessitated the construction of several theological "systems" to explain the dual nature of appearance and reality, God and man, good and evil, heaven and earth. Buber's *I-Thou* offers a significant alternative to such systematizing. Because the prophetic tradition for the Jews has always been an ontological one, not a metaphysical one, there has been no theological development in Judaism comparable to that in Christendom. The Torah still stands as the norm of man's relationship to Yahweh, to God, and there is little or no need for further speculative thought; as a matter of fact, such speculation for the Jews borders on the sacrilegious because of its presumptuousness. However, it is not unimportant to notice here that Martin Buber speaks out of the Hasidic tradition in Judaism, which opposed the Hellenization of Judaism in the third century A.D., and which militantly opposes the domination of rabbinic legalism—the form of idolatry to which Judaism is most prone.

Buber begins, as does Heidegger, by attacking the traditional Western theory of knowledge which assumes that the primary problem is overcoming the polarity which exists between myself and the world, i.e., I can't *know* the world in-itself, I can know only my impressions of it or my own construction of it. To such a problem and to such related ones of subject-object dualism, Buber responds by suggesting that they are pseudo-problems. These problems arise because one assumes that the identity of the *I* is self-evident—that we all know who we are simply in the act of being. René Descartes' affirmation which emerges from his process of doubting, "I think therefore I am," is a classic expression of this identity faux pas. To say "I think" is to beg the question of identity. The conclusion is contained in the premise. For Buber, *I* is a differentiating symbol whose correlative terms are either *It* or *Thou*, the world or another. Reality is dynamic and contextual, never static and atomistic. I can know only who I am and what I am in terms of my contextual involvement. Isolation can never be the condition for identity.

However, it is just at this point that there is an essential difference between Buber and Heidegger. For Heidegger, identity is bound up with the possibilities and potentialities in *being*. *Existence* is the realization of one's potentiality as *Dasein*. But it is just here that Buber takes issue with Heidegger. Heidegger's understanding of existence is monological not dialogical: "The man of 'real' existence in Heidegger's sense, the man of 'self-being', who in Heidegger's view is the goal of life, is not the man who really lives with man, but the man who can no longer really live with man, the man who knows a real life only in communication with himself."[32]

Both Buber and Heidegger have made valuable contributions toward the development of a new theological expression which we have termed the "third movement" in contemporary theology. Their thought has become the basis for a new phenomenological description of ontology and, as such, provides a new vocabulary for attempting to understand the central mystery of the Christ-event. Chapter 2 of this book is a development of Buber's basic insight: the *I-Thou* encounter. Chapter 3 is a discussion of time and history, which begins with Heidegger's observations concerning time and being.

This book, however, is not the first systematic attempt at theology within the third movement. The contemporary German theologian Gerhard Ebeling has already developed a theology incorporating many of the insights of both Buber and Heidegger. Although I am convinced that Ebeling's theology stops short of the radical demands inherent in the contributions of these men, much of what follows here will not be incompatible with Professor Ebeling's thoughts.

Ebeling accepts Buber's *I-Thou* encounter as the basic structure of our human condition: "To speak of God as the one who encounters us is clearly to speak of the reality of God. For how else should reality be experienced except in an encounter?"[33] However, Ebeling accepts this structure with certain modifications. For Buber, the *I-Thou* relation (with man or God) is a creative encounter out of which something genuinely new emerges in terms of *who* I am. For Ebeling, the *I-Thou* relation (preeminently with God in His Word) is more a revelational event in which I *dis*-cover my essential identity:

> What is transmitted as word of God can thus be understood as word of God only when it finds in man and his world the context into which it announces something hidden; nor can this be just anything that happens to be hidden, but must be that which ... renders a decision concerning the humanity of man. ... The word of God seeks to verify us where our being in the world is concerned. ... It takes seriously what is meant by *identification* in relation to the humanity of man. Where man is concerned, identification is verification.[34]

My authenticity as a human being is confirmed in the *I-Thou* relation.

The *Thou* who confronts me in the word is, of course, *the* Word, Jesus who is the Christ. It is at this point that Heidegger's contribution becomes important to Ebeling. The transition from the Word of God to the word of God, from the Christ to Jesus, from God's Word to human words, is made possible by the fact that reality is peculiarly and essentially related to its linguistic expression. The "word-event" contours and constitutes all human existence. Ebeling states: "Language is the body of our spirit,"[35] which is strikingly like Heidegger's contention that language is the "house of being." The force of such a claim is ontological, so that it is possible for me to say that not only does God come to me in His Word, but also that He comes to me in His word, and that the two are one and the same: "When the Bible speaks of God's Word then it means here unreservedly word as word—word that as far as its word-character is concerned is completely normal, let us not hesitate to say: natural, oral word taking place between man and man." But, as Ebeling's critics have pointed out, such a narrow definition of "word-event" leads either to a poverty of human expression about God or to a self-destructive inconsistency of terms, both of which Ebeling seeks to avoid.[36] As well as these difficulties in precisely determining the nature of the "word-event," Ebeling likewise has not clearly defined the limits or nature of the *I-Thou* (subjective) encounter, particularly vis-à-vis the *I-It* (objective) relation. In some instances of *I-Thou,* the dependence upon the Other seems to constitute a social or psychological expression of encounter rather than an ontological one. In that case (at least from Buber's perspective) Ebeling's total concept could be reduced to *I-It,* but such a reductionist position is certainly not Ebeling's intent.

It is also not clear that Ebeling's phenomenological approach to the "word-event" remains consistent and thereby escapes the classical metaphysical stance. The limitations of man's encounter with the Word made flesh should preclude any "absolute" metaphysical statements by Ebeling about the nature of God—other than the reality of His presence within the word. But in developing his ideas on soteriology, Ebeling retreats to the mysteries of Chalcedon: "In Christ we do not have to do with a substitute for God, but with God himself. And the sacrifice offered by him is not a substitute for full surrender, but is itself the complete surrender, love in its totality." In this one assertion all the paradoxes, contradictions, and mysteries of "Two-Nature Christology" return. Ebeling's mention of the Incarnation has the same effect: "If we take seriously the fact that God turns to man, claims him, addresses him, then it is meaningless to ask how he can do this in a way that man can understand. For this turning to man is God's humanity. His Word which is directed to man is as such a human word. There is no trace of a difference."[37]

Professor Ebeling's theology, while so instructive and insightful in its exploration of the communication of faith, does not provide the basis for a new Christology, an alternative to the classical concept of Incarnation. If we are truly to take advantage of the insights which Heidegger, Buber, and the existentialist tradition have provided—particularly in escaping from the confinements and limitations of classical metaphysics—then it is necessary to redefine what we call "reality" in terms of the new ontology.

Therefore, beginning with the "human condition," we must seek to understand and to describe man's relation to man, world, and God in terms of the experience of identity, time, history, reason, and revelation. Then we will be ready to look again at the nature and meaning of the Christ-event. From the traditional, or Barthian, stance, this would appear to be another instance of "natural" theology, of anthropocentric thought, but such claims merely expose the fact that the critic is truly unaware of the nature of the new ontology and the fundamental contribution of *I-Thou* encounter to contemporary thought.

The interpretive historical sketch which I have just made provides the context out of which the rest of this book is developed. It is no longer possible to accept, simply on the strength of tradition, the old orthodoxy as being Absolutely True. This conclusion is drawn not only on the basis of internal argument—the limitations imposed by such philosophers as Hume and Kant—but also on the new ontological insights of much contemporary thought. Nor is it possible to accept the half-way measures of the Liberal tradition, a scaling down of theological claims to meet epistemological criticisms while maintaining the same metaphysical stance. If the contributions of the third group of scholars are taken seriously, then the theological task must be begun from a new point of departure. It is my belief that the basic position of Martin Buber has provided us with just such a point. Some of the thoughts and consequent development in Buber's writing are not as relevant to this study as others, but I would like to acknowledge my indebtedness to his thinking.

2

The Human Condition

I am here and now. It might seem that one would have difficulty arriving at a more basic or self-evident statement about the human condition than that—I am here and now. It seems to be the minimum claim, the least comprehensive denominator. Yet that short sentence is the cryptic summary of this whole study, the present chapter of which is a consideration of the word *I*.

For centuries, we have assumed that the one thing we did not have to worry about was the identity of the *I*. We might have to worry about its proper development, its achievements, its possibility of full and mature expression, but not its identity. Even when we were not sure who we were, our problem was not that we were essentially characterless, identityless; rather, our dilemma was discovering that genuine person we knew we must be underneath our acculturated self, behind our "public" self, or beyond all the confusion of daily life—the *real* me. Plato was so convinced of this, he imagined us choosing our identity before birth; life became simply the living out of this choice under the conditions of temporal limitations. For Christians, such essential identity was thought to be bestowed by God in the gracious act of creation. The act was gracious not only because it was God's, but also because it placed upon man the moral and spiritual responsibility of self-fulfillment, i.e., the responsibility of freedom. If we would only act as God originally intended, our life would exhibit that serenity which is possible only through the security of true self-knowledge. The Eternal God had chosen us from all eternity. Such election permits development but presupposes essential and immutable identity.

Many modern philosophers, as the selected review of the late-nineteenth early-twentieth centuries in chapter 1 has indicated, believe the identity problem is much more complicated and less self-evident than classical metaphysics or traditional Christianity has supposed. One such philosopher is Martin Buber, who believes that we need a whole new approach to the problem. Consequently, we shall have a rather extended look at his analysis.

For Buber, one begins to understand identity, his own and others, within the ontological context of *being,* which for man means within the *act* of existing. Such human existence, for Buber, is not like the radical isolation of Heidegger's *Dasein* ("being-there") which focuses on self-consideration in the quest for meaning. Buber believes that "all real living is meeting," that "in the beginning is relation." He understands this relation to be threefold:

> Man's threefold living relation is, first, his relation to the world and to things, second, his relation to men—both to individuals and to the many—, third, his relation to the mystery of being—which is dimly apparent through all this but infinitely transcends it—which the philosopher calls the Absolute and the believer calls God, and which cannot in fact be eliminated from the situation even by a man who rejects both designations.[1]

It is Buber's belief that *I* is a differentiating word of identity. It makes no sense, indeed cannot be spoken, without the correlative words *Thou* or *It* through which and with which I establish my identity.[2] The word *I* which I apply to myself is, therefore, not one of sheer identity, sheer uniqueness given in terms of some Absolute bestowal or creation. Rather, it is the term which gradually emerges because of my involvement in the primary relations *I-Thou* and *I-It*. The *I* which emerges from these relations is that *self*-consciousness which I indicate by using the word *I*, that identity-in-relation which I presume when I say such things as: "*I* did that" or "*I* am not he" or "*I* love you."

Though man's "living relation" is threefold, which includes a relationship to God, his relationship to the world is twofold and is characterized by the two primary words just indicated—*I-Thou* and *I-It*. That is, Buber has recognized that there is a radical qualitative difference between my relationship to others in terms of intimate personal encounter and my relationship to things. Such a dichotomy should not raise the specter of Immanuel Kant, the advocacy of two separate but ultimately related worlds or realities. Buber believes that he avoids Kant's dilemma not by the Hegelian logical ploy of identity-in-difference but rather by accepting the mystical paradox of identity experienced in the nature of existing itself.

> Formative power belongs to the world of *Thou:* spirit can penetrate and transform the world of *It.* By virtue of this privilege we are not given up to alienation from the world and the loss of reality by the *I*—to domination by the ghostly. Reversal is the recognition of the Centre and the act of turning again to it. . . .
> For this double movement, of estrangement from the primal Source, in virtue of which the universe is sustained in the process of becoming, and of turning towards the primal Source in virtue

of which the universe is released in being, may be perceived as the metacosmical primal form that dwells in the world as a whole in its relation to that which is not the world-form whose twofold nature is represented among men by the twofold nature of their attitudes, their primary words, and their aspects of the world.[3]

This point will arise again when Buber considers the related problems of freedom and necessity and will be dealt with more extensively at that time.

But it is not enough to say that my relationship to others and my relationship to things differ. As it stands, that statement is misleading, for it is possible for my relationship to another person to be of *It* character. When I treat another human being as an object, a unit of political power, a source of economic potential, a statistic for survey, then that human being has become an *It*. This *It*, however, may become, again or for the first time, a *Thou*. Such an assertion on Buber's part supports his contention, mentioned earlier, that he views his position as genuinely different from that of Kant or Hegel. This transition of *It-to-Thou-to-It* could only be possible in a context in which *being* is ontologically (existentially) understood. Before further comment, however, a closer look at the primary words *I-Thou* and *I-It* needs to be taken.

Buber calls the encounter of my *I* with another person's *I* a "subject to subject" relationship, or (from within the relationship itself) an *I-Thou* encounter. It is this experience which informs me *who* I am rather than *what* (*I-It*) I am. The *I-Thou* relation, therefore, is the most fundamental human relationship of all, beginning with an unborn child in the mother's womb: "The ante-natal life of the child is one of purely natural combination, bodily interaction and flowing from the one to the other." Strictly speaking, ante-natal life is not conscious *I-Thou* (though some psychologists would not balk at such an assertion) but is the natural matrix which Buber calls the "a-priori of relation, *the inborn Thou*."[4] General endorsement of this contention can be found in many philosophers, e.g., Gabriel Marcel, Paul Tillich, or John Macmurray. For Gabriel Marcel, it is a matter of "preliminary notions": "I concern myself with being only in so far as I have a more or less distinct consciousness of the underlying unity which ties me to other beings of whose reality I already have a preliminary notion."[5]

Buber's claim receives specific support from Erich Fromm within the biological-psychological context:

> *Symbiotic union* has its biological pattern in the relationship between the pregnant mother and the foetus. They are two, and yet one. They live "together" (*symbiosis*), they need each other. The foetus is a part of the mother, it receives everything it needs from

her; mother is its world, as it were; she feeds it, she protects it, but also her own life is enhanced by it.

In the infant I-ness has developed but little yet; he still feels one with mother, has no feeling of separateness as long as mother is present. Its sense of aloneness is cured by the physical presence of the mother, her breasts, her skin. Only to the degree that the child develops his sense of separateness and individuality is the physical presence of the mother not sufficient any more, and does the need to overcome separateness in other ways arise.[6]

The infant, at the moment of birth, would feel the fear of dying, if a gracious fate did not preserve it from any awareness of the anxiety involved in the separation from mother, and from intra-uterine existence. Even after being born, the infant is hardly different from what it was before birth; it cannot recognize objects, it is not yet aware of itself, and of the world as being outside of itself. It only feels the positive stimulation of warmth and food from its source: mother. Mother *is* warmth, mother *is* food, mother *is* the euphoric state of satisfaction and security.... The outside reality, persons and things, have meaning only in terms of their satisfying or frustrating the inner state of the body. Real is only what is within; what is outside is real only in terms of my needs—never in terms of its own qualities or needs.[7]

Buber, of course, is mainly concerned with the religious implications of man so considered in terms of his primary relationships. "The spiritual reality of the primary words arises out of a natural reality, that of the primary word *I-Thou* out of a natural combination, and that of the primary word *I-It* out of natural separation."[8]

Although Buber calls both words (*I-Thou, I-It*) primary, it is obvious that for him *I-Thou* takes priority in both origin and importance. Because the prenatal relationship with the mother is a pure expression of the "a-priori of relation" and that this is symbolic of my "a-priori of relation" with the cosmos, all other relations follow from this as either direct expression or as derivative expression: "The first primary word [*I-Thou*] can be resolved, certainly, into *I* and *Thou,* but it did not arise from their being set together; by its nature it precedes *I*. The second word arose from the setting together of *I* and *It;* by nature it comes after *I*."[9] In terms of personal identity, one can understand why Buber insists upon this priority; little in terms of personal identity seems to happen to me when I encounter my desk or my subway tokens, but often strange and exciting things happen to me when I encounter another person because each encounter has the potentiality of radical reorientation for me. I rarely expect that from my encounter with things. However, later in the chapter, I shall take issue with this priority. I do not think it can be supported by a genuine ontology of *Being*. Likewise, such a radical separation of *I-Thou* and *I-It* would tend to counter Buber's contention that he has avoided the Kantian error of separate worlds.

First, let us look specifically at the word *I-Thou*. When Buber calls this a *word*, he means that it is fundamentally an expression of *being*, a single condition of *being*. Part of that fundamental expression or condition and, at the same time, symbol of the totality of that expression of *being*, is the articulation of the words themselves. This, of course, does not mean the specific words *I* and *Thou* per se, but any words which convey that fundamental relation. "Primary words do not describe something that might exist independently of them, but being spoken they bring about existence. Primary words are spoken *from the being*."[10] What Buber is offering us is not a contradiction but an acknowledgment of symbolism as a generic part of *being*. So everyone who is in love needs and longs to hear the words *I love you* from the loved one—because such words are part of, and symbolic of the totality of, the expression of *being* we call "love." In the words of Martin Heidegger, "language is the house of *Being*." Perhaps it should be noted here that love is undoubtedly the finest expression of what Buber considers the *I-Thou* relation. When I say "Thou" to another, I am never, in effect, speaking that word or term in isolation—as though my *Thou* could be a thing—rather, I am always meaning, if not saying, "I-Thou." "*I-Thou* can only be spoken with the whole being." It is an act of love.[11]

It should be noted that for Buber *love* is more than just a sensation or feeling. It is an event of metaphysical significance for which Buber finds Jesus' life a pertinent example:

> Feelings accompany the metaphysical and metapsychical fact of love, but they do not constitute it. The accompanying feelings can be of greatly differing kinds. The feeling of Jesus for the demoniac differs from his feeling for the beloved disciple; but the love is the one love. Feelings are "entertained": love comes to pass. Feelings dwell in man; but man dwells in his love. That is no metaphor, but the actual truth. Love does not cling to the *I* in such a way as to have the *Thou* for its "content," its object; but love is *between I* and *Thou*. The man who does not know this, with his very being know this, does not know love . . . Love is responsibility of an *I* for a *Thou*.[12]

Because the *I-Thou* is spoken with the whole self, there are no bounds (other than the implicit physical or intellectual ones) to such a relationship. Bounds suggest some form of projected objectification on the part of the *I*, some separation consciously acknowledged; the *I-Thou* experience is totally engrossing. It knows no bounds; my *Thou*, says Buber, "fills the heavens."[13] In a less poetic way, one can say that within the *I-Thou* experience consciousness of and with the other has displaced any isolating self-consciousness. The transcendent *I*, the elusive *knower* that can never be known, is totally and completely involved in the encounter, so much so that the *I* which emerges from this encounter is other than the *I* which began that meeting. A development, though it may be ever so slight, has taken place, because the *I-Thou* encounter is a creative thing. Anyone who has loved and /or loves knows the continuing validity of this. It should also be noted that the word *love* as it is being used here is not restricted to romantic love—that erotic love with healthy libidinal overtones; the word also includes that love which exists within families and between friends, which may exclude the physical or sexual encounter. In short, love is an ontological event: an active, creative event. That such a creative experience takes place has been witnessed to by poets, librettists, and novelists since the beginning of time. For most of us, it is simply self-evident.

Two things should be noted at this point. One is that such an all-engrossing *I-Thou* experience, such an existential moment, is usually not a lengthy thing, nor does Buber consider it so. While such an experience is "outside" of what we normally call clock time—so that the encounter may have been one minute or one hour, which of these we never know until it's over—it still *takes* time, and because of the intensity of the experience, it is usually limited. Though a man may be completely in love with his wife, to whom he has committed himself both publicly and privately through the institution of marriage, that still does not alter the fact that some ninety percent of that life is lived in the realm of *I-It,* the realm of social and personal responsibility—children's meals, paying bills, and civic participation are all part of the world of *It*. It is likewise true that the *I-Thou* encounter is not spatially significant in itself. This, of course, does not mean that the encounter takes place in some "fifth dimension" or "twilight zone"; it simply means that the participants are unaware of their spatial context or its significance until the encounter is past. The instant an individual has become conscious of and responsive to his physical surroundings in a spatial way, he has moved into the world of *It*.

The second thing to note is that such an *I-Thou*, totally engrossing, creative experience does not seem to occur only with other human beings. It can happen with Nature as well. Buber believes that it is possible for me to have an *I-Thou* relationship with a tree, for example. This, he insists, does not mean that the tree ceases to be a tree or that he can describe with any words what the nature of the reciprocal relation with a tree is like.

He simply witnesses to the fact that at certain times and certain places, what we ordinarily think of as objects of nature can confront us with the intimacy of the *I-Thou* meeting. While it is difficult for most of us to imagine such a thing happening, this may be true because of our refusal to be "there" for such an experience, i.e., to credit its possibility. For Viktor E. Frankl, an Austrian psychiatrist, this possibility became real in the life of a young woman facing death in a concentration camp in Nazi Germany:

> This young woman knew that she would die in the next few days. But when I talked to her she was cheerful in spite of this knowledge. "I am grateful that fate has hit me so hard," she told me. "In my former life I was spoiled and did not take spiritual accomplishments seriously." Pointing through the window of the hut, she said, "This tree here is the only friend I have in my loneliness." Through that window she could see just one branch of a chestnut tree, and on the branch were two blossoms. "I often talk to this tree," she said to me. I was startled and didn't quite know how to take her words. Was she delirious? Did she have occasional hallucinations? Anxiously I asked her if the tree replied. "Yes." What did it say to her? She answered, "It said to me, 'I am here—I am here—I am life, eternal life.'"[14]

For most of us, Buber makes sense, if at all on this point, in the realm of animals. Many of us unashamedly champion the cause of genuine encounter with our pets, though we may do so with no little sentimentality attached. However, no less a naturalist than Konrad Lorenz would support the contention.[15]

Along with the categories of Nature and other human beings, Buber likewise includes our life with what he calls "intelligible forms." By this, Buber seems to mean those experiences and /or conditions of life which inspire us to paint, write, dance, act, or take artistic pictures, i.e., to respond in a personal and creative way. These intelligible forms are not simply products of the imagination; they are forms which confront us and demand our effective power for their expression. Consequently, Buber considers our response an "act of being" which involves both sacrifice and risk—the sacrifice of exclusive devotion to the act and the risk of total exposure which such creation demands of the artist: "The work does not suffer me, as do the tree and the man, to turn aside and relax in the world of *It;* but it commands. If I do not serve it aright it is broken, or it breaks me." In this third sphere of *Thou* relation, we find ourselves in a context (or relation) "which does not use speech, yet begets it. We perceive no *Thou,* but none the less we feel we are addressed and we answer—forming, thinking, acting. We speak the primary word with our being, though we cannot utter *Thou* with our lips."[16]

In all three of these spheres of *Thou,* the relation with the *Thou* is immediate. It is not qualified by any preconditions, classification, or foreknowledge. The relation is also mutual but without any purpose, goal, or advantage, though the result of such a relation may in fact serve any of these things. It is only in and through such meetings that I become who *I* am. Such a becoming does not so much imply a growing solidity or singularity as it does a growing maturity. That *I,* who I am, is more than just a social construct. An identity which I am accorded by society is a classification which is objective not subjective, which is past (insofar as it is already formulated) and never present. My *I* which is a present or potential *Thou* can never be so classified, for it is the expression of my *being* and thus forever renewing itself. For this reason, we have the sometimes disconcerting experience of knowing ourselves to be "a different person" in different situations. Such variation does not mean that we are schizophrenic or emotionally unstable; under the conditions previously described, it simply means that we are responding creatively within a given *I-Thou* relation. Thus, in a very real way, I am one person with my mother, another with my wife, another with my son, yet another with my friend. All of these relationships, meetings, both *effect* and *affect* me. In terms of *I-Thou,* the relationships are effective; in terms of *I-It* (my continuing timeful relations with these persons), such encounters are, in retrospect, effective and productive of "character" and "personality."

Buber summarizes the *I-Thou* relationship this way:

> Man meets what exists and becomes as what is over against him, always simply a single *being* and each thing simply as being. What exists is opened to him in happenings, and what happens affects him as what is. Nothing is present for him except this one being, but it implicates the whole world. Measure and comparison have disappeared; it lies with yourself how much of the immeasurable becomes reality for you. These meetings are not organised to make the world, but each is a sign of the world-order. They are not linked up with one another, but each assures you of your solidarity with the world. The world which appears to you in this way is unreliable, for it takes on a continually new appearance; you cannot hold it to its word. It has no density, for everything in it penetrates everything else; no duration, for it comes even when it is not summoned, and vanishes even when it is tightly held. It cannot be surveyed, and if you wish to make it capable of survey you lose it. It comes, and comes to bring *you* out; if it does not reach you, meet you, then it vanishes; but it comes back in another form. It is not outside of you, it stirs in the depth of you; if you say "Soul of my soul" you have not said too much. But guard against

wishing to remove it into your soul—for then you annihilate it. . . . Between you and it there is mutual giving: you say *Thou* to it and give yourself to it, it says *Thou* to you and gives itself to you. You cannot make yourself understood with others concerning it, you are alone with it. But it teaches you to meet others, and to hold your ground when you meet them. Through the graciousness of its comings and the solemn sadness of its goings it leads you away to the *Thou* in which the parallel lines of relations meet. It does not help to sustain you in life, it only helps you to glimpse eternity.[17]

There are references at the beginning and end of this quotation which refer to or imply another sphere of *Thou* experience which has not yet been mentioned in this text: the *Eternal Thou*. This sphere shall be discussed after first considering the second of the two primary words, *I-It*.

When I pronounce the word *I*, I am acknowledging at the same time either the context of *Thou* or *It*; I can never pronounce the word *I* in isolation, de novo, for even those moments of seeming solitude, reflection, or introspection are acts dependent upon past *Thou* encounters or *It* experiences. The imagery, the vocabulary, the values are those I have inherited and accept or are prefigured by those against which I now take my stand. *I* am who I am and what I am in terms of my interaction with my contextual world.

The world of *It* is the world of transitive verbs, the world of objects and my relation to them. It is not simply one of external objects such as rocks, chairs, and municipal governments; it is also the world which I imagine, will, feel, and think. Such a world, whether it be perceived or thought, is always limited, bounded by other finite perceptions or thoughts. In objectification *things* are fixed and limited by the very act of thought-particularization. I am never *one* with such objects as I am with my *Thou*. I place myself next to such objects, or, if such *Its* happen to be my thoughts or opinions, I recognize that I *possess* such objects which I can inspect, change, recall, remove, or ignore, almost at will. This world has to do with *what* I am but not with *who* I am. Even our vocabulary supports such a qualitative distinction. For example, I "break" a law (*It*), but I "betray" a person (*Thou*). There is more than just a priority of importance implied in these words, a matter of degree; there is a distinction in kind. It is the basis for the ironic distinction which so many dramatists use; for example, Hamlet knows that the revenge for his father's death (the *It* demand of the world) has, in the final analysis, nothing to do with the lost *Thou* relationship which he had with his father. What he knows he must do as Prince has no bearing upon *who* he is as Hamlet. Tragedy results when the priority or nature of the *Thou* and *It* spheres are reversed or confused. The fact of tragedy because of this possible confusion is another indication of the separate but related worlds of *Thou* and *It;* it is a "dramatic" denial of the Kantian dichotomy.

The world of *It* arises for me with my first conscious act of *I*, that is, my first self-conscious act. When the *I* begins to emerge from its primitive and initial *Thou* relation with the world (at this early stage mother and world are indistinguishable and all is *Thou*),[18] it begins to know itself as distinct from the world about it, and self-discovery begins in a new and different way—as anyone knows who has played games of hide-and-seek with infants. However, as Buber notes: "This happens in a 'primitive' form and not in the form of a 'theory of knowledge.'" At that moment when human consciousness establishes a perception as object, "the barrier between subject and object has been set up. The primary word *I-It*, the word of separation, has been spoken."[19]

The word of separation is not uninformative. The *It* world has much to tell me about myself and itself. It teaches me the possibilities and limitations of my body relative to other things and other bodies— that I can stand so much heat and so much cold, that I can eat this and drink that, that I am stronger than this but weaker than that. It also teaches me about the relative possibilities and limitations of my mind, talents, and proclivities—that I am an amateur photographer, not a Steichen, Porter, or Adams. It is from this world that I receive, test, accept, or reject standards, values, norms, ideologies, dogmas, ideas, skills—all that education can provide, whether it be formal or from the school of "hard knocks." It is the world of cause and effect, the world of the computer, of Greenwich Mean Time, of customs and taxes, of "eating and drinking, dung and death."[20]

The *I-It* world is also the world of other people who are not *Thous,* though, of course, the potentiality is there. This does not mean that the *It* status is a demeaning one, a matter of second-class citizenship. (The *It* category for people, particularly my casual acquaintances like Bill my barber and Benny my butcher, requires special consideration and will be discussed later in the chapter.) The world of *It* is the world of citizenship, social concern, political activism, and cultural achievement, and as such has an integrity of its own. When this world of public concern, values, and organization is challenged by the intrusion of a *Thou* relationship, then a situation which we call "conflict of interest" arises and compensation for that *Thou* relation must be made. A judge, for example, will disqualify himself from sitting in judgment over a member of his own family. The value of justice, of equality before the law, cannot be maintained in an *I-Thou* relation which obliterates all objective judgments. Any man who accepts public office accepts, at the same time, the obligation to maintain an objective *It* relationship in the function of that position. The world of *It* is a necessary part of man's self-expression even though it is not sufficient in itself. "And in all the seriousness of truth hear this: without *It* man cannot live. But he who lives with *It* alone is not a man."[21] *I-It* and *I-Thou* are both primary words.

As with the world of *I-Thou,* Buber provides the following summary of the world of *I-It:*

> He [man] perceives what exists round about him—simply things, and beings as things; and what happens round about him—simply events, and actions as events; things consisting of qualities, events of moments; things entered in the graph of place, events in that of time; things and events bounded by other things and events, measured by them, comparable with them; he perceives an ordered and detached world. It is to some extent a reliable world, having density and duration. Its organisation can be surveyed and brought out again and again; gone over with closed eyes, and verified with open eyes. It is always there, next to your skin, if you look on it that way, cowering in your soul, if you prefer it so. It is your object, remains it as long as you wish, and remains a total stranger, within you and without. You perceive it, take it to yourself as the "truth", and it lets itself be taken; but it does not give itself to you. Only concerning it may you make yourself "understood" with others; it is ready, though attached to everyone in a different way, to be an object common to you all. But you cannot meet others in it. You cannot hold on to life without it, its reliability sustains you; but should you die in it, your grave would be in nothingness.[22]

Thus identity and self-consciousness emerge from the two primary words which are fundamental to life, but there does seem to be a difference between *I* which emerges from the *I-Thou* relation and that *I* which is the result of the world of *It.* The *I* of the *I-It* relation is characterized by its individuality, its ability to perceive, use, and function in the public world. This *I* achieves its "identity" by differentiating itself from other individualities. It is an individuality "concerned with its My—my kind, my race, my creation, my genius." Such an *I,* Buber believes, "is the spiritual form of natural detachment."[23] The aim of this self-differentiation is to experience and to use the world, to get the most out of "life" while it lasts.

By contrast, the *I* of *I-Thou* is not intent on self-differentiation or individuality at all. This *I* emerges as person, as sheer subjectivity, i.e., not even a consciousness of *my* subjectivity—which would be in the category of *It.* This subjectivity emerges not by detachment from others but by entering into relation with them. The *I* of the *I-Thou,* states Buber, is "the spiritual form of natural solidarity of connexion." The relation of the *I-Thou* encounter is its own end, its own reward. It is self-authenticating and self-fulfilling. In short, it is what Buber calls reality: "He who takes his stand in relation, shares in a reality, that is, in a being that neither merely belongs to him nor merely lies outside him. All reality is an activity in which I *share* without being able to appropriate for myself. Where there is no sharing there is no reality. Where there is self-appropriation there is no reality."[24]

This seems to imply that for Buber the world of *I-It* could not be included in what he terms "reality." But this is not the case. Again the priority of the *I-Thou* relation is used to bridge the gap. When I am no longer participating in the *I-Thou* relation and am conscious of my separation from the world, the reality of the shared (*I-Thou*) world remains present to me in terms of an experienced potentiality for reunion. This is possible because of what Buber calls "the province of subjectivity in which the *I* is aware with a single awareness of its solidarity of connexion and of its separation. Genuine subjectivity can only be dynamically understood, as the swinging of the *I* in its lonely truth."[25] Any man who has experienced separation from his family or loved ones because of professional or military obligations knows perfectly well of this *I* in its "lonely truth." Again Viktor Frankl's experience in a Nazi concentration camp provides us with a moving corroboration of the point. Long separated from his wife, he tells of walking to a forced work detail with a fellow prisoner:

> And as we stumbled on for miles, slipping on icy spots, supporting each other time and again, dragging one another up and onward, nothing was said, but we both knew: each of us was thinking of his wife. Occasionally I looked at the sky, where the stars were fading and the pink light of the morning was beginning to spread behind a dark bank of clouds. But my mind clung to my wife's image, imagining it with an uncanny acuteness. I heard her answering me, saw her smile, her frank and encouraging look. Real or not, her look was then more luminous than the sun which was beginning to rise.
>
> A thought transfixed me: for the first time in my life I saw the truth as it is set into song by so many poets, proclaimed as the final wisdom by so many thinkers. The truth—that love is the ultimate and the highest goal to which man can aspire. Then I grasped the meaning of the greatest secret that human poetry and human thought and belief have to impart: *The salvation of man is through love and in love.* I understood how a man who has nothing left in this world still may know bliss, be it only for a brief moment, in the contemplation of his beloved. In a position of utter desolation, when man cannot express himself in positive action, when his only achievement may consist in enduring his sufferings

in the right way—an honorable way—in such a position man can, through loving contemplation of the image he carries of his beloved, achieve fulfillment.[26]

But loneliness is not the final character of such subjectivity. Between each *I* and *Thou* there is evident a spirit which can be identified with neither of them, an awareness of that reality which is realized when an *I-Thou* relation is established. It is the expression of at least partial fulfillment of the a priori, inborn *Thou*. Subjectivity, through this spirit, is made aware of The Subjectivity who is God: "The extended lines of relations meet—in the eternal *Thou*."[27]

> Every particular *Thou* is a glimpse through to the eternal *Thou:* by means of every particular *Thou* the primary word addresses the eternal *Thou*. Through this mediation of the *Thou* of all beings fulfilment, and non-fulfilment, of relations comes to them: the inborn *Thou* is realised in each relation and consummated in none. It is consummated only in the direct relation with the *Thou* that by its nature cannot become *It*.[28]

This relation, then, becomes the final and fundamental source of my *I*, my identity. It emerges out of my encounter with God Himself—a point which Buber and Kierkegaard would share. In such a way, the sterility of predetermined, foreordained identity is avoided. I am not, in such circumstances, *what* God made me; I am, rather, who I choose to be standing in the presence of God. I am not made in the Image of God; I am made to image God. The noun has become a verb, symbolic of the fact that the relationship is a living one. I do not know God's Being; I encounter God's *Being*. God is not a passive principle in my life but an active creative force. My relationship with the *Eternal Thou* is creative for me just as are my relationships with human *Thous*, only with the *Eternal Thou* this creation brings with it a sense of fulfilling, a consummating expression of subjectivity, or *I*.

Although the *Eternal Thou* is the ground and possibility of all our encounters, this is an assertion I can make, a belief I can avow, only after the fact. That is, there is nothing coercive about my relationship with the *Eternal Thou*. This is not to imply that the "order of knowing" somehow precedes the "order of being"; it is simply to imply that knowing is a reflexive function of subjective *being*. The very character of grace is presence, not coercion. God confronts me, but I must respond by stepping into direct relationship with Him. "Relation means being chosen and choosing," and such choosing is done with my whole self.[29] There is nothing in the *It* world which can prepare me for such a choice or which can make it easier. I am not closer to such a spiritual experience by rejecting the world of sense experience, nor am I given some advantage by having clever or profound ideas. All of these things belong to the world of *It* and cannot lead from *It* to the *Thou*. Buber's rejection of natural theology at this point is as radical as Karl Barth's. "Everything," writes Buber, "that has ever been devised and contrived in the time of the human spirit as precept, alleged preparation, practice, or meditation, has nothing to do with the primal, simple fact of the meeting."[30] The mystery is in God's presence, the quality of *Thou* present through all things yet not in all things. It is analogous to the human sphere of *I-Thou* relation. Love is not brown eyes, yet through those brown eyes love becomes expressive—but in such a way that the eyes become incidental to the meeting. Robert Rosthal, writing in the "Translator's Introduction" of Marcel's *Creative Fidelity,* summarizes a similar stance of Marcel's:

> Being itself is indefinable, and the Absolute Thou, God, whom Marcel identifies with being, is not the object of a rational theology: any attempt to prove his existence or define his nature is futile. It is in the mutuality or reciprocity of personal relationship, of which fidelity is the supreme example, that we gain access to being, that we can have some intimation of the Absolute Thou.[31]

Buber continues his discussion of God and the world:

> Men do not find God if they stay in the world. They do not find Him if they leave the world. He who goes out with his whole being to meet his *Thou* and carries to it all being that is in the world, finds Him who cannot be sought.
>
> Of course God is the "wholly Other"; but He is also the wholly Same, the wholly Present. Of course He is the Mysterium Tremendum that appears and overthrows; but He is also the mystery of the self-evident, nearer to me than my *I*.
>
> If you explore the life of things and of conditioned being you come to the unfathomable, if you deny the life of things and of conditioned being you stand before nothingness, if you hallow this life you meet the living God.[32]

Although many believe that Buber becomes a pantheist at this point, I do not believe that the charge can be fully substantiated. What is being affirmed is a mysticism which more implies a doctrine of continuing creation than a pantheism. In any strict pantheistic scheme, even the world of *It* would be an encounter with God.

The exclusive, all-encompassing nature of the *I-Thou* relationship which I share with another is also characteristic of my relationship with God. The distinction rests in the fact that my human *I-Thou* encounter always ends by resolving itself into an *I-It*. The cosmic inclusion by which everything is perceived and understood, which is characteristic of the human *I-Thou* relation, ceases to be operative or relevant in the *It* world of multiple proportions—as the shared moment of adoration with a child turns to anger and action when he carelessly wanders into the street. However, in my *I-Thou* relation with God, unconditional exclusiveness and unconditional inclusiveness are one. In terms of this true relationship, I do not renounce the world but am able to comprehend it on its *true* basis—that is, as an expression of creative order. Here, Buber is once again in danger of abandoning his ontological stance and appealing to a deus ex machina solution to the problem of synthesizing the worlds of *I-Thou* and *I-It*.

At this point, one is almost dramatically aware of one of the differences between Buber's thought and traditional Platonic metaphysical idealism. Within the Greek tradition, the divine properties of God's omniscience, omnipotence, and omnipresence—in short, God's perfection—would preclude the kind of relationship which Buber claims for the *I-Eternal Thou*. Buber's *I-Thou* relation is time-full; it is *now*, and it is a true relation within which action and reaction, or (more accurately) genuine communion takes place. The terms *time-full* and *now* (as opposed to *timeful* and the *present*) are used to indicate a condition of awareness other than *clock time*, a meta-time which transcends the self-distinctive passage of moment to moment. More will be said concerning this in chapter 3.

My subjectivity is confronted by the Subjectivity of God. Thus God *can* be angry, joyful, pleased or displeased, loving or wrathful with me as I respond or do not respond to his presence. Consequently, we need God and God needs us; "You need God, in order to be—and God needs you, for the very meaning of your life." The world is part of divine destiny; "there is a becoming of the God that is."[33] The world and man participate in the expression of divine meaning—not in essence as the Gnostics would suggest, but in responsive action as suggested by a doctrine of creation. With this in mind, we can see why Martin Buber has found such friends among the "process" theologians. However, it is important to consider carefully the use of words here. To bring together *destiny* and *becoming,* the *Eternal Thou* and *the God that is,* does not mean that Buber has slipped back into the metaphysical dualism that has plagued Christian thought for such a long time—the futile effort to combine Greek monism (with its absolutes) with Hebraic monotheism (with its *God who acts*). That is, *destiny* does not suggest, Here is a goal or end toward which God is moving and which, upon arrival, is total, complete, perfectly realized Reality. It is, I believe, closer to Buber's intention to assert that destiny is better understood as *nature* than *end*. God's nature is to *be* and to *be with*; ours is to *be with* God. In the same way, *Eternal* applied to God does not suggest so much timeless perfection (which would, of course, permit no change) as it does a continuing actualization, a continuing timefulness. This will be given more extensive consideration in chapter 3.

It might be helpful at this point to note that Buber does make a distinction between *destiny* and *fate*. As opposed to *destiny, fate* is that word which we use to describe the course of life determined not by the *Eternal Thou,* but the world of *It*. For those who either reject the *Eternal Thou,* who have refused to make themselves available for that encounter, or for those who claim no awareness of Him, the alternative *fate* becomes some variant of the world of *It*. I can consider it the power of cause-effect, Nature, or some irrational power of destruction—whatever *it* is, my life is finally and ultimately controlled by this force. When I subscribe to such a belief, I resign myself to the thought that I have little or no control over what happens to me. Such a subscription precludes any "reversal," any appeal to a final subjective Reality. It is this stance I have taken if I state: "When my number's up, my number's up," or "If the bullet has my name on it, there's nothing I can do," or, euphemistically, "That's the way the cookie crumbles." It is true that when I have taken my stand within the world of *It* I have relieved myself of the responsibility of fulfilling my destiny; of responding creatively in the presence of God, which is an awesome task demanding my total involvement. But when I lose my *destiny*, when I deny its reality or validity, I have to pay the price of my loss of ontological freedom which is irrelevant to the world of *It*. Only in the face of destiny am I free to define myself, to *be* myself. In the realm of *fate* that freedom is taken from me. I am exposed to suffering the consequences of life. Even for the nihilistic existentialist who speaks of radical freedom, my encounter with Nothingness forces me to choose my own *essence*. However, existential freedom is relative, conditioned by fate. Any thought of genuine choice is an illusion. The essence I choose is simply the temporary mode of self-expression—like Camus' Sisyphus pushing his ever-returning stone to the top of the mountain, I must *consider* myself happy, but I can never *be* happy. The fact that I believe in such fate does not assure its reality or any reality. It is only the imaginative expression of my self-will.

> The unbelieving core in the self-willed man can perceive nothing but unbelief and self-will, establishing of a purpose and devising of a means. Without sacrifice and without grace, without meeting and without presentness, he has as his world a mediated world cluttered with purposes. His world cannot be anything else, and its name is fate. Thus with all his sovereignty he is wholly and inextricably entangled in the unreal.[34]

For Buber, to deliver the life of *Thou* over to the world of *It* is simply a tragic mistake; it is, as the early Greek tragedians were well aware, the realm of tragedy. When subjectivity and sensitivity, self-consciousness and love, are governed by necessity, objectivity, and indifference, tragedies are bound to result.

To give primacy to the world of *I-It* is not only the source of tragedy, it is also the ground of evil. *I-It* is not evil in itself; as a primary word it is most necessary to life and its effective expression. It is only when *I-It* assumes the ontological priority, the authority, and role of *I-Thou* that it becomes the source of evil—when, for example, face-saving or pride prolong a war at the needless expense of human life, or when repressive conformity to custom or opinion deprives one of his individuality or creative expression. The misuse of *I-It* is evil for two reasons: it reverses the natural and created priority of the *I-Thou* over the *I-It,* which results in the kind of tragic conditions previously described; and it robs a man of the possibility of true fulfillment, of the reality of his own *I,* of authentic subjectivity.

It is in terms of the previous understanding of fate and destiny, necessity and freedom, *I-It* and *I-Thou,* that Buber attempts to overcome the problem of Kant's bifurcated world:

> If I consider necessity and freedom not in worlds of thought but in the reality of my standing before God, if I know that "I am given over for disposal" and know at the same time that "It depends on myself," then I cannot try to escape the paradox that has to be lived by assigning the irreconcilable propositions to two separate realms of validity; nor can I be helped to an ideal reconciliation by any theological device: but I am compelled to take both to myself, to be lived together, and in being lived they are one.[35]

Buber believes validity of such a position must rest not in an appeal to some transcendent Truth—that would be self-defeating; the validity, rather, is to be found in the consistency of living itself. It is found in the continuous confrontation with the *Eternal Thou* who never ceases to be *Thou* for us, the One who can never be expressed but only addressed. It may be that I can believe myself to be estranged from God or remote from God or even alone, but what I know is not the absence of God but self-withdrawal. Such a withdrawal may make it seem as though God is not there, that the world is comprised of two separate realities, but this experience soon exposes itself as a distortion of reality or demands that we drop the *I-Thou* dimension of life altogether. Such an experience, because of Buber's basic dialogical position, must be considered a psychological aberration rather than an ontological shift. The experience of self-withdrawal is one phase of the natural pattern of "reversal;" any abandonment of *I-Thou* is an invitation to tragedy, cynicism, and isolation.

Thus far in this chapter, I have considered the basic insights of Buber's theological position concerning identity. Much more could be said about all the points, and, of course, any extended study of Buber would include many more considerations. Enough has been written, however, to give us a common vocabulary and base for the consideration of a new theological position which uses Buber's distinction between *I-It* and *I-Thou* as a point of departure. It is this assertion of primary words which comprehends and employs the theological insights of the most revolutionary of the nineteenth-century movements. It takes *Being* seriously in its time-full sense; it recognizes human limitations; it is sensitive to those priorities which seem to govern the lives of all men. However, before drawing out the implications which such insights have for theology, I shall suggest some modifications of Buber's thought, which I believe necessary.

As stated at the beginning of the chapter, reality is my *being* here and now. It is important to note at once that this is not a solipsistic claim. The phrase *my being* is not the claim of sheer individuality or aloneness. *My being* (or my life) is never lived in isolation nor am I ever conscious of any isolation as personal uniqueness. I *am* within context. More truly, I emerge out of context and consider the *I* which emerges as the expression of a potential which could only be realized through such a context. *Who* I am and *what* I am are thus developed out of the nature and extent of my interaction with *my* world, i.e., that world into which *I* have come through some creative act for which I can assume no responsibility or knowledge. *Who* I am emerges from my intimate and personal relations with those who address me as *Thou* and whom I address as *Thou; what* I am results from my interaction and experience of the things of this world, those things with which I am juxtaposed or which I possess, control, or contact. For Buber, as we have noted, there is a radical qualitative distinction between these two spheres of life, with priority being accorded to the *I-Thou* relation both in time and importance. The *I* which emerges from the *I-Thou* finds itself within the context of *It* with the ability to focus on any instance of *It* at hand—whether that is a physical object, an idea, or even a feeling. All this is possible for Buber because he maintains that my prenatal situation is that of an a priori potential *Thou* which only begins to realize its potential for individuality in the initial union with and subsequent separation from my mother. The difficulties of such a position are apparent: How can the initial separation of the *I* from its *Thou* be explained? How can I experience that for which I have no potential or nature? If Buber's *I-Thou* priority can be maintained, how can both *I-Thou* and *I-It* be primary words?

I think one must begin by maintaining that there is in that mysterious creative event which I am, an a priori *It* as well as *Thou;* that both are evident when I am still in the womb; that what I receive through the umbilical cord is as basic a context for me as my prenatal personal identity. My active *Being*—my *is*ness—is as evident in the world of *It* as my *am*ness is in the world of *Thou*. The nature of such *being*, or at least the nature of the expression of *being*, may vary, but priority can only be a relative, maybe even arbitrary thing. Though an exact correlation is difficult to make, it appears that Gabriel Marcel intends to make a similar point by referring to human existence as "incarnate being," i.e., that affective unity which I have with my body: "To be incarnated is to appear to oneself as a body, as this particular body, without being identified with it nor distinguished from it—identification and distinction being correlative operations which are significant only in the realm of objects."[36] Incarnate being is being-in-the-world; it is a participation, not a relation or communication.

I think it is evident that there is such a world of *It*, of things, organizations, and ideas, the experience of which is radically different from my relation to another in love. But each of these worlds exists with its own nature and character. The world of *It* is the world of cause and effect, of natural laws, of mathematical relation, of census and consensus; the world of *Thou* is one of personal identity, unity, oneness—a world in which cause and effect, time and place have little or no meaning. The world of *It* is the world of my physical body which needs food and sleep; which responds to drugs and medicines or selectively responds to the surgeon's knife; which breaks when I subject it to too much stress; which dies predictably and unavoidably under specified circumstances of alteration, deprivation, or ingestion. To *be*, my body must respond faultlessly to the world of *It*, for without it I simply *am* not. On the other hand, my *Thou* operates seemingly with total disregard for my *It* body. Love is not only blind to the world of *It* —it usually is deaf and numb as well. In fact, there are times when my total disregard of my body, because of my involvement with a *Thou*, may lead to injury or death.

This observation points beyond itself and indicates that the situation is not one of simple disparity. It does seem possible for the world of *I-Thou* to intersect the world of *I-It*. When that powerful and personal relationship which we identify with love does exist, it seems to exert a kind of natural priority over the *I-It*. Heroic epics, from the *Iliad* on, have witnessed to the power of love—its creative and destructive force. What actually happens is not a cancellation of the *I-It* world by the *I-Thou*—only chaos would result from that—but the course of cause and effect is altered by the introduction of a new or modified cause. The effect of such an injection is not to disrupt the nature of the causal principle but to deny it total determinism. It is to provide new power or motivation in terms of a new identity, so that when I then place my *I* into context with an *It*, the direction of that encounter is altered accordingly. The radical form of this for religion, of course, has been the conversion experience, that which reverses my direction on the Damascus road because I am a "new" man. My identity has been altered or deepened because of my encounter with God; consequently, my way in the world of *It* has been altered: my thoughts cease being self-centered, my actions display generosity rather than greed, my motivation has shifted from fear to love. We need not take so dramatic an instance to make the point; even the agonizing experience of stopping smoking, drinking, or taking drugs can be the result of a change in who I am, whom I love.

More clinically, just on the basis of my physical body I am able to see or feel the effect which the *I* can have on the normal context of cause-effect relationship. Contemporary psychology and medicine have alerted us to the fact that it is not uncommon for the *I* (more, that is, than just the physical operation of the brain) to control the health and /or sickness of the body. It is possible, according to psychosomatic medicine, for me to worry myself sick. It is also possible for me to retard or speed my recovery from an illness by determination of my will. In a more conscious way, the advocates of yoga claim that by concentration I can actually control certain functions of my body, e.g., the rate of my heartbeat. Though the contexts of *I* and *It* are readily distinguishable, evidence is such that I cannot deny they are interrelated.

Even on a less personal level, we can see this in operation in governments and institutions which express corporate human interaction. One of the reasons for changing administrations or personnel is that we know that we are altering the cause-effect syndrome for a particular situation. When the Democrats or Republicans have been in office for twenty years or so—it's "time for a change." The alteration comes not from a change in the Constitution or even in laws so much as a change in the *identity* of the political leadership. Identity is more the product of *I-Thou* than *I-It*. This effect is nowhere more evident than in the Supreme Court and is the reason for the most elaborate of procedures followed in selection. The law of the land is determined by the interpretation of these men; as the court changes, so does its interpretation of the Constitution.

But the relationship within such an infrastructure of *Thou* and *It* is not one-way. While the *I* can impose itself upon the world of *It* and can alter the pattern of cause and effect, there is evidence that the world of *It* can affect the identity of the *I*. Such evidence comes to us from a variety of sources. Psychologists and physicians now believe that the cycle of extreme manic-depressive reaction may be caused more by chemical imbalance than by some previous mental trauma. Tranquilizers and lithium have already enabled physicians to control the extremes of this condition—a very dramatic incursion of the world of *It* into the world of *I*. We also know that severe depression can be the result of physical disease such as mononucleosis or the effect of the postpartum reaction after childbirth. We are told by users that certain drugs such as LSD and its variants are "mind-blowing," i.e., they are capable of altering for good or ill the personality of the user. More evidence is suggested by the recent hypothesis that human behavioral patterns are directly influenced by the number of *Y* factors in our genes. And, of course, what man does not fear the onset of senility which cripples mind and body?

In some mysterious way, the contexts of *I-Thou* and *I-It* are interrelated. Each can affect the other, each can alter the other, but neither can totally control or eliminate the other. Such a situation does seem to suggest that *both* contexts are primary ones and that both participate in the expression of my *being* here and now. However, it precludes the Kantian dichotomy because it recognizes my knowing or acting simply as expressions of my *being,* not as metaphysical "orders" which prescribe it. *Being* is naturally and necessarily interrelated; it is possible for the worlds of *Thou* and *It* to affect each other and, to follow the lead of Buber here, to even become one another. My *Thou* is not permanently a *Thou*—such an existential experience cannot be sustained: when my wife is giving a dinner or planning a trip, life is all "business"—my *Thou* has become an *It*. The reverse transformation is, of course, true; *Its* can become *Thous*. Any new person to whom I am introduced is first of all an *It* with whom I may later share the relation of *Thou*. Love at first sight is more the gift of fantasy than reality.

This last observation, the interaction of *Thous* and *Its,* raises the genuine and very difficult problem of identity. If it is true that the *I-Thou* and the *I-It* relations are primary ones, both must tell me about myself, about *my being.* If it is true that the experience of each of these relations is qualitatively different, how is it possible for me to avoid a kind of ontological schizophrenia despite the evident interaction? The answer in part lies in a further clarification of these experiences. The *It* context controls more than just the relation of my body to the laws and forces of the physical world, my response to gravity, heat, light, and oxygen. The *It* world also includes the socio-political-economic world within which *I* live the majority of my life and through which I learn about *what I am.* That is, *what* I learn about myself in this context is more than what chemistry, biology, and physics can tell me. It is also what the "social" sciences—sociology, psychology, economics, and politics—can tell me. One point to note here is that human behavior is so consistent, so much the product of psychological patterns and social "laws," that the system of cause-effect is operative to the degree that the word *science* is applicable. But in all of these experiences of pure science or social science, I am dealing with an abstraction of my *being;* for while these disciplines can inform me "in general" or "on the average" what I am, they cannot tell me *specifically* what I am or take into account the differences who-I-am may make in what I am. In education we often find students whose college board scores and high-school records definitely indicate *C* work in college, but who actually do *B* work. We call it "overachieving," although it is really an expression of identity. Here the spheres of *Thou* and *It* tend to converge.

Our response to the world of *It* is further complicated by the fact that the context of *It* is not uniform, but takes on the character of the interactants. My relationship to an *It* house or an *It* law, e.g., gravity, is different from my relationship to a person who is an *It*, i.e., one of the general public rather than my *Thou*. In both cases (house or person), the character of the *It* relation remains: it is objective to me and operates on the cause-effect principle governed by time and /or space. Yet, the nature of these two cases is so different I am apt to treat them as two separate contexts.

In short, there seems to be room for a general or casual relationship with another person which one can designate *Me-You*—a category which falls within the context of the *It* world.[37] Such a category recognizes the dynamics of rational and emotional responses which characterize human relationships, as opposed to the relationships of inanimate objects. The *Me-You* relationship has its own character, no little part of which is its universal human potential for being *I-Thou*. The *Me* character is that which I have by accident of birth—that I was born of these parents with these particular convictions and ideas, in this country, at this point of history, in this year, etc. Such coincidental contingencies have shaped my basic approach to life, my language, my values, my ethics, my religion, my way of life—even my palate. Through a variety of educational processes, I have become what I am. It is commonplace to hear someone declare that to have fought in a war, to have lived through a depression, etc., leaves an indelible mark upon one's character and thought—upon his *I*. However, the point is that far more subtle things than wars and depressions affect what I am. There are some people in our culture, for example, who seem to fall totally into the category which sociologists call "other-directed" people. Religion, values, attitudes, vices, virtues—all are dictated by the pressures of parents, peers, society in general. An extreme instance of such an analysis might be as follows: my minister "gives" me my faith, the Republican party my politics, Kiwanis my civic responsibility, American Legion my fun and foreign policy, United Fund my charity, television my life-style, and so on—H. Richard Niebuhr states that it is more true to say that I am lived rather than that I live.[38] It is very possible to spend one's entire life being a *Me*.

But because *Me* (or *You*) is an expression of the "It" category, it is objective; it is something extraneous to that intimate personal experience which I reserve for the words *I* and *Thou*. Yet because *Me* is an accepted expression of identity, it is also subjective. That is, though an individual may be a *Me* living in a world of other *Mes* who share all his contingencies, traits, values, and thoughts, he still knows that he is a *Me*. He can stand at a distance from his *Me*-self and analyze it even though that is a painful and disillusioning project at times. In fact, it is sometimes so painful to realize that there is so little unique about us—that we truly are other-directed—it takes a counsellor or psychologist to help us retrieve some sense of individualized identity. But what about that *I* that does the knowing in this case? Simply by the fact that it knows the *Me*, it is no longer identical to the *Me*. *I* transcends the *Me* in its unselfconscious subjectivity. As some writers would suggest, this *I* is the active knower who can never be known. However, if our thesis is correct, the definition cannot be left that vague.

Under the circumstances previously described, it is possible to say that I can have an *I-Me* relationship with myself, though the "relationship" under such circumstances is simulated, not real. Very often the internal dialogues which I hold with myself seem to be of this structure. When I question my actions, values, and beliefs, my *I* seems to play the role of interlocutor in the search for an appropriate self-expression. By this I do not mean what has historically been identified as my conscience. Conscience is the conditioned moral sensitivity held and expressed by the *Me*-self. There are times when the action upon which I decide is contrary to my conscience. Anthropologists and psychologists have given us enough information about the conscience and its education and /or development for us to completely rule out that it is my "true" self or, more absolutely, the undeniable voice of God. I do not mean to imply by this that conscience is not a powerful standardizing judge of my actions, a powerful censor of my thoughts. What I want to imply is that I experience my conscience; that I recognize that I am in relationship with my conscience as I am with my *Me*-self. Consequently, my *I* must be something other than conscience or the *Me*-self. Very often, when my *I* is acting as the interlocutor in the *I-Me* context, what I am searching for is not a new or more developed expression of the *Me*-self but rather that expression of the *Me*-which-I-already-am which will best meet the *It* context. Conscience is a relational function of the social self, and its "content" is acquired.

There are three implications, at least, concerning the structure of relationships which can be drawn from these observations. The first is that it is possible for me to have an *I-Me* "relationship" that is creative and that will result in a new or modified expression of the *Me*-self. Such a change or genuine alteration can be the result of an earlier and corresponding change in an *I-Thou* relationship which I share with another or with God. My understanding and response to the world and my participation in it are a reflection—passively or actively—of *who* I am. When *I* effect such a change in the *Me*-self (as opposed to simply letting the changes be imposed upon me by outside pressures), it is an attempt to give myself a more adequate or relevant self-expression in the *It* dimension of my *being*. This may result in minor alterations of my social or political stance or in radical changes in my whole life-style. Joining a commune or a religious order, or initiating a program of self-analysis could each result in a radical *I-Me* alteration.[39]

The second structural implication concerns the possibility of a *Me-You* relationship. In fact, there never can be such a human relationship so exclusively confined to the *It* dimension of *being*. However, the *Me-You* relationship, as symbolic of our public and formalized life, is so prominent in our day-to-day existence that we are inclined to give it independent status. It is the world of human laws and customs, manners and public morals, standards and causes, organizations and corporations, of, in short, cabbages and kings. But when my acculturated self (*Me*-self) is in relation with a *You*-self, I am always aware, consciously or subconsciously, of the context, the rules of the particular game. The *Me*-self can never totally divorce itself from the *I*, although we tend to live a large percentage of our lives in gamesmanship. Within the *Me-You* category, the relation is never totally inclusive and must be ontologically superficial. Of course, it is true that many people attempt to exist on a *Me-You* basis, but that could hardly be called *living*. The existential element is totally excluded from such an other-directed life. Another way of stating the same point is to note that the *Me*-self, as an acculturated self, is in the past. It is caused and effected. Although it seems to exist in the present, its expression is prefigured. The Zem Zem always act like Zem Zem; they have done it for years. . . . The *I*, on the other hand, is existential, is *now* and as such is open and free. Such openness and freedom in the realm of identity terrifies many people, for if there is no present *Thou* in their lives to whom to relate, only the existential abyss, the void, seems evident to them. Consequently, they flee back to the safety of the *Me*-self, behind which they hope they can successfully hide, both from others and from themselves. These are the people who say: "It's best not to ask these questions of identity," or "I just keep busy so that I don't have to think about such things." For such people, life is inauthentic; it is an endless struggle to submerge self-awareness, to suppress the authentic self, the *I*. Psychiatrists' offices, hospitals, and bars are filled with people who have not been successful in such a flight from reality.

The third implication of the ontological nature of the *I-Me* relation is that there can never be a sustained *Me-Thou* or *I-You* association. For another to be my *Thou*, I must be open and responsive in such a way that the relationship is subject to subject, i.e., *I* to *Thou,* which transcends the public, acculturated *Me*-self. *Thou,* as we have noted, is a word of intimate, not casual, relation. If I put another off by my adherence to models of politeness or by refusing to respond to their genuine offer of meeting and self-exposure, then the *I-Thou* cannot take place, and the intimacy implied by the word *Thou* cannot occur. The relationship remains in the *It* world, primarily an expression of *Me-You.* If the *Me-Thou* and *I-You* encounters can be said to happen at all, it is as momentary gestures or invitations to move into a meaningful relationship.

Thus the possibilities for a relationship with another person seem to be summarized symbolically in the following way: *I-It, Me-You, (I)me-You(Thou),* and *I-Thou.* We shall examine each of these in turn. I can have an *I-It* relation in which I simply regard the other as a thing with which I am in contact. This is to disregard his or her personal commonality with the rest of mankind. I judge that this was the case for those responsible for the attempted genocide of the Jews in Germany and is the case wherever prejudice—particularly racial—occurs. Other instances of this *I-It* relationship take place, at least symbolically, when certain of my dealings with the state or government are put on a computer basis. This is manifestly true for such standardized matters as taxes in which a certain percentage of my income, as with all incomes, is turned over to the government for its operation, but it can also be true for welfare and relief relations with the government which in the name of *Me-You* concern, often do carry the stigma of the *I-It,* a relation which the recipients find degrading and embarrassing. Reformers then try to bring such relations to at least the next level, the *Me-You* relation.

The *Me-You* relationship, which we have discussed at some length, is the relation of people in terms of their cultural contexts. This is true for individuals and for those corporate groups which represent us as individuals. On the corporate level, it is the relation of Britons and Americans, of Republicans and Democrats, of Blacks and Whites, of Rich and Poor, of the Educated and the Uneducated—or, for that matter, any group which assumes a set of common characteristics, styles, or causes. The *Me-You* category is the proper one for public officials and their constituencies, or of public corporate entities which take the public's humanity seriously; it should characterize the relationship of cordial concern and common need between nations or within the United Nations; it is all the relationships of responsibility between government, citizens, etc. This is a good and proper relationship within the major category of the "It-world." It is only destructive or harmful when the "individuality" of the participant is totally accounted for by such a relationship, when the existential *I* is totally repressed in order that conformity or security may be totally achieved. Then the *Me-You* relationship becomes inauthentic because it is being asked to express that which by its nature it cannot include—that thinking, critical, restless person *who* I am. When my action or life is not part of this sheer corporate structure of the public world, then my relationship is of a different nature and should be called an *(I)Me-You(Thou)*.

The *(I)Me-You(Thou)* relationship is that in which I acknowledge that the other to whom I am related is not a statistic or a cultural collage but my potential *Thou*.[40] I meet such a person in terms of his context as he meets me in terms of mine, knowing at the same time that there is more to this other than just his public expression of self. But this context also has to do with myself. In such a relationship, I am existentially aware of my *Me*-self; I am aware of my public postures, values, beliefs, and talents. The point is that I am aware that *I* am more than just the sum of these things; that meaningful as they are, they may change, be sacrificed, or be reinforced by the life which *I am now*. *(I)Me* existence is transitional; it belongs to the *It* world but is potentially *Thou;* it is in the present but is potentially in the *now* (timeful but potentially time-full); it is here but is potentially nonspatial. For example, when I say to one with whom I share such a relation, "I'll meet you at the Park St. station at 3:30 P.M.," time and place are considered factors necessary to my negotiation within the *It* world of cause and effect. But I am likewise aware that it is the meeting which is of importance to me, not the time or place. For such a meeting, my *I* is never fixed in a "Me" category though it is expressing itself through one. I may say to my friend, "How are you?" Under the circumstances just described, the question is ambivalent. My friend can either respond, "Fine, thank you," which greets me but at the same time holds me off at arm's length, or he may decide to tell me how he is. If he decides to respond truthfully, the *You* relationship moves into *Thou* and awaits my responsive reaction. The fact that one could do several variations on the theme—I could ask my original question of greeting in such a way as to preclude any intimacy—only shows the fluid state of such a relationship. *(I)Me-You(Thou)* seems to be the natural structure of genuine human relationship. It acknowledges that objective, corporate relationships do exist and may minimize my existential involvement; it also acknowledges that an *I-Thou* relationship could occur, which could creatively alter who I am and permit me to know the deepest sense of self.

It is the identity created in the *I-Thou* relation and incorporated into my self-awareness which gives me the security to make myself available to another whom I may meet in the *(I)Me* context. Without the experience of *Thou*, without love, I am defensive and distrustful and find it exceedingly hard to "risk" myself in such a relationship in order to permit the development of an *I-Thou*. Without the security of love, I resist letting any relationship get beyond the *Me-You* involvement. I can live well enough under these conditions, but life, in the last analysis, will always seem empty, unfulfilled, and—perhaps in the end—even absurd.

The relationship of depth is the *I-Thou* encounter, though *communion* would perhaps be a better word if we could rid it of its connotations of softness and sweetness. The *I-Thou* is most accurately described by Buber and those who follow his lead as love.[41] It is that experience of encounter in which my attention is not focused on myself but on my relation to the other. The experience of love is the experience of care, respect, responsibility, and knowledge—much in form and way in which Erich Fromm describes these qualities in his book *The Art of Loving.*[42] But I would go on to suggest that within the *I-Thou* relation itself, which is an existential moment, I am aware only of the ecstasy of the encounter for which Fromm's terms are abstract descriptions, analytically separable but existentially indistinguishable. What I discover in the *I-Thou* encounter is that my identity is rooted in love which incorporates these four characteristics. Consequently, care, respect, responsibility, and knowledge are (or should be) involved in both *(I)-Me* and *Me-You* relationships to the degree that my personal identity is involved in each. Gabriel Marcel makes the same point in terms of responsibility: "I claim to be a person insofar as I assume responsibility for what I do and what I say. But to whom am I responsible, to whom do I acknowledge my responsibility? We must reply that I am conjointly responsible both to myself and to everyone else, and that this conjunction is precisely characteristic of an engagement of the person, that it is the mark proper to the person."[43]

I should care for all men, be respectful of all men, be responsive to all men, and know all men. Obviously, human limitations prescribe severe limitations on such a universal potential. Accordingly, I respond to others in keeping with the nature of my relationship to them. For example, as a human being, I wish to aid those whose homes and communities have been destroyed by such disasters as hurricanes and floods, and I respond to this need on the *Me-You* basis through nationally or internationally organized relief organizations. To the needs of my students and friends, I respond on a more immediate and personal basis, the individual responses of *(I)Me.* Under these circumstances, I do what I can in terms of all other responsibilities I have accepted. In the existential experience of love, however, there are no limitations, no relative claims; the one claim—at the moment—is complete. Under these circumstances, man often does that which seems absurd under more objective conditions, e.g., the sacrifice of his life to redeem a situation which is hopeless. Such extremity, however, is confined to the moments of intimate encounter, of *I-Thou* relationship. Once the relationship has moved into the *(I)Me* context out of the *I-Thou* relation, more objective considerations are taken into account. Before an individual sacrifices himself in a hopeless situation involving his friend, he remembers his obligations to his wife and children, to his other friends who depend upon him, his obligations to society and the potential of his own self-expression.

A conclusion we can draw from this is that the line dividing the *(I)Me-You(Thou)* from the *I-Thou* is so fine that it is practically undetectable or undefinable. When the transition to *I-Thou* occurs, it is a creative thing, having to do with my identity; after such an encounter, I am never the same person I was before it took place. This is even true within a continuing relationship such as a marriage. The marriage relationship does not remain static any more than other human relationships. Either it is moving in depth to a new and increasingly meaningful identity-in-relation, or it is withdrawing into an ever-increasing *(I)Me* context of convenience, perhaps even into the *Me-You* relationship which the normal conditions of marriage strain in terms of necessary (or expected) intimacy. In the *Me-You* stage, the marriage is usually heading for divorce. The expected intimate gestures and expressions of love and the reality of the impersonal *Me-You* relationship cannot happily coexist for any two given people. The emotional and intellectual strains preclude the security and confidence needed for an authentic marriage of exposure and trust. But the point we must consider at the present moment is this: the most intimate, meaningful, totally complete relationship an individual has is that of the *I-Thou*. It is generally preceded and followed by the *(I)Me-You(Thou)* relationship. The difference between the two periods of *(I)Me* relation is one of intensity, enhanced by anticipation or memory, and one of identity which emerges from the encounter.

A man's *(I)Me* relation with his wife should always be on the verge of breaking into an *I-Thou*, so that the event can happen a "hundred" times a day, provided you have enough hours together. Family life is a life of *(I)Me-You(Thou)* which each shares with each other member of the family; there is a mutuality in love (care, respect, responsibility, and knowledge) which is continually leading various members of the family into an *I-Thou* encounter. Of course, the process of "falling in love" is much the same: the *(I)Me* relation I share with another is finally consummated in an *I-Thou*; I return to the structure of the *(I)Me* relation, but the dynamics of the relationship are different because *I* am now different.

A side note about a common tragedy could be mentioned here. Because the *I-Thou* is the basic fulfilling relationship of our lives, we often, in a desperate effort to "achieve" or "find" it (neither of which, as Buber indicates, can we do arbitrarily), fantasize such a relationship on the basis of the incomplete care, respect, response, and knowledge of the *(I)Me* relation. This is particularly true under the emotional extremities of our sexual relationships. The orgasmic identity is taken to be the *I-Thou* encounter, when in fact it is only the sometime response to, or expression of, the *I-Thou* relation. There are, obviously, times when the sexual has nothing to do with the depth of intimacy involved in the *I-Thou*—Buber's *I-Thou* with a tree could be a classic example. The general confusion of experience and expectation between sex and the *I-Thou* has led to many unhappy and premature marriages.

But we are at the point now where we can no longer avoid the difficult problem of identity involved. We have claimed that the *I-Thou* experience is a creative one which has to do in a very basic way with *who* I am. We have likewise said that in the living of our lives, we are in a constant state of transition between the *(I)Me-You(Thou)* relation and the *I-Thou* relation. The *(I)Me* context is not a creative one in terms of *who* I am, though it does seem to affect *what* I am and what I do; but at the same time, I am aware that such a relation could change, could become personally creative. The *I-Thou* is always potentially evident in the *(I)Me* relation. The question of identity is this: Is there a continuity in terms of self-consciousness which exists between the *I* of the *(I)Me* and the *I* of the *I-Thou*? Am *I* the same person who "yesterday" was acquainted with a woman but "today" love her as my wife? If the *I* of the two experiences is one, then are not the two experiences merely different in degree rather than in kind? Or, if they are different in kind, then am I not caught in the Kantian dilemma of basically unrelated worlds?

That my expressed self-consciousness within the two contexts may be only a difference in degree has been eliminated by our initial acceptance of the qualitative distinction between *I-It* and *I-Thou;* that there may be a self-conscious continuity between the two contexts is not necessarily precluded by this fact. Such a continuity must be grounded in that which is *prior* to either relation if the Kantian dilemma is to be avoided. Thus it is important to look at the condition we call self-consciousness.

When I say that I am "self-conscious," what do I mean? Am I conscious of my total self? The very fact that I can be conscious of myself, i.e., objectify or view myself, shows that I am also in some way "outside" myself looking in. There seems to be what we have previously called the transcendent self, the active knower who does the knowing and therefore can never be known itself. Even the sentence structure—the double indication of *I*—denoted this. If there is such a transcendent self, can it be said that this self is truly coexistent with the self that is known? If that be true, then it seems that we are again caught in the Kantian dilemma, for in coexistence as opposed to identity there would never be any possibility of *knowing* whether the two *I*'s are one; the opacity of the transcendent *I* would simply preclude any attempt at identification. Therefore we would have to conclude that the social self (the objective, contingent *I*) simply expresses a reality that is ontologically distinct from the transcendent *I*. In this case, even the word *coexistent* becomes inappropriate, for if we could apply the word *existent* to each of these expressions of *I*, we have merely shifted the burden of distinction to *that* word; the condition of distinction would remain. There is still a further problem if we want to think of the two *I*'s in this transcendent-social way: we are left with the problem of claiming that one of these *I*'s is "more real" than the other. However, as with consideration of *coexisting,* such a distinction would merely mean that we have shifted the burden of argument to the definition of the word *reality*. To do justice to both *realities* is simply to find ourselves back with Kant. To eliminate one reality is to declare one "self" as merely appearance or as imaginative projection, neither of which possibilities seems in accord with our original ontological analysis.

It would seem that the previously discussed dilemmas about self-consciousness result from two things: they are structured, implicitly if not explicitly, by the Greek metaphysical distinction between appearance and reality and therefore inherit all the logical dilemmas that go with that stance; and it is perhaps the case that our earlier phenomenology is incorrect, that the new ontological consideration of *being* is excluded. With this in mind, let us take another look at self-consciousness.

What do I mean by the term *self-conscious?* Does this mean that I am conscious of me, of an objective, contingent self as was suggested earlier? I do not think that is the case, at least as far as the identity of the *I* is concerned. When I say to myself, "Look at you. Sitting there thinking. Is that who you are?," I realize that such self-consciousness in fact destroys the *self* of which it is supposed to be conscious. That is, the self doing the sitting and thinking no longer *is* at the moment that I begin to think about such sitting and thinking. The radical timefulness of my act precludes the duality implied by formal logic. One conclusion I must draw from this is that the ambiguity of formal logic is the result of its being an abstraction from reality rather than the expression of reality; logic is an expression of thought, not reason—a distinction which will be further explored in chapter 4. It might appear that one is caught here in some form of infinite regress—that I am thinking about thinking about thinking ad infinitum, but such speculation is not the result of the experience itself, but of the old metaphysics which could consider The Reality and thereby support mind-mirroring regression. If we take the act of *being* seriously, then the thought of my thinking is not an act of infinite regression but is the existential expression of my self; the previous thinking-self simply *is* no more except as a memory, which, after all, is present but only as a functional abstract.

The significance of this argument is that there can be only one genuine self, not two. There is not a transcendent self and an objective self. My experience of self is never so pure a distinction as either of those terms lead us to believe, nor is it ever so dual. The ontological experience is that self-consciousness is not a reflexive term. Rather, I know or *am* myself most authentically when I am *not* "self" aware. That is, self-awareness in the sense that I try to assess my character or personality is a kind of meaningless tautology of consciousness trying to catch hold of its own shadow and endeavoring to consider that shadow substance. Such self-awareness is an abstraction from reality, constructed out of memory and imagination, which can only tell us superficial and obvious things. For this reason, self-analysis in any depth is finally impossible. I am what I am *now* in the context of encounter in which I presently find myself, whether that be *It, You,* or *Thou.* In this light, one can be sympathetic with Sartre's judgment that "I am what others say that I am" as much as what I "know" or "think" myself to be. That consistency of character or pattern of behavior which I observe in my past actions is always "observed" from the vantage point of *now* which is beyond or outside of that consistency. I know that my *I-Thou* is never consistent; it is only creative, open, free, and unique. I know that my *Me-You* life is almost always consistent in keeping the cause-effect world within which it operates; however, I know that such a consistency can be changed when I so determine—as alcoholics so dramatically and courageously have shown in AA rehabilitation. Thus I move from self-consciousness, the intense experience of *my-being* in *I-Thou,* to self-awareness, the domination of form, law, and cause-effect action in *I-It;* but I am *self-conscious* in both cases. It is simply the nature of my awareness which is different. This is not a solution by semantics although it may at first appear so because it necessarily involves the presuppositions of the act of knowing.

The distinction between self-consciousness and self-awareness is ontologically genuine. It is phenomenologically apparent but experimentally indistinguishable. The potentiality of individuality, or what we could call the a priori integrity necessary for personal *being,* is sheer nonreflexive consciousness which becomes defined (in extension and limitation, in quality and quantity) as *I* or *self*-consciousness *within* the context of encounter. This nonreflexive consciousness is sometimes mistakenly or prematurely called "I" or "the radical I" or the "unique I" prior to encounter, but such designations ignore the encounter-implications inherent in such a claim. I believe that this is the mistake which H.R. Niebuhr makes in *The Responsible Self* when concerned about the same identity problem: "The radical action by which I am and by which I am present with this body, this mind, this emotional equipment, this religion, is not identifiable with any of the finite actions that constitute the particular elements in physical, mental, personal existence. In my social, ego-alter existence, I know that this intensely private experience of selfhood is not solipsistic" (p. 112). "How?" is the immediate response to such a claim. However, since this book was published posthumously, it would be wrong to state that Niebuhr would not have dealt with this problem in later revisions.

Thus self-consciousness becomes the prior condition of awareness, so that the term *self-awareness* is shorthand for *self-conscious awareness*—the awareness of *my-being* within the contexts of *Thou* and *It*.[44]

At first, this argument seems to put us back into the Kantian dilemma, but that is only if we neglect the fact that self-consciousness is prior and common to my awareness in each context. However, unless we can make a distinction between the types of awareness, we are denying that there is any qualitative distinction between the *I-Thou* and *I-It* encounters. To distinguish between my objective relationship to my desk and my subjective one to my friend is not difficult to do, but the problem becomes acute when dealing with the distinction between *I-Thou* and *(I)Me-You(Thou)* relations. Although the *(I)Me* relation is ontologically subsequent to the *I-Thou* relation, it is best for purposes of explication to begin with the *(I)Me* experience. The *(I)Me* experience of self-awareness is one of individuality and uniqueness. Although I have chosen and now execute a life-style, I am aware that I have so chosen and *am* so "freely." If my life-style is common to many, or at least commonly understood by many, I am still unique in and through such a contingency. What I have called the "*(I)Me* self-awareness" is the existential self-awareness; the self making, in its radical freedom, its own choice of expression or life-style in terms of its encounter with the world. This does not deny, however, any earlier or original *Thous* whose encounters have been formative for me, but it asserts that there are no *Thous* who are immediate to my life at the present moment. That I *must* choose under these conditions is part of my awareness of the radical timefulness of my life, my *being;* what I *may* choose is dependent upon my historical and biological contingencies. In any event, in the *(I)Me* existential experience I know myself at that moment to be radically and immediately central, alone, the Archimedean point of my universe. The world is *my* world as I see it, understand it, and react to it. It is not that I control it—or can even effectively shape its destiny; it is simply that I am the focus of meaning—the world's and mine. The character of this experience develops in divergent ways, depending upon the nature of the prior *I-Thou* relationships out of which the *(I)Me* has emerged. If my experience with *Thous* has been one of betrayal and rejection, then my existential response will be defensive and bitter, and I shall reject with mistrust any new overtures to encounter. If my experience with *Thous* has been frequent and meaningful, then my existential response will be open and altruistic, and I shall encourage any overture to encounter.

In the case of the negative development, the *(I)Me* nature is suspicious of *Thou* pretensions of the world and reacts accordingly. It is because this is true that we fear for our lives, our civilization, when any one man controls nuclear force in the world—that one man who may say, "Unless I can have my way, no one will have any way at all." But our illustration needn't be so dramatic. Many of us, most of us no doubt, have done destructive things, even affecting our own welfare, in order to prevent another from succeeding in some noble or generous cause. As the old adage has it, mankind is always ready to cut off its own nose to spite its face. For this reason, we all "take satisfaction" in another's misfortune or demise. After all, his meaning, in the last analysis, has no meaning for us. Or if it does have meaning for us, we then lament *our* loss, not his. The self-awareness of the *(I)Me* is isolated and defensive. In the final analysis, the world and those in it are against me. If we can understand this radical defensive isolation, then we can understand Winston Smith's action in Orwell's novel *1984*. When man is forced to face the "rats" of this world, he faces them in and for himself; all other relationships with the world and others assume a subordinate role. What remains is *my* world, *my* struggle, *my* meaning.

If this is the case, that self-awareness is isolated, defensive self-expression in *(I)Me*, why isn't the world in chaos? Why aren't we all out to cut each other's throats? History and politics have offered us several plausible reasons. One is fear: although I secretly know that I alone am important, that my life alone has any meaning, I recognize that others are stronger than I am, or are more intelligent, or are more powerful in a variety of ways; consequently, I shall so act as to get the most out of my relationships; I shall preserve as much meaning as possible for my life; I shall "cheat" or exploit the situation only when I can do so with some safety. Life for such a person is a struggle within a dangerous and threatening hierarchy; he must determine just where he is in that hierarchy and just what the limits of his self-expression can be. Such a life is precarious, yet there are few if any of us who do not know just exactly what I am writing about. We only need to think of the corruption within society about which each one of us knows—and says nothing—to know the power of the argument. To talk about, to reveal such corruption, would mean self-destruction. Consequently, since "Number One" is at stake, we keep silent. After all, we argue, what good is a safe, clean world if we are not around to enjoy it? The Mafia has prospered on such a philosophy for years, as have military and dictatorial powers.

Another reason for lack of chaos in such an atomistic world of meanings is that of cooperation, the social contract theories. In short, we need each other in order to survive in any meaningful way. I cannot take time to teach and write unless someone else is out growing crops and raising beef cattle. What both of us desire is, after all, the common good. No matter what we do in the way of work, no matter whether we agree or disagree on any given issue, both of us cooperate to achieve the best for all. Love is not a necessary ingredient.

A more cynical approach toward a similar result—community survival—is posed by those who champion enlightened self-interest. As long as another does not prevent me from "doing my thing," that is, achieving my meaning or expressing it, then I don't care what he does. If farming is his vocation, great. This is the position of enlightened self-interest in which Ayn Rand tries to interest us. Her books have had great appeal to many simply because she tacitly acknowledges that the world of men is basically selfish, that meaning is individual, and that self-interest imaginatively followed is the best road to survival. While such a position does have much to say about how many people live much of the time, it has little to say about the experiences of generosity and love which we have also had and which are radically distinct from the motivations of self-interest.

Without discounting the at least partial validity of the points of view which I have briefly developed, let us now turn to the more *Thou* responsive development of *(I)Me*. Even though such self-awareness is existential, self-centered, and defensive, there do seem to be acts and conditions which would indicate that the person performing those acts does so not out of self-interest but out of honest generosity and altruism. Of course, it is possible to argue that when a young college student joins the Peace Corps or VISTA, he does so out of an extended self-interest because of a sophisticated understanding of the relationship of personal and corporate self-interest; it is likewise possible to argue that such a person acts out of some sense of guilt, e.g., the exploitation of the poor, or of underdeveloped countries; or he may act in such a way to receive the acclaim of his peers or his elders—his reward in praise not service; or, most insidious of all, he may act magnanimously out of a sense of superiority. All of these are possible; all do and have occurred. However, it would be wrong to say that all acts of generosity and altruism are so motivated. I think that these acts which we consider truly beneficent are the reflection of the *I-Thou* context out of which one participates in the *(I)Me* world. That is, my generosity toward another—even though I now stand at the center of my own universe—is related to the fact that I have, at an earlier time, participated in an *I-Thou* relation with that person. In fact, it may be that I have participated in an *I-Thou* relation with another but now, because of that previous experience, treat this new relationship within the *(I)Me* as potentially *I-Thou*. To have known love is to know that love is possible and potentially "there" in every relationship. I believe that Søren Kierkegaard had something like this in mind when he wrote that if you would know any man—all his past disappointments, his hopes, his dreams, his fears—you would love him to death no matter who he was. *(I)Me* relation is not the relation of love, but it can express itself out of the context of prior experiences of love. The self-awareness expressing itself in terms of *(I)Me* does so as one who has loved and expects to do so again.

We are now in a position to look at the subjective self-awareness of the *I-Thou* context. In the *I-Thou* relation, which we most commonly think of in terms of the ecstasy and/or intimacy of love, my self-consciousness is most keen in and through the intense awareness of another who is open and responsive to me. It is in such an experience that I consider myself most "alive" and "full of life"—though such terms are only applied in retrospect. The self-consciousness of the *I-Thou* relation is an awareness of communion, of community, of unity; it is the awareness of a commonality with (but not a duplication of) another. But just *there* rests the difference between the *I* of the *I-Thou* and the *(I)* of the *(I)Me*. In the *(I)* of the *(I)Me,* self-awareness means individuality, aloneness, isolation; in the *I* of *I-Thou,* self-awareness means mutuality, community, union with another. Instead of *being* meaningful over against the void or the abyss of nothingness or meaninglessness of the *It* world, I *am* meaningful with another. In the first instance, the *(I)* is fixed, bracketed from the world as indicated—a potentiality which at the moment is not actualized. Although, under such circumstances I may alter *what* I am, I cannot alter *who* I am; that is a creative process which I alone cannot accomplish, no matter how much I study or do. In the second instance, the *I* is not bracketed or fixed but is open and creative so that each encounter is a deepening experience of self-consciousness. Because of this fact, true love expressed through the convention of marriage which encourages the maximum exposure, is an ever-deepening and more meaningful experience. Marriage may also be the occasion for bitterness because of the same exposure, where animosity rather than love characterizes the relationship.

The distinction between the *(I)* and the *I* is not one of sheer self-consciousness or continuity but rather in the nature of its expression. The *I* is creative and open, the *(I)*, static and complete. However, more needs to be said about the interrelation of these two *I*'s. The objective self-awareness which I *am* in the world of *It*, i.e., my self-conscious relation to the world of ideas, things, powers, and people, is that which I bring to that world from my previous *I-Thou* encounters. *Who* I am as a person-in-community becomes apparent to me as I withdraw from the *I-Thou* relation and find that my relationship to the world of *It* has changed. Reflection upon the experience of *I-Thou* cannot change me, but it can give me a sense or an understanding of the change that has already taken place. Reflection in terms of objective self-awareness for the *(I)* is always "after the fact." Consequently, the richness of my life, even in the world of *It,* can be measured by the nature and number of the *I-Thou* relationships in which I participate. The man who is starved for love and affection, whom the world has "kicked" about, rejected, or ignored, responds with a pathetic and thin life. He finds the world cruel, cold, exploitative, and destructive; he responds in kind. The child who suffers early rejection by his parents is handicapped emotionally, for those *Thous* who ordinarily provide the stability and meaning for his life are withdrawn from him. Some believe that bitterness and distrust experienced at an early age are impossible to overcome completely. On the other hand, warm and generous responsiveness, availability for encounter, can encourage just the opposite expectancy in a child. In such a pleasant situation, an affirmation of life, a warmth toward all people, an openness, an inclusive humanism occurs. The problem is, of course, social as well as familial. How do you provide a context conducive to trust—particularly if the child must be reared in the bitterness of a ghetto experience or in the suspicion of radical political unrest or war? We are all aware that the sins of the fathers are visited upon the children, and the aforementioned are certainly some of the ways that it happens.

When the focus of my consciousness has shifted from the context of *I-Thou* to that of *(I)Me-You(Thou),* I am able to discern a number of important things. The first, and by implication the most immediate, is that my most intense awareness of self comes in the *I-Thou* encounter, but the most "complete" expression of *being* occurs in the context of *(I)Me.* The *I-Thou* relation, just because it is virtually all-consuming in its mutual responsiveness, excludes an awareness of the "ordinary" *It* experiences of time and place, cause and effect, appearance and relation. The *I-Thou* concerns my spiritual self as opposed to my existential or social self, that self which can be described only retrospectively and in terms of relation and *being* rather than in terms of individuality or essence. The *(I)Me,* because it is the expression of a correlation of the spiritual, existential, and social selves, is the more complete. It involves me consciously in both the *Thou* and *It* worlds. In such circumstances, my existential experience may be dominated by either *It* or *Thou,* nothingness or love; but it is still a radical experience in which I respond to the world of *It* by affirming a life-style; I do this in the presence of my memory of previous life-styles and previous *Thou* encounters. Because this state of self-awareness is a correlation of the two worlds, the result is always a shifting, changing, compromising one. There are those, for example, who are unwilling to alter their life-styles and therefore undergo a loss of freedom in a physical sense. Conscientious objectors who are forced to choose jail rather than military service fit into this category. Of course, the converse is also true. There are many who will change their life-styles in order to preserve their physical freedom, a fact which can be documented in many countries of the world where rule by military power is in effect. Which of these components of the *(I)Me* awareness should have priority or precedence is an old and noble question. Dostoevski in his imaginative "Grand Inquisitor" section of the novel *The Brothers Karamazov* suggests a natural priority of the *(I)* over the *Me,* the existential over the social, the spiritual over the physical. He makes the point negatively, in terms of the fear of freedom, but the priority is unmistakable. I think that we can agree that there is an ontological priority, a priority of *being* in terms of subjective self-awareness, but it would be wrong to say that there is some absolute metaphysical priority involved. The *(I)* is prior to the *Me* and at least in part its creator through interaction with the *It* world. Because the priority is an ontological one of *being* rather than a metaphysical one of structure, the authenticity of self-expression may change from context to context, for I am who-I-am-in-context. The *(I)Me* is the more complete expression of self because the intensity of the *I* awareness is modified by need for recognition of the primary *being* of the *It* world.

Another point which becomes evident when the focus of my consciousness has shifted from the context of *I-Thou* to the context of *(I)Me-You(Thou)* is the recognition of limitation. Each of these contexts has its own form of limitation which has already been implied though not explicitly stated. The *I-Thou* context while intense, free, and creative is withdrawn from the *being* which is causally expressed in the world of *It. I-Thou* is utterly impractical even though it is indispensable in terms of my identity and meaning. On the other hand, the *(I)Me* context is practical, full of common sense, aware of time, place, and social structure. Yet its limitation is that it is tied to the past in terms of identity and cannot creatively cope with the critical problems which arise concerning who I am; it cannot provide me with the ecstasy of love without which I am, as Buber suggests, not a person. It should be noted further that though there are mutually excluding limitations within each of the contexts, this does not mean that there is an implied change of self-consciousness which automatically occurs when an individual moves from one context to the other; actually there is only a change in focus: from the context within which *I am* with another [*I-Thou*] to the context within which I stand alone and comprehend all other [*(I)Me*].

One also learns from his movement between the two contexts that their interrelationship should encourage him to extend as much love in terms of respect, care, responsiveness, and knowledge into his *(I)Me-You(Thou)* relations as is "humanly" possible. Through openness and personal availability and because of the dignity and sense of worth one accords another, the potentiality for the *I-Thou* encounter is ever present. Of course, in cases where critical judgement is necessary, e.g., a teacher in a classroom situation, a judge in court, a politician with government appropriations to dispense, such potentiality must be checked to prevent personal preference from distorting public responsibility. On the other hand, outside the realm of public responsibilities, there is no reason to doubt (granting the limitations of time) that any man is my potential *Thou*—even those whose ideas I oppose. It is just for this reason that some historians believe Queen Elizabeth I's ministers prevented her from ever meeting Mary, Queen of Scots. Despite their differences, the establishment of an *I-Thou* relation between them would have changed the course of history. Such potential has much to say to race relations in the world today. I cannot hate or totally reject one who is my potential *Thou*. Prejudice demands that I keep another on the level of *You(It)*, not *You(Thou)*—which, of course, is my own impoverishment as well as his.

One further insight which comes from this movement between contexts is that as *I-Thou* relations recur or are renewed, the possibility of further recurrence is enhanced. I suppose this is the process which we call "falling in love" or establishing a deep friendship. As we become more open, trusting, and available we find that we move into the *I-Thou* context more frequently and with less personal tension. Each time the experience is more rewarding and creative provided that the increased openness and trust are there. In the case of marriage, we acknowledge to ourselves, to our *Thou*, and to all others that our relationship has become so strong, so creative, and so constant that we cannot even identify ourselves without reference to the other; that the creative relationship has so affected each that it has effected a commonality which must be recognized and expressed privately as well as publicly. In these circumstances, I assume full responsibility for my *Thou* as my *Thou* does for me; priority for my attention and focus for my identity have been established. Of course, the fact that this has happened once does not mean that it cannot happen again. Widows and widowers often have equally gratifying second marriages. There is a danger, however, when an individual makes himself too available for another *Thou* whose relationship could in any way rival an established marriage. The new *I-Thou* will also be creative and mutually effective, and the result will be an identity crisis. Marriage means radical care, respect, responsibility, and knowledge. Such radicalness does not imply exclusiveness, but it does imply priority and discipline. My human limitations—as well as my sense of identity—are such that I cannot possibly respond to more than one person at a time in that intense and thorough way. Total responsibility means total attention, and total, by definition, means one. This does not mean that one cannot love children who result from such an *I-Thou* relation. Children are loved in a particular way—out of the mutuality of that *I-Thou* relation which was their origin. The responsibility, care, respect, and knowledge are deep and strong yet not of the same nature as the intense, radical relation which one shares with his *Thou*. It is as though the children participate now as portions of an extended *I-Thou* relation. With children, the relationship is unequal and compassionate; with one's *Thou* as spouse, the relationship is mutual and passionate. In reality, the parent-child relation is the most intensive form of *(I)You* relation we have. As the child grows older, *I-Thou* usually develops, but if the initial husband-wife relation is sound, the new *I-Thou*—while strong—will never replace it. It is not a matter of desirability but of limitation. I am only capable of one such intense and defining *I-Thou*. Such a natural exclusiveness because of focal-limitation is the reasoning behind the idea of celibacy in many religious orders. Total devotion to God as my *Thou* precludes the rightful responsibilities I would owe to wife, husband, or family. Whether such practice should be (or even can be) institutionally mandatory is an important point, but is outside the scope of this study.

Any discussion of the *I-Thou* encounter would be incomplete if it did not go on to discuss one's relationship with God, which Buber and many others would consider the basic *I-Thou* relation. Although this is not new—this sense of a personal relation with God—it does become new when such an affirmation is permitted to stand by itself without the aid of the traditional Greek metaphysical structure. Consequently, we must seriously adopt the attitude of Pascal, who wanted to know about the God of Abraham, Isaac, and Jacob and not about the God of the philosophers. The plea is for a relationship with the living God, not for an understanding of the scope of divine sovereignty. We have to do not with God who is The Truth, The One, The Reality, The Perfect-Actualized-Eternal, but with the God who responds to Moses or to us by saying "I am that I am." God is never known by the mind. He is only known through encounter. Any knowledge about God is simply an abstraction, an imaginative portrayal through inadequate and misleading terminology: the God who creates man with freedom of choice, with responsibility, would deny it by His own omniscience and omnipotence; the God who creates all things *essentially* good is compromised by the presence of evil. "When we speak of God it is not of God that we speak" writes Gabriel Marcel. "I have always had the conviction that the attributes of God as defined by rational theology: simplicity, immutability, etc., have value only if we succeed in discovering behind them the qualities of a Thou which cannot be construed as a him without being denatured or reduced to our absurd, human proportions."[45]

What I am aware of is the sense of *being,* not only my own *being* but of that *Being* by whom I am addressed. I am aware of the God who acts, who responds, who says *I AM*, who expresses Himself as *Being.* That is, my responsiveness to God is not unlike my responsiveness to other *Thous.* What I become aware of with another is his presence, or more accurately, our presence. I do not *find* him but am aware of meeting *with* him. Only after the experience do I reflect upon who he is in distinction from myself. So is my experience of God. My awareness of God is not an awareness of Him—out there somewhere. It is more an awareness or sense of presence, a sense of community, of identity. It is the awareness of what Rudolph Otto called the *Mysterium Tremendum*—but it is more than just an objective awareness, for I feel that I am actually participating in the *Mysterium Tremendum.* It is the awareness of what Schleiermacher called the "feeling of absolute dependence"—but is more than the feeling of sheer dependence; it is dependence *upon Being-Itself,* the *Thou* who is creator of heaven and earth.

My sense of *being* is never one of just *am*ness; it is always one of personal intensity, of *I-am*ness. But this, we have seen, is an expression of the primary word or condition *I-Thou.* The sense of dependency in human relations is not one of helplessness but of mutuality. I am dependent upon my *Thou* who is responsive to me and who is, in turn, dependent upon me. Such is the corporate nature of *being.* In my relationship to God as my *Thou,* my sense of dependency is there, but it is the experience of ontological dependency in terms of *being,* i.e., life itself, not in terms of bestowed personal identity. The fact of my *self*-consciousness permits me to acknowledge my dependency and at the same time be independent of it. That is not a contradiction; it is a condition of creation, of my experience of *being:* I cannot account for my *being,* but I know I must account for my specific identity. My experience is not that God has endowed me with a given personality or character but that given the potential to *be* within a certain context, I must be responsive and responsible. Even my experience of encounter with God bears this out. The relationship is not one of absolute law which permits me no choice, but one of grace within which I must choose. God does not create me in some static image, or even his own; my experience is that I am free to meet Him, to "image" Him, or to refuse to be available to Him in an *I-Thou* context. Should I choose the last alternative, the loss is mine and God's, but for me such a loss is self-destructive, for God it could be only tragic.

Such an experience of the presence of God is available to me not only directly in the mystery of immediate confrontation, but also in and through other expressions of *being:* through *I-Thous* which I may have with other human beings, as well as through *I-It* experiences. A more complete explanation of this will be found in chapter 4 when we shall be discussing revelation. Nevertheless, through these experiences, certain things become evident. First, all *being* is expressive of God, contingent upon God. No form of *being* is self-sustaining or self-perpetuating; that remains a mystery bound up with the nature of *Being-Itself*. For example, I can no more will myself into the future than cause can guarantee its effect. That I-am-now and it-is-now is as much of an affirmation as I can make. The consistency, nature, and presence of *being* is dependent upon Him who addresses me as *Thou* through *being* in all its forms. Just as in my human *I-Thou* relation I am led beyond the physical aspect of the person to an encounter with the self, so I am led beyond the created order to the Ground of Being, to God Himself. In each case it is an experience of self-consciousness with another, which in retrospect I call creative identity.

Second, it is through acknowledgment of God as my *Thou* that my life achieves that experience which is variously labeled fulfillment, security, consistency, or maturity. Only God can satisfy that innate, a priori need for *Thou*. Undoubtedly, this is what St. Augustine knew when he wrote that "our hearts are restless until they rest in Thee." The *I-Thou* relationship grants me that consistency of character, of which the relativities of various other *I-Thou* relations seem to deprive me. It is this relationship which can sustain me in a world in which no other *Thous* are available because of isolation, imprisonment, martyrdom, or disfigurement—religious history is filled with such witnesses. In such cases my self-conciousness is my awareness of God. Such a self-conciousness is not only possible as the mystical experience of God; it can also prove to be the ground of human *I-Thou* relations. That is, in the security of my identity before God, I am able with freedom to make myself available for the *I-Thou* relation with others. We have mentioned earlier the risk involved in the *I-Thou* exposure in which one's identity is at stake, but when *who*-one-is is sustained by his relation to God, then what he risks with another is tragedy, but not destruction.

The question may arise, how is it possible for me to have an *I-Thou* relation with God and with another human being at the same time? While it is possible to have an *I-Thou* relationship with God in which I am aware of the exclusiveness of that relationship, the understanding of the exclusiveness of my human *I-Thou* relation involves me in a sense of wonder, beauty, joy, affirmation, and mystery which point beyond themselves to the *Being* of God. That is, the *I-Thou* relationship with God can be known in and through the human *I-Thou* as its ground and possibility. The relationship with God always remains a possibility for me, available when all other relationships have withdrawn, and it remains with me when those human relationships are reestablished.

Martin Buber calls the divine *Thou* the *Eternal Thou*. However, the implications of the word *Eternal* are metaphysical and carry the sense of

God being beyond time: perfect actuality. We have discussed the difficulties of such a view, so explicit in Greek idealism, and we have argued for thinking in terms of God's *Being* (verb) rather than God's *Being* (noun). Consequently, I will henceforth use the term *Eminent* to indicate the *Thou* of God. To do this involves us in a discussion of time and history, the topics of the next chapter.

3

Time and History

Time and history have always been two of the most difficult questions with which the philosopher and theologian have had to work. What is *time?* What does *the present* mean? What is *the past?* Where is the past now? Why must I change to a spatial metaphor to talk of the past or future? What has the past to do with the present? Does it do more than merely precede it? Does the past control the present and therefore the future? Where is the future? Does the relationship between past, present, and future mean that all time is eternally present? What *is* eternity?—or is that statement a contradiction in terms? If eternity stands beyond time, over time, or under time, then what is the relation between time and eternity? What about reality? If reality is one, perfect, and therefore total actuality, can time be anything more than mere appearance? Is it perhaps a condition of human understanding and perception as Kant suggests? Is time really divisional—an infinite series of points—or is it duration, a continuous flow? Does time control history, or does history control time? Is history merely the recording of sequence or does its meaning elude time? Is *kairos* ("the right time") of a different order than *chronos* ("clock time")? All of these questions are part of the critical focus on time and its meaning for our lives. To understand ourselves and our world we must understand time, for it is time that conventionally marks the moments from our birth to our grave. But it is not just that; it is the experience of every man who after an exhilarating hour, day, or vacation says with wonder and dismay, "Where did the time go?" We all experience time, the passage of time, the awareness of time beyond time, the glimpse of the timeless, the eternal. We recognize that time is part of the time-space continuum, one vector of human life and expression with which I am intimately involved with the physical world; but we know, too, that it is more. . . .

Most of the previous questions are contextual ones. That is, they arise out of an assumed metaphysical position which has actually determined the nature of the question being asked: how is it possible for the experience of time to be understood in terms of the fixed and eternal world of Reality (or God) and the changing and transient world of appearance? Given such a context, the questions are prescribed and the answers prefigured. If we set this metaphysical assumption aside, however, and begin with a new ontological approach to the phenomenon of *being,* the analysis will prove to be different. If we do not find answers to the previous questions, we may discover contexts within which they have become irrelevant.

Being, as we have argued in chapter 2, is twofold in its expression: it is subjective and objective, represented by the basic symbols of *I (Thou)* and *It.* This expression reflects the twofold experience of my self-consciousness: my subjective self-conscious awareness[1] in terms of my encounter with another "subject" and my objective self-conscious awareness[2] in terms of my encounter with an "object." Both of these encounters are primary, which indicates the commonality of *being* (in terms of the sheer givenness of the encounters), the individuality of *being* (in terms of the self-awareness and *other*-awareness of the encounters), and the unity of *my being* (in terms of my *self*-conscious participation in each encounter). However, we find that such a description of self-conscious *being* in terms of subjective and objective encounter is incomplete, for the dynamism of the experience has been ignored—the dimension of action and reaction, of continuance and change. This dimension we call "time"; it is, as such, an expression of *being* as fundamental and primary as the symbols *I* and *It.* Consequently, time should not be incongruous with the interrelatedness of *I* and *It* but rather should be expressive of it.

The structure of our language, which reflects and symbolizes our *being,* is helpful at this point. The experience of dynamism is symbolized by verbs which describe the state or relation of the subject and/or object involved. The condition which we call *"am*ness" is always *I-am*ness (subjectivity); what we call *"is*ness" is always *He, She,* or *It-is*ness (objectivity). *You-are*ness is the coordinate experiential symbol represented by the form *(I)Me-You(Thou)*—the form implied in the majority of our human encounters as discussed in chapter 2.

Therefore, *being* is twofold in its verbal expression and this expression reflects the same self-conscious priorities exhibited in the subject-object relations. My *being* is *I-am*ness. Consciousness of *being* in terms of "time" begins with this ontological assertion. Human life in its most fundamental and primitive form, most completely realized in infancy, is an experience of *I-am*ness. Life is assertion, action, extension, development, meaning; that is, life begins as a continuum of self-consciousness which is centered in my *Thou* encounter with mother and the world. Encompassing *I-am*ness is where we begin: life is *now,* which is a totalizing act of awareness. But into this world of total inclusion and time-full[3] extension, a second kind of awareness begins to intrude. It is not the awareness of self but the external (at least self-consciously unaccounted for) imposition of sequence; the awareness of conditions we call "then" and "yet," "before" and "after," "was," "is," and "will." It is a regularity which seems to structure my life rather than vice versa. No doubt, this begins with the regularity of the "two-o'clock feeding," the schedule for naps and sleeping, the recurrence of day and night. The daily routine of living soon makes us aware that there is another world-dynamism than that of our *self*-consciousness, though obviously not totally extraneous to that consciousness.

From such natural and early experiences we receive our initial experiences of what we now call "clock time." Martin Heidegger believes that our sophisticated chronometry begins with primitive man observing not only the patterns of human needs and functions—hunger, sleep, and pulse—but also the regularity of days and nights, the movement of the moon and stars, the tides, the seasons. The further subdivision of such natural periods of recurrence into hours, minutes, and seconds is a matter of convenience and spatial conformity and symbolism: the circular movement of earth around the sun is symbolized in the circularity of the clockface.

"Time," symbolized by the clock, seems to be an expression of *being* in which I participate, which is objective to (other than) my self-consciousness yet not so alien to it that no awareness is possible. Because it *is* an expression of *being* I know it to have the *presence* of an encounter, but because it is objective to my self-consciousness, I think of it as *present* rather than as *presence*. The repetition and order of such present encounters give me the experience we indicate by the words *before* and *after*, *then* and *yet*. But these words are words *out of the present*. The point of reference, the point of orientation, is the present without which a word such as *before* becomes meaningless.

Through these observations, we learn that *being*, whether it has to do with I-*am*ness or It-*is*ness is *now* and/or present. Though we can symbolically speak of the past and the future, there is no other "time" but *now* and the present; "time" is the *expression* of *being*. Thus for "time," as for *Thou* and *It*, my life is twofold, with the act of knowing providing an epistemological priority but not an ontological one. The priority I am referring to here is the primacy of the self-conscious over the unconscious or subconscious. Because of the interaction of these expressions of *being*, it becomes evident that any priority or primacy is only a matter of self-conscious orientation and not of essential or metaphysical order. "Time" as *now* is the sense of presence, of subjective identity and meaning; "time" as present is relativity and objective change, sequential and repetitive. Each of these must be considered separately and then the two coordinately. Because clock time, as matrix for scientific methodology, has become such an important factor in contemporary life, it will be most helpful to begin there even though such a beginning presupposes my *self-conscious now* and permits the use of spatial metaphor.

One *is* in the present. That is not only where he *is* in the beginning, that is where he always *is;* the present is the context of change. The present cannot be totally comprehended because one is always objectively (never subjectively) within it, but he can provide some explanation of it by observing it from the outside (subjectively) in terms of the related experiences we call "past" and "future." When I speak of the past, I do so as of the present in terms of present memories, present forces, present effects. The only thing which sustains the past, therefore, is the present. The past in fact could not "exist" without the present to sustain it. Such an observation becomes evident if we imagine a civilization of ancient times all of whose artifacts and memorabilia have been destroyed. Were this to be the case, i.e., no present evidence to sustain it, such a civilization would not "exist," could not be called to mind, discovered, or fantasized—even as much as Atlantis. What we call "the past" is only that which is continued in some form in the present. More specifically, the past is that which *is* no longer in terms of its own expression of *being* but *is* presently dependent upon related expressions of *being*. What we call "the past" is a mental construction of convenience which does not exist spatially any*where*—although we use spatial metaphors, as mentioned earlier, for descriptive purposes. Nor does *the past* exist in any Time-Continuum which has some sort of independent metaphysical stance; it is the observation of "clock time" out of the subjective *now* which gives the impression of setness, position, fixity, and of metaphysical reality to what we call past events. The category of "Pastness" per se as differentiated from *the past* is part of the descriptive category of change, necessitated by my subjective sense of the continuing present. Pastness is the designation of no-longer-presentness. The particular events of which I become conscious in the present retain their *It* (objective) characteristics; however, because *I* am conscious of them (in my self-continuity), they appear as in *the past,* as fixed and as inviolable as my identity. Of course they are not, for the only fixity is in the nature of the interrelationship of the subjective and objective expressions of *being*. The events, as ideas or memories, can change, fade, or disappear. Their theoretical fixity remains dependent upon the nature of knowing, not upon the content of knowing. This does not mean that the past is unimportant or simply imagination. The past is a reflection of the epistemological priority in my *being* which comprehends both the significance (continuity) and insignificance (meaninglessness) of sheer sequence or change.

The future is much the same in its dependence upon the present, yet different in its relation to *being*. There *is* no future; there is only the present and our projections or anticipations from that present. It is the remembered stability of the presents now past, the remembered, observed, and recorded movement of cause and effect over a long period of time (of "recorded history," we say) that encourages us to predict the future or project our plans, hopes, and dreams—all of which *are* present—"into" the future. The future, therefore, is simply an imaginative speculation about life and times sanctioned by the experience of stability in the past. The fact that we do not *know* the future, that we do not go "out on a limb" is not that the future is too complicated to decipher; it is that the future does not yet exist. Of course it is true that the consistency and stability of the past, which I am at present considering, are what give me the confidence to leave home in the morning fully expecting to find it, my wife and family there when I return. This is good and seemingly certain; we must believe it, until disaster strikes, and we are rudely reminded that the only reality there *is* is present.

The observation may be made that what we have considered about the future thus far have been events within the future, not the future itself. But such a point does not destroy the argument, it simply changes its focus. Our awareness of only what is timeful is our awareness of the present; it is the awareness of a condition we call *is*ness—the awareness of continuation and change. There is nothing in *that* experience itself which speaks of or indicates the future. *Is*ness as continuation and change is simply the mysterious root fact or basic expression of *being*. It is always tied to events; it is never a thing-in-itself, something within which *being* participates—that is the old metaphysical trap which considers *being* as an intellectual construct and must then go on to ask, "Does it exist?" *Being is; being* is *is*ness. This can only mean that the future as such is a present imaginative projection of eventfulness based upon present memory for *both* content and form. Nothing grants me the prerogative or privilege of going beyond that. What we call the "present" is the edge of *is*ness spatially symbolized by the continuous sweep of the second hand of a clock.

Perhaps two issues frequently cited in support of the reality of the future ought to be considered briefly here: the destruction of the planet earth and death—*my* death in particular. What can we make of those scientific theories which assure us that the years of the earth are numbered? It is true that some scientists suggest a great freeze, others a fiery holocaust, but what they do agree on is that it will end. I do not think we should make too much of the fact that our scientists cannot agree on the nature of the end—as we say, "That should straighten itself out in time." The point to be made is that both theories (or any others) are imaginative projections based on present data, including those data which continue as the present "from" the past in the form of artifacts or ideas harbored by the brain. The probability, the belief of such a theory of destruction is present. It does not come to us out of the future; it does not come to us as a certainty out of the past. It comes to us in the present and will continue to do so, modified by whatever experience we have in the present and in the present in relation to the past. I assume that the scientists are right, but the reality and probability of such an assumption are present, not in the future or in the past.

Death is a more dramatic argument if only because it is existential; it is about me. It is more visceral than theoretical, and the argument runs something like this: the one thing I am certain of in this life is its eventual termination, my death. The fact that I am alive at present, and that I "know" I will be dead later, assures me of the reality of the future. After all, it is that assumed terminal event which gives my life its importance, if not its meaning. The anticipation of death means that each moment must count, for the expected number of moments is limited. As Professor Joseph Haroutunian remarks: "A person is one whose lifetime determines the times of his life."[4]

But the only validity of this argument is the validity of probability. The assurance of my death is a belief I have accepted upon the evidence that no one to my knowledge has failed to die yet. Even Jesus died on the cross. Consequently, it seems logical to the point of unquestionable belief that death will come. But of singular importance is the point that my death is a matter of convinced probability, not necessity. To make this claim is not to deny man's temporality but to preclude any "fixed" nature. Part of the problem in this issue is that our priorities have been mistaken. What is assured is the present and only the present, and even that is mysterious. The fact that *I am* does not mean that I can will myself into the next moment, as we have noted before. The real mystery is not death, but life, and I control neither one. I believe that good health habits may extend my life or that suicide will end it, but neither of these can ever be more than a present assumption. The fact that we are dealing with probability rather than necessity is corroborated by the many religious myths of resurrection or reincarnation found in the world religions. Even the finality of death is not a sure thing. The future which is the projection of my mind, is still a mystery comprised of marks from the past, guesses, and imagination.

Such present timefulness with its references to past and future covers only a portion of our lives. Much of our lives, in fact all of our self-conscious life, is lived outside such a "time" sequence. Consciousness of the "time" which we have been considering thus far is secondary; that is, self-consciousness is removed from that process, that *is*ness, which we have identified as present time or clock time. The fact that we can identify it, observe it, and analyze it shows that in some sense we are removed from it; time is objective to us in the same way the *It* world is objective to us. We can wear its symbol around our wrist, but we cannot consciously *be* it. Self-consciousness is of a different order. I believe that this is what T.S. Eliot meant in his poem "Burnt Norton" when he stated that "to be conscious is not to be in time." As one who is self-conscious, I am not only free of such calculated immediacy of *being* but also incapable of comprehending it in any direct way, although a portion of my life is obviously governed by it. What I am conscious in (not of) is *now,* which is different from the present. The present is the moving continuous edge of *being* objectively and relationally understood; the *now* is not understood as present but as the sense of presence; it is identity in expression with the world or with another. *Now* is the world of I-*am*ness in which *being* is expressed in terms of continuity, rather than it-*is*ness in which *being* is expressed in terms of change. When my self-consciousness is focused in my *now* world, the present slips by unnoticed, so that suddenly I say, "Can it really be *that* late?" Hours become moments, and moments hours. The ordinary standards of objective relational time simply do not apply. *Now* is qualitatively governed by authenticity and meaning, not quantitatively by age or minutes. It should be apparent that "time" of both kinds is part of the new ontological understanding of *being.* Consequently it is coordinate with our analysis of *I-Thou* and *I-It* and can be best further discussed with this in mind.

As a human being who understands himself to be both an unconscious and a conscious being, the nature of sheer physical relation—e.g., between atom and atom, rock and rock, object and object—has no meaning other than observable consistencies and conjectured laws of change and relation. However, the fact that I can apply such consistencies to my own physical and social *being* permits me to orient myself and the world in that *is*ness which consciousness calls "the present" as opposed to "the past" or "the future." An interesting point to observe here is that my symbolic orientation in that *is*ness is constructed out of the experienced consistency of previous presents, which, consequently, appears to be an orientation out of the past. Time, clock time, is the expressed and experienced relation between present and presence.

*Is*ness in terms of its sheer *being* is only *is*ness. There is no orientation "within" the present, for the present is simply the present. But when the mind, through memory, retains for the present other experienced presents, and a pattern of relations among them begins to emerge, e.g., the movement of the stars, the tides, day and night, the pattern emerges or *is* as a present intellectual observation, although its content *is* no longer. The continuing consistency of my observation, day-night, day-night, day-night, encourages me to apply this observation out of the interrelational *past* to the present: this is day, and from my past sequential experiences I assume that night will follow; it is 12 o'clock noon, midday, and I assume that it will be right to call the next hour 1:00 P.M., one toward midnight. But what I am actually applying to the present is the structure of a closed system, consistent within itself. My assumption and belief is that this consistency will continue to be an evident structure in the present, an assumption which differential calculus continues to support. But just to state this indicates the intricate nature of my relationship to time. From an *I-It* encounter (the imposition of sequence upon my consciousness), an awareness develops which becomes, in the form of an idea, part of my life-style. I then impose my own symbolism from that life-style upon the continuing sequence. In terms of our designations for *being*, my timeful expression is therefore *(I)Me-It*.

Thus the timefulness of the *It* world is the presently imposed structure of the relation between *past* presents. From this I am able to ascertain what *is*, but to ascertain this is not in any way to explain the mystery that *is* is or how *is* is. Even our way of thinking of clock time is indicative of this: because clock time is *past*, a closed system (minutes, hours, days, and seasons are repetitious; each effect becomes an efficient cause), time is divided into units of convenience. However, because such units are imposed, they are symbolically numbered sequentially to indicate progression as well as repetition. Only in the sequence of years does the subject-object paradox implied by the *(I)Me-It* relation appear. The years do not repeat and are thus symbolically unique, though the seasons do repeat and thus symbolize measure and order. In terms of clock time itself, the present inexplicably *is*, and is therefore unique, though its form is apparently past and therefore repetitive. All our natural sciences as sciences are grounded in such consistency, in the past; our social sciences are grounded in the paradox of the past and present. What natural science endeavors to do is to seek out the universal (or consistent) nature in the particular and must assume (though it can never establish) that such past universals are consistently relevant to the present. Thus we almost come to the conclusion that on any occasion when clock time is relevant or effectively employed, we are in part dealing with the past.

But it appears that movement out of the past is something of an illusion. If we begin where we know we must, with the present—the only reality that *is*—then we must recognize that through the *is*ness of the present the past emerges. The present does not flow out of the past. The past is simply that present which has ceased to *be* present except in terms of those marks and memories which continue. The present is productive of the past, though we seem to have discovered this in reverse. By examining the marks and memories we *have* of past *presents* we discover patterns, consistencies, and relationships. Because these existed earlier, we once argued, such patterns must exist in the present. Our ontological understanding of reality must make us reverse this; it is the continuing consistency (i.e., coherence) of the present which enables us to see and to utilize the consistencies of the past. It is the reality of the present which governs the reality of the past and makes it comprehensible. To say that the past is the only real thing we *know* is simply to fail to acknowledge the presupposition of the present inherent in such a claim.

Let us summarize what we have said thus far about clock time and *being*. Clock time is an abstract expression of *being* devised out of present observation of the consistencies of events which are no longer present except to record or memory, but which once were present. Because these consistencies are not ontologically interior to consciousness, i.e., not subjective, but are spatially exterior to consciousness, e.g., the movement of the stars, the turning of the earth in relation to the sun, or the beat of my pulse, "time" can be accurately expressed in a spatial relation; movement through space is symbolically the passage of time. But the fact that we can talk about the "passage of time" obviously indicates that we do so outside of conditions of clock time. Even though I recognize consistencies in myself—the need to eat, to sleep, to breathe—my very awareness of "time" indicates that I transcend the symbol at the same time that I am subject to it. Though the *being* of my physical existence is subject to the present and therefore to the consistencies of relation governed by that present (e.g., every seven years, without conscious direction, my body cells replace themselves; or when I am burned, I cannot reverse *being's* expression and not be burned), the *being* expressed in terms of my consciousness is not so ordered. In terms of what we have said earlier, consciousness in objective actuality is only present but in subjective comprehension suprapresent. Therefore consciousness can only be partially "in time." We could say that consciousness per se is time-full but not in clock time. Clock time, as we have seen, is a construct of the *past* although its reality is rooted in the ontological expression of *being,* the present. Consciousness, because it belongs in one of its dimensions to the present, to the ontological expression of *being,* can comprehend clock time and can be aware of its own partial involvement with it; but because consciousness is of the present and yet an expression of the *now,* it cannot be completely confined to what, by definition, is an abstract, closed system *self*-devised.

The *It* world, the world of science and technology, is the world regulated by and expressive of clock time. It is the world in which physical *being* seems to express itself in terms of a continuing consistency which is the nature of its identity. The authenticity of the *It* world is expressed in this consistency, any violation of which now leads us to suspect our observation and not nature. Such human assurance is the product of centuries of observation; in fact, we have become so convinced of the fidelity of consistent physical expression that we have, as we did with "time," ignored its origin. We have claimed that the past controls the present and therefore the future; we have claimed, in support of this, that every event, object, or state is an effect *produced* by some prior cause; that everything (understanding the word *thing* in its broadest possible context) has something antecedent to it and responsible for it, although that seemingly involves us in a closed system.

Actually we have been dealing with an ambiguous situation as though it were a singular or simple one. *Cause* and *effect* are simply expressions of convenience used to describe events (the continuous expression of *being*) already artfully delimited by the device of clock time. We speak of *a cause* or *an effect* as though it were some discontinuous, discrete unity of identification on the one hand, and, on the other, as though each were somehow mysteriously and necessarily related to the other as corollary. But the reality of the matter is something else, as this study of time indicates. *Being* as timefully expressive is continuous *is*ness. Therefore, if we employ the traditional sense of causality (i.e., responsibility for, related and prior to, determinative) within the new ontology, then *cause* (as continuous *is*ness) is always in the present and *effect* (as contingent *was*ness) is the past! This is the reverse of the ordinary conception of cause-producing-effect in which the effect is present and the cause is past. What we are witnessing in timefulness is the consistency and continuity in the expression of *being*. It is the reality of the present which makes possible the "reality" of the past. What seems sequential in terms of development and emergence of the present out of the past, the effect out of prior cause, is directly dependent upon the continuing consistency of present *being*, i.e., any radical break in that consistency would bring into question only the reality and relevance of the past rather than reality as present.

Over a period of such consistent timefulness—and in keeping with our useful but artificially discrete units of time: seconds, minutes, hours—we have mistaken repetition for causal reality or for at least its partial expression. For example, when I clap my hands, a noise follows. This has happened so many times that I now believe that the clapping of my hands is the *cause* of the subsequent noise. Actually I am anticipating an in-the-past consistent physical expression of sequence and am confusing that anticipation with the existential expression of *being* without which there could be no sequence, only sheer or static actuality. Ignoring for the moment the practicality of our former understanding of cause and effect, this reversal—time-cause as present, time-effect as past—is the only way we can understand the existential events of novelty and creativity which, by the fact that they occur, should warn us of any closed system of prefiguration or determinism.

Nevertheless, for "all practical purposes," we will no doubt continue to employ the categories of cause and effect, as previously understood, in the routines of daily life, but such an employment is an act of faith: that the present will indeed continue to conform to the past, that the inexplicable consistency of physical expression in the past *is* present and will be. When the ecologists tell us that we are destroying our world, and perhaps already have—i.e., it may be too late to remedy the damage— they are speaking out of the present, from which vantage point they view the past, and then, in turn, speculate about the future. It is the consistency of natural expression now which permits them to "read" the danger signs in the past and to count on them for the future. But the important point to remember is that their assurance is actually in the present, not in the past or future.

When we move from the physical sciences into the social sciences the problem is somewhat different. To the consistency of physical objects, events, states must be added the consistency and inconsistency of human behavior and the ability of human willfulness to affect more than simply itself. The studies in economics, history, political science, psychology, and sociology give us ample evidence of this. The vacillation between consistency and inconsistency reflects the introduction of self-consciousness into the equation of *being*. One way of observing this change is in terms of the metaphors of time. Clock time effectively (if not genuinely) expresses the world of *It:* the relationship between *It* and *It*, its presence, its consistency. However, clock time is no longer totally adequate to express this new equation, for self-consciousness is not *in* clock time. Thus in the social sciences, we are in the middle (or transition) area, somewhere between *I-It* and *I-Thou*.

Insofar as the social sciences deal with the world of *Me-You*, they are sciences, and the social consistencies which they chart are seemingly as valid as any physical law. The predictability of most human behavior is (for any defender of human free will) an awesome thing. Predicted grade averages in college is a good example of such human consistency. Most college admissions officers will affirm that by applying a weighted formula based upon the verbal and quantitative results of the high school applicants' Scholastic Achievement Test and upon the high school scholastic records, it is possible to predict the grade average at the end of the students' freshman year within one percentage point. Such predictability cannot be applied with total accuracy to each member of the class, but it does apply to the class as a whole.

In such a *Me-You* relationship, clock time is still valid as an adequate metaphor of the expression of *being*. But where self-consciousness enters and the relationship becomes *(I)Me*, it appears that more than one kind of "time" is at work. Insofar as I am involved with a life-style, or am functioning as an other-directed self, or, more prosaically, am just letting the world push me around, I am in the world of *It* and the metaphor of clock time is still applicable. Under these conditions I can be studied, surveyed, and polled with accuracy and precision. However, when the expression of self is genuinely *(I)Me* as described in chapter 2, then a different kind of "time" is involved, namely identity time.

In order to make the distinction as clear as possible when we are discussing the different kinds of "time," I shall use different words for each. Actually, it would be more correct to say that we are not talking about different kinds of "time" so much as of different kinds of experience or living which we are attempting to describe by the symbol *time*. If one of the most essential qualities of *being* is its expression metaphorically described as "time," then we must be careful to make the necessary distinctions in terms of the nature of that experience. When we talk of the *It* world, the world of things and forces, we call the interaction of these things and forces "timeful," that is, they take place in the present or are related to the present in terms of past and future as described earlier. When we are talking of the *being* of the *Thou* world, the world of my self-consciousness, the experience of "time" is different. "Time" is no longer a matter of seconds, minutes, or years marking the experience of sheer continuance, of "cause and effect," of interrelatedness, of movement within the applicable categories of beginning and end. If we have used present, past, and future to describe the *I-It* experience, then some new nomenclature must be used for the consciousness of self. Consequently, the terms of the *I-Thou* experience will be designated "time-fullness" rather than timefulness, "now" rather than the present, and "*am*ness" rather than *is*ness. Each of these changes needs to be explained.

If we use the word *timeful* to describe the continuous experience of *is*ness, it is to describe a context in which that continuous experience is marked by regularity and order. It is to describe a context for which clock time is a relevant symbol. It is to describe a context for which sequence and development can be objectively recorded. The word *time-full* has a different connotation. This word describes a context in which clock time is no longer relevant, a context within which measurable sequence and development are no longer possible. "Time" in the sense of seconds, minutes, and years is irrelevant, but "time" in the sense of the *expression* of *being* is very much in evidence. All this is true because time-fulness has to do with *what* I am, but time-fullness has to do with *who* I am. Time-fullness is the nature of the *I-Thou* encounter in which "time" (clock time) and "place" are of only peripheral importance—out of focus and "out of mind." What is at stake in the *I-Thou* encounter is my identity, not my daily schedule or routine. Within this context we do not say,

"My identity is. . . ." That is to talk of identity in terms of the *It* world—much the way I would say, "I am an American" or "I am a Christian." Within the context of *I-Thou,* my *being* is expressed simply in terms of "I am." Thus to say that my experience is time-full is not to eliminate clock time from my life, but it is to indicate that clock time is irrelevant to my identity as a person, as a *who* rather than a *what.* More positively stated, my *being* is as much a continual, full expression of my self-consciousness which remains *self*-consistent as it is of my objective self-awareness which constantly changes according to the order and nature of that physical *being.*

Before comparing the terms *is*ness and *am*ness, it might be well to point out that the discussion of this difference, itself, is a matter of *is*ness, of objectivity, rather than of *am*ness, of subjectivity. *Am*ness is ontological in a way which precludes any discussion "about" it; my identity, in terms of my self-consciousness, cannot be anything but self-expression. To talk about it in a book is to be once removed from the reality of it all. Ontological identity can only be indicated by inadequate symbols, symbols which indicate *that* it *is,* not *who* I *am.* This linguistic paradox is resolved in terms of our ontological experience, not in terms of logic.

The structure of language itself is a partial and symbolic explanation for our use of *am*ness with time-fullness and *is*ness with timefulness. *Am*ness always indicates personal identity and expression; the subject is subjective. *Is*ness always indicates identity of the other or another in an objective way. Both words (*is* and *am*), of course, are verb forms—present, active, indicative . . . of *being*—but there seems to be a priority involved. *He is, She is,* and *It is* are derivative expressions; that is, they are always spoken or thought with an implicit reference to the *I* context. They express something objective to myself which I can never *be* but can only experience secondhand, so to speak. Thus the metaphor of "time" is relevant. The third-person singular represents clock time which I can comprehend, observe, or calculate but in which, as a self-conscious person, I cannot participate. *It is* necessarily presupposes *I am,* but *I am* does not necessarily presuppose *It is.* Because I have a body, *I am* is involved with *It is,* but the epistemological (not ontological) distinction remains. Thus *am*ness is different from *is*ness; *am*ness involves my identity, my *Thou* encounter; its character is continuous identity rather than continuous change.

The third change in the description of "time" is the introduction of the term *now* for the *present. Now* is the word by which we will distinguish the subjective expression of *being* from the objective but unconscious experience of *being.* As with our terms *am*ness and *is*ness, the objective term—*present*—presupposes the subjective, the observer, but the *now* does not presuppose the *present* although it does and can comprehend it.

Thus to be correct, I must always speak of *the* present from the point of view of my self-consciousness; I cannot speak of present as though I *consciously* participated in it. I can theorize that my body or thoughts are present in an objective way to other objective things and forces, but I cannot existentially know what that means, for consciousness, as we have seen, imposes a qualitative distinction. The objective relations of *being* present can only be considered descriptively, never confessionally. Because language is so imprecise and because it is always in the process of change, it is difficult to find terms which will carry the exact meaning desired. Consequently, the word *now* as the word to describe the subjective, self-conscious, confessional expression of *being* as identity is somewhat arbitrary. *Now* in popular usage also has its correlatives, *before* and *after,* just as *present* has its own: *past* and *future,* but popular usage does seem to favor the aforementioned distinction. When we hear about the "Now Generation," the users are referring to more than clock time; the overtones of identity are unmistakable.

When all three of these ideas are brought together—time-full, *am-ness,* and *now*—we have the basic description of the *I-Thou* encounter. It is true that when *I* am encountered by another *I,* in such a way that *I* become deeply involved with who that other *I* expresses rather than what he is, my experience is so ecstatic, deep, and creative that all objective and physical considerations recede to the point of insignificance. These moments of encounter or love are the most critical and memorable we have because they have to do with who we are. We often think that it is in these moments that we are most alive, most truly fulfilling life or *being*—"This," we say, "is what life is all about." Of course, this does not mean that moments of trauma induced by changes in our physical or objective world are not important or memorable. The destruction of war, the loss of sight, imprisonment—many factors can dramatically change our lives—or at least the way we have been used to living our lives; but it is the loss, destruction, or betrayal of love, the *Thou* relation which is the most devastating to us. This certainly is the idea, if not the context, for the New Testament injunction by Jesus, "Do not fear those who kill the body, but cannot kill the soul. Fear him rather who is able to destroy both soul and body in hell" (Matthew 10:28).[5]

It is in and through the *Thou* experience that we understand the *now. Now* is the expression of my meaningful *being.* But to say that is not enough. What makes my *being* meaningful is identity, my *who*ness which I express as my *I-am*ness. This *being* is of a different character from my physical *being,* so that my sense of what is "time" is different. This is one way of saying that *being* is prior to "time" as either *is*ness or *am*ness. *Being* is the basic, root expression, and clock time and identity time are simply the two ways we have of distinguishing it. Because of the nature of knowing, *not* because of the nature of *being,* there is a definitional priority between identity time and clock time. However, the derivative nature of clock time is a matter of human epistemology, not the ontology of *being.* It is necessary to understand this in order to understand the difference between the character of identity time and clock time. Clock time is regular, orderly, repetitive, objective, and continuous. As opposed to this, identity time is continuous, unitary, flexible, unrepeatable, and subjective. Neither of these lists is meant to be exhaustive, but each is descriptive of *being.* In the first instance, *being* is timeful, in the second, time-full.

We do need, however, to explore the time-fullness of *being* further. To say that I-am-*now* is a statement of my identity, my self-consciousness. Primarily such self-consciousness is not subject to clock time; it is only secondarily or structurally so. That is, I can speak of someone's self-consciousness at the present and, again, in the future; but when I do this, I have artificially made an object of that person's self-consciousness by referring it to sequential events of clock time. The reference is to the change in events, not a change in self-consciousness. When I attempt to apply this objectification to myself, i.e., my own self-consciousness, what I am considering is *not* my self-consciousness but only my social-consciousness, my objective self-awareness in terms of others and the world, my *Me*-self. When I attempt such an inversion, the artificiality of the process is patently clear—I am playing with ideas about myself, I am not existentially involved in them. Because my self-consciousness is not mainly governed by clock time, I cannot say that it changes (i.e., is subject to any discontinuity of selfhood), for that would imply a chronology foreign to my own self-consciousness. I know, for example, that I *am* the same one who as a boy begged for pennies from my neighbor Mr. Finney, who fell in love with a girl named Jane and then another named Joyce, who preached the Word, who teaches. The chronology, as the verb changes indicate, refers to the events, even to life-styles, but not to my self-consciousness. I am one and the same; I am *now* in all of these events. I do not change, but that does not imply that identity is total and complete actuality, that my identity is completely fixed at birth as some idealists, Christian and non-Christian, would have it. Even the language is deceptive and dangerous in such an attempted definition, for words like *total* and *complete* give a quantitative and therefore objective and timeful connotation implying change. I do not change, but I do mature; I do extend myself in depth and in breadth through my encounters with the *Thous* of my life. The spatial metaphors in this continued attempt at description are just as culpable as the temporal ones, but the limitation is in language which, itself objective, necessarily involves us in implied contradiction. I *am,* in short, perdurable.

My self-consciousness is *now.* If I try to prohibit this expression by denying the *now,* by substituting clock time for identity time, by living through memory in the past, by living in anticipation in the future, or by avoiding or denying any further *I-Thou* encounters, then I am actually trying to escape from life. Such a life is not a successful denial of identity or of self-consciousness—the attempt at denial would be self-defeating because it is obviously self-contradictory—but such a life can be characterized as stagnating or moribund. Oneness remains, but my meaning and authenticity as a person are being jeopardized.

There are two extreme situations concerning self-consciousness which may be definitionally helpful to consider. The first has to do with psychological and /or physical maladies. When I have the experience of *being* two (and by this I do not mean the dialectical process of thought), then society does not commend me for excellence but says that I am sick; I am suffering from schizophrenia. Such abnormality is destructive of *being,* not its expression. Or again, as we get older and our powers of mind begin to diminish, identity remains even in the limited expression of senility, though senility can rob us of any creative function in the world and can curtail the scope of our self-awareness. But all these maladies simply emphasize the identity context. We fear that these things may one day happen to us because we know *we* shall be there to experience or suffer them. Meaningful life is that life in which identity in depth and maturity is achieved, that life in which our self-consciousness is made beautiful in love. To not achieve this, or to lose it, is the condition of tragedy.

The second extreme situation concerning self-consciousness is the process of thought reform or ideological reform termed "brainwashing." When one has been subjected to such a process, is his self-consciousness really changed; is he destroyed as a person or the person he used to *be?* That such might be the case is more the product of popular misunderstanding and poor science fiction than fact. What actually occurs in the person who is subjected to thought reform is a radical and intense personality change, an identity shift, a change in self-awareness (in terms of others and the world) rather than a change in self-consciousness. The loss of self-consciousness would actually defeat the purpose of the action—the "witness" of this particular person to the "new truth," a witness which includes a confession against the "old truth." The experience of ideological reform is an intense, personal one, not unlike a religious conversion except that this alteration of self-awareness is occasioned by coercion as well as the inner enthusiasm of evangelistic exhortation. The fact that "heroic rejection," "recovery," and "renewal" are all possibilities is a good indication that the continuity of the *I* remains even under such violent conditions.[6]

A clarification in light of a claim made earlier is necessary at this point. In describing the *I-Thou* encounter, it was observed that, in one sense, I am a different *I* with every *Thou* encounter which I have; this is true because each encounter is a creative one from which I emerge a different person. What has this to say, therefore, to the understanding of *now* which has been previously discussed? First of all, we can say that it is not a contradiction of *now* even though, with an obvious sequence of *Thous*, we have become involved with clock time. To emerge a "different person" from the *I-Thou* encounter is not meant to indicate radical change or loss of self-consciousness, but only development in depth or breadth. That is, I bring to each encounter that I have the identity which is mine because of all my previous encounters. Perhaps a theoretical distinction would be helpful in explanation. In and through a number of *I-Thou* encounters, my self-consciousness remains constantly and consistently *that*, but my self-awareness in terms of others and the world, my identity, deepens and is enriched. The gift of self-consciousness within encounter in the *now* remains *now* for me, is me, and continues to be me in the continuous expression of myself. The meeting of an old and very dear friend can substantiate this for us. After being apart for years, we find that those years have not in fact separated us at all. We were *now*-together in an *I-Thou* relation; we are *now*-together in that same relationship. It is only in the objective occurrences of our lives that we find any strangeness, and good conversation can soon fill in those gaps. If such an encounter and reunion does not occur, I then suspect that the original relationship was not a deep or meaningful one of *I-Thou*. Many relationships which seem deep are personally superficial but do reflect the common depth of mutual concern about a common cause or external event.

My confrontation with God as my *Thou* is little different. It is both *now* and present, and it has to do with personal identity. Within the relationship, I am aware of the presence of God in encounter with my own self-consciousness, my identity. With God, my identity (and therefore my meaning) is intensified and deepened, and, because that encounter is continuously available, it continues to *be* meaningful to me even when other relations fail. The relationship to God does not mean that all other relationships are inconsequential or redundant. Much of the variety, richness, and depth of personal expression is denied me if I cut myself off from other *Thous*. On the other hand, these other *Thous* can never fully compensate for that particular relationship in depth which is my relationship to God, though such a judgment can be made only after the fact. In that encounter, which we shall discuss in chapter 4, I "know" my *Thou* to be my creator as well. God is therefore not only *now* for me but also present in terms of *being*. His *Being* and my contingent *being*. Because of this intimate twofold relationship, the history of man's agony over his awareness of God's presence has been twofold. When a man of faith enters into a period of doubt or despair (what mystics and existentialists have long called "the dark night of the soul"), it is not God's *Being* which is in doubt but the immediacy of His personal, creative presence. God is *now* for such a man, but He does not seem to be present; the tension between these two conditions of *being* is what produces the agony, the questioning, and the doubt—all of which have to do with himself and his response to God, not with God's reality or His response to the man. There are others for whom "God" seems to be present in the witness of *Being-Itself*[7] and in the lives of others, but for whom He is not "real." He does not seem to confront them as their *Thou*. God may be present, but He is not *now*. To ask whether God is present is to ask the confessional question: "What have I done?" The agony for God in this case is the agony for reunion, for an awareness of grace, for forgiveness. Those who are asking whether God is "real" are actually asking the fundamental question: "Who am I?" The agony for God in this case is the agony for meaning, for fulfillment, for identity, not simply for God's continuing creative presence.

Thus far we have talked about time in terms of the extremes of experience: *I-It* and *I-Thou*, *is* and *am*, clock time and identity time. The more difficult task lies ahead in that area where these two come together and in which most of us live the most of our lives. The question of the nature of *(I)Me-You(Thou)* must be answered. As noted in the last chapter, the *(I)Me* context is that from which I have chosen a life-style (engineer, college professor, doctor, clergyman) in order to live in the world and with the world community. Insofar as my life is an expression of that life-style, it participates in the *It* world characterized by objective relationships, by clock time, by other-directed nature and activities. However, insofar as *I* have chosen this life-style and stand as its judge and critic, I am participating in the *Thou* world characterized by subjective relationships, by identity, by creativity and initiative.

It may be well to note that it is superficially possible for man to live his life in the *It* world where present and final responsibility seemingly rest on other people and objective forces; this is a life consigned to fate rather than one of fulfilling a destiny. Under these circumstances, *now* becomes unbearable and the *present* is threatening. Therefore man flees into the past or into the future—both fantasy worlds—in hopes of escaping the *present* and *now*. The tragedy of such a life is its complete lack of reality, its complete denial of potential. The appeal of such pseudo-security is so great that usually only great personal tragedy, an existential moment, can "bring" such a person back to an acceptance of responsibility. Even so, the reorientation in *now* is an agonizing process, for there has usually been little or no preparation for such responsibility. What I am describing here is the extreme case, but some such refusal to cope with "reality" is true for most of us. In fact, those who want only the old way, the old songs, the old hymns, the old values are participating, partially at least, in the escape from the present, from *now*. Not only individuals but corporate units can do the same. The factories which try to maintain the old methods, towns which try to forestall new and better methods of governance, communities which try to prevent social changes from occurring, all are trying to escape the responsibility of the present. If they persist, as we have witnessed so many doing, they begin to fail, die, or sometimes violently explode. The fantasies of the future are no better than the fantasies of the past; both misunderstand the timefulness of *being*.

However, normal human-life expression, from which vantage point we call the previously discussed avoidance patterns "escapism" or "abnormal behavior," is lived in the *(I)Me-You(Thou)* context described in chapter 2. Within this context, both the time-full and timeful aspects of *being* are expressed. However, because they are qualitatively different, they do not vie with each other though they both contour the expression of *being*. To the extent that I am living in the *You* world, the *It* world of corporate structures, laws—human and natural—order, regulations, civic or national responsibilities, I am a conscious participant in the clock-time existence of hours, deadlines, projections, studies, coordinates, ad infinitum. While, as noted before, I cannot consciously *be* clock time, I can use it as one of the coordinates of my life and am aware of the fact that my own physical life is an unconscious participant in such clock time. Insofar as I am living in the *I* world, the world of self-consciousness and identity, I am in the context of *now*, of self-expression in relation to *Thou* or to Nothingness. My *Thou* may be another or God; my rejection of *Thou* is my acknowledgment of Nothingness.

In the ordinary course of events, therefore, when I am not in the ecstasies of the *I-Thou* experience nor simply responding without critical assessment to the pressures and patterns about me, I am involved in expressing my identity in terms of the *present* context. *Now* comprehends and utilizes the present; the reverse is not true. Whether I live ten, twenty, fifty years—or for eternity (an imaginative endless stretch of *being* in this case)—makes no difference; my self-consciousness is perdurable. For this reason, as children, we could not imagine the world existing without us or going on without us. The stretch of our identity is in terms of *now*, and *now* does not know itself as restricted to clock time. As we get older, the mystery remains, but at least as adults we know that it is a mystery. Not only birth and death are mysterious, the sustainment of *being* so parenthetically enclosed is also mysterious.

I do not know what death means in terms of self-consciousness, but I am able to anticipate what it means to my physical expression of *being*. Consequently, I order my life accordingly. That does not mean that *clock time* controls the *now* (only death can tell us about that relationship), for it is possible for me to forfeit willingly the anticipated remainder of my physical life for someone or something sacrificially. Another way of stating that is to acknowledge that identity is stronger than conformity. Luther, in defying the Church, said: "Here I stand. God help me I can no other." The priority of decision is with the *now*. If my life becomes totally other-directed, it is because I have permitted this to happen. It is the decision not to decide which is an act of self-betrayal. Nevertheless, it must be noted that even though identity time has priority over clock time, identity time cannot violate or prevent the expression of clock time. I cannot stop clock time, much as I would like to, nor can I make it run backward. Clock time is the continuously present expression of objective *being* which I may choose, at my own physical peril, to ignore; but that choosing has nothing to do with my actual *being* in that dimension. This poses something of a dilemma—the coordination of self-expression in terms of identity and self-expression in terms of my physical *being*— which mankind has ingeniously solved by such contrivances as alarm clocks, bells, buzzers, and chimes, all of which are designed to make us aware that there is a reality whose *present* expression we cannot totally ignore. Thus life in the *(I)Me* context shifts back and forth in its focus between personal meaning and public meetings, identity and itinerary, self-consciousness and schedule. Each "time" makes its claim as the self-expression of my *being*.

Often in our conversations we indicate the nature of the focus which is dominating our lives at the moment. For example, someone coming out of a concert hall after a stimulating and exciting evening and saying "That was great!" implies several things. Because of the use of the past tense, he is employing the concept of clock time. He is acknowledging that the execution of the concert is over; he can no longer hear it even if he can "hear" it in his memory. By implication, he is acknowledging a distance between himself and the concert; he greatly enjoyed the performance; he did not participate in it; it did not become a *Thou* for him. While he was listening to the music, he and it were *present* but he was alone in his *nowness*. By stating his appreciation in the present, even though he uses the past tense, he acknowledges a present appreciation in terms of memory. The experience, however, is still objective to him in terms of identity.

If someone should come out of that concert and say "That is great!" instead of "That was great!" it could mean the same thing phrased in a less accurate way. On the other hand, such a person could be saying that the concert did encounter him as a *Thou,* that it was a creative experience which effected an identity development. This person is expressing present appreciation for a past event, which is perhaps the only way we can symbolically convey that we're dealing with identity time and not clock time. The concert is meaningful *now* for him, his life, and his identity. The experience has not become simply memory, as it did in the first instance, although it has moved into the past in clock time. What will eventually become memory for him will not be the concert, but the eventfulness of the concert for his life—a memory which will include the music, of course.

Such experiences happen to us with people as well. We meet in the course of a week hundreds of people on the street, but the possibility is always there that one whom we may so meet will become not simply *present* to us but *now* for us. This person changes our lives by affecting our identity, not by exerting some external force or law to which we respond externally. When that occurs, the focus of our *being* is on the *now* and the present becomes insignificant in its continuous expression. For the most part, the adjustment of focus between the present and *now* is simply part of the expected expression of *being;* the movement between the two "times" is an expression of a desirable balance in life. To exclude either context is self-destructive: one cannot function as a member of human society if his awareness is confined to *now;* his life can be only meaningless if lived exclusively in the present.

One further question must be answered before extending our phenomenological analysis of the nature and relation of *being,* in both its time-full and timeful expressions, to God. Is it possible to have a memory—which we have treated as objective—of my *now* existence? Insofar as *now* is my intimate self-consciousness, there can be no memory, for memory implies clock time, which such self-consciousness excludes. Yet it seems to be the case that we remember *when* we were such-and-such a person or *when* we loved so-and-so. These memories, however, are not of our self-consciousness but of particular expressions of identity which were eventful and therefore timeful. The condition of *who* we are remains always with us. As we stated earlier, my self-consciousness does not change although it does seem to mature, so that my sheer identity in terms of self-consciousness is always *now* and always, in one sense, complete. Albert Speer, Hitler's personal architect recently released from Berlin's Spandau Prison, poignantly reflects on the implications which can be involved in such identity-events:

> I kept that old sketch [an architect's draft of the Prachtstrasse] framed there, while writing my memoirs, just to remind myself how far megalomania can really go. And not only Hitler's. If you ask me if I was the ambitious and driving young architect who

drafted that mad plan, that small sketch on the wall, I shall answer, "Yes, of course." But if you ask me the far more searching question as to whether I am that same man today, I must answer that I don't honestly know. This troubles me often in the evenings. I have been looking for the answer in the works of the Swiss theologian Karl Barth, but I just don't know.[8]

What has my relationship to God got to do with time? Though we shall concern ourselves with revelation specifically in the next chapter, we have already established that the nature of my subjective relationship to God is that of *I-Thou*. God "stands" over and against me as my *Thou*, the *Eminent Thou* with whom I reach my most complete expression of personal identity. By definition, this seems to involve me in saying that God is primarily *now*—outside of clock time. Symbolically man has always tried to express this by speaking of God in eternity, in heaven, or "above" the earth. "Our Father, who art in heaven . . . Thy will be done (present-future orientation) on earth as it is (*now* orientation) in heaven." God is always addressing me within the context of the *I-Thou* relation so that my response to Him is always one of self-conscious identity, but it also is one of self-conscious responsibility within the *It* world. The fact that I move in and out of this relationship, thus into the world of clock time, is what gives my relationship to God a sense of the sporadic or intermittent. The fact and effect of the relationship are involved with clock time; the nature of the relationship is involved with identity time. The use of "time" is not an arbitrary determination but is descriptive of the immediate implications of the relationship itself. Because the relation is *I-Thou*, God is experienced as personal confrontation, as the presence of *Being*. Such an experience is time-full, as any self-conscious confrontation is. The presence of *Being* is just that—a sense of *presence*, not principle. This time-full expression of *now* has no place in the Platonic idealism of Greek metaphysics.

Thus far the relationship to God seems to be a mystical one, a matter of direct and personal confrontation with God *now*. But the experience of the presence of God has always been broader than that. In fact, in much religious history and literature, man is first made aware of the presence of God through an *I-Thou* encounter with another person or the physical world, the beauty of nature, the awesomeness of natural power. These are not God but have been the occasions for an awareness of God. When such an experience occurs, I am aware that I am being addressed by God, i.e., somehow I know that my identity is bound up with the experience. It is a sense of the presence of *Being* in which the *present* has been superseded in the act of encounter by *now*. Because such an experience often comes in and through the natural, physical world, I can acknowledge the same dual expressiveness of God's *Being* as I find in myself. God who is *Being,* who expresses Himself as my *Thou,* also addresses me through the stability of the unselfconscious identity of the physical world. Though God is *now* and is always *now* he comes to meet me through that order which is present. The present is the mediator for the *now,* just as the physical person whom I meet can mediate the *Thou* who addresses me in terms of my identity. The implication of this for "time" is clear: *now* is the larger, more profound expression which includes within it an awareness of the present, and an ability to affect the course of events in the present, while in its facticity remaining bound to the present.

Because the *now* is other than the movement and change of the present, and can comprehend the interaction and infrastructure of natural identities, which we call orders or "laws," it is possible for human will, as an expression of identity, to alter the course of events in the present. It is not possible to truly alter natural identities, though it is possible for one to rearrange them in such a way as to produce new relationships and new products. But two points should interest us here. One, although identity is beyond timeful reality, it can impose itself willfully in a timeful way; if identity were totally subject to time it could only *be* present. It could then never utilize the present. Two, we should notice that because clock time is present, so that the time-cause is present and the time-effect past, such alteration is possible. Otherwise a natural determinism, with no ambiguity or paradoxical tension, would preclude any genuine change, creativity, or uniqueness. Likewise, the future is not fixed but remains a potentiality of the present, the expression of hope, imagination, and will.

Of course, such a view of time directly affects that discipline which we call history. If time is understood as *now* and present, then our understanding of the nature of events must reflect this perspective. In terms of classical metaphysical Idealism and its heirs, history is the record of appearances which point beyond themselves to the one timeless Reality; or, for one like Hegel, history is the dramatic and dynamic unfolding of the Absolute Idea; or, for some Christians, history is the record of man's progress (or lack of it) to the Kingdom of God; or, for some Communists, history is the dialectical process by which man will reach the humanist ideal of a classless society; or, for some pragmatists, history is the record of man's attempts to achieve a better life for himself, a guide to what to do as well as what not to do. However, what all these views of history assume is some point of fixed reference called "reality" which the recording of events substantiates or exposes. Even those, like Marx, who wished to leave history open to the future, to the creative act, in the end failed to do so by finally appealing to a fixed metaphysical reality or resolution. The radical concept of time changes all this.

Before going further, however, there are some definitional matters to clear up. The word *history,* as we all know, is ambiguous. What do we mean by *history?* Does history refer to the events themselves—so that we can talk about the force or power of history? Or does history refer to the objective recording of an event, i.e., George Washington was the first president of the United States, so that there is no history where there is no spectator? Or is history an interpretation, a source of meaning for my life? Part of the confusion about *history* as an academic discipline is that it has been thought of in each of these ways. Consequently, to avoid confusion, we must settle on one definition of *history,* and the rest will need other verbal symbols; or, like Carl Michalson, we must add adjectives such as *worldly, existential, biblical,* and *eschatological* to it to differentiate meanings.[9] Part of the confusion about *history,* however, is caused by the ambiguity of time in idealist metaphysics, the conflict, in some form, between time and eternity.

For the purposes of this study of time, we shall begin by viewing what happens to these expressions of *history* when "time" is understood to be the expression of *being, now* and in the present. If *being* is timeful, then by definition everything that happens (and has happened) is (or was once present). The world is occurrence; the world is happening; the world is expression. On this basis, and on this basis alone, all things, all happenings, are of equal note or importance. In terms of time and occurrence, it makes little difference whether I am dropping a paper gum wrapper or an atomic bomb; in terms of sheer *is*ness, there is no difference. Let us simply call this "occurrence" and mean any present thing, action, or state of *being.* This is not history; it is the totality of *is*ness observed or unobserved. When such an occurrence becomes meaningful for me, i.e., affects me directly or indirectly in terms of *what* I am or affects me directly in terms of *who* I am, then that occurrence becomes an "event." Such an event can be solicited (as when I purposely commit myself to some action or to some friend) or unsolicited (as when I am unwittingly or unwillingly involved in some traumatic experience, e.g., a depression or war, or when I become "involved" because of disease, accident, or action of another). An event is an occurrence which, for any one of a number of reasons, has become the focal center of my conciousness and thereby singled out for attention. The line of demarcation between occurrence and event is subtle to the point of being indistinguishable. An event can be present or *now* depending upon whether it is objective or subjective in nature.

History, therefore, is the term we shall use to describe those occurrences which human understanding confronts, selects, and orders as noteworthy for its life and times. History is the personal record of meaningful occurrences which we have called "events." While occurrences (as happenings) take place in the present, in clock time, in the world of *It,* events may be either present or *now, It* or *Thou.* History is grounded in the *now* as the expression of my identity. Who I am determines what priority I give to events. History is the expressed relation of identity time to clock time. Thus history is dependent upon my ontological stance. In other words, it is my life *now* and in the present which partially governs whether a particular thing or happening is merely an amorphous occurrence or whether it is an event, but it is totally my responsibility for the meaningful ordering of those occurrences which do become events for me. If I ignore a particular happening because of my life *now* and in the present, that happening will (if confined to my experience alone) disappear with the present. It will completely disappear if no traces of its *being* or expression persist with the continuing present. It is true that many occurrences are lost forever, as if they had never happened, simply because they were not selected by someone as meaningful events.

There are occurrences which, because of their general nature, become general events. World War II is such a significant event. Many people the world over related meaningfully, often tragically, to this occurrence. To them, the war was not an amorphous happening but a catastrophic and meaningful event which dramatically affected their identity and life-style and perhaps threatened their physical *being.* Due to the nature of war and to the physical and economic upheavals (let alone the personal ones) many effects of the war are still with us and very much in evidence. Consequently, since meaningfulness is so general, the event has been included as part of mankind's general history. It achieved that position not because it happened but because it became meaningful to so many; its effect on an individual was not confined to the present but often became a part of his *now.* As part of the *now,* his identity, the event holds an importance and place which the passage of time only indirectly affects.

The fact that history is involved with such subjective and objective interaction, with both time-fullness and timefulness, is supported by the observation that even those large events such as World War II are subject to an almost infinite number of interpretations. The war means one thing to the French, another to the Germans, the British, the Americans, and the Russians. When occurrence is selected for eventfulness, it is usually because of the identity which I bring into the context of that occurrence. This is true of community or general identity as well as individual identity. I am sure that the Germans understand, *now,* the battle of Stalingrad in a totally different way than the Russians understand it. In other words, there is no such thing as objective history. There is objective occurrence, even objective eventfulness, but history involves my self-conscious identity, or a nation's corporate-conscious identity—

although this corporate-consciousness is something of a myth, a symbolic statement to identify a general consensus rather than a real consciousness.

This point also becomes clear in dealing with the phenomenon of the "generation-gap." If one has lived through the depression days of the thirties, which became eventful for a great number, it becomes very difficult to explain or excite the youth of the seventies in this event. For most of them, affluence has deprived them of any sensitivity to those happenings which became so meaningful to the older generation. Consequently, the event, for them, is only a reflected occurrence and is dismissed. If the depression is not dismissed, it is only because the youth must still deal with an adult population which still "lives" the depression, or because they must deal with an economic situation which does affect them in the present and which does, at the same time, bear the unmistakable marks of the thirties. One hundred years from now, who knows what the history of the depression will mean or be? Our current experience of historiography leads us to believe that the interpretation will be markedly different.

This leads us to another observation about our ontological view of history. Because history is an expression of our selection and ordering of events and because it is involved with our identity, we can understand why the work of the historian is so important and never complete. History is always changing and developing because we are always maturing and developing. While it is true that the passage of time permits us to gather more and more present data about a particular event in the past and therefore permits us to get a clearer picture, a more complete competence, it is likewise true that time, clock time with its continuous abundance of happenings as well as identity time with its ever-deepening expression, gives us an altered perspective on the event itself. The occurrence in the past has not changed; because it is past, it cannot; but we have "grown" and therefore the meaning of the event for us has consequently changed. One need only follow the fascinating history of the Civil War in America to observe this. The longer we spend collecting and organizing data concerning the event, the more accurately we can reconstruct and analyze it, but its meaning for us as American citizens faced with racial crises, geographic prejudices, and continued privations is giving the Civil War a totally "new" history. Some Civil War historians believe we shall have to rewrite the textbooks on the war because of what has happened to us through the study of Black history. Not only do we have new data to consider; we also have an enriched identity.

Black history itself is a case in point. It is the emancipation of the Black person in America which has created a Black history. Black history has not created the Black person. What for many have been occurrences have not become events. The tragedy, of course, is that many occurrences in the past, simply because they were not recorded and therefore left no mark for the present, are simply lost. There are imagination and speculation which in themselves are helpful, but they cannot be classified as history.

This brings us to another point which is of importance. While the ground of history itself is only *now,* history need not be only of the present, although it must concern itself with that which is present. Again Black history is a case in point. While it is an expression of Black identity which is *now* and present, Black identity is *now* and presently interested in its roots, its past. While Black history cannot recapture occurrences in the past, it can partially recreate them in terms of events. Even though occurrences are no longer present in full execution, one can, from the marks and memories which still are, make them eventful, meaningful.

History is a study produced and encouraged by age and experience. The longer we live and the deeper we involve ourselves in life, the more relevant history becomes as a discipline or expression of self. Most of us have had the experience of taking a young child to a "historical site," or a museum, or to an art gallery in which the child is bored to death; he would much rather be at the zoo where something is going on, *happening.* His view of those things which for his parents are part of eventful living is simply that of occurrence. There is no identity association yet. When that does occur, the museum becomes a new world, a *now* and present experience. This, no doubt, is what is meant by the phrase *a sense of history.* A sense of history is a mature sense of identity which sees the interrelatedness of *being,* the continuity in human affairs that affects and has affected man's identity. I suppose this proves to be a good working definition of a historian. Of course, a historian can be simply a good technician, a cataloguer of others' insights and identity expressions; but most historians bring to the awareness of historical method an identity of their own which enables them to be as much a critic and creator as a cataloguer.

This view of time and history has important implications for Christianity whose adherents think of it as a historical faith. For many, such a claim has indicated a proof method. If the fact of Christianity could be established, then Christians could have the assurance of the truth of the faith, and since history is *in the past* such a faith would be irrefutable and unassailable. That such has never been the case seems to be more an indictment of such an understanding of history than a rejection of Christianity. Few men today would deny that Jesus of Nazareth lived at the beginning of the first century. Present literary evidence in terms of early documents and accounts far outweigh speculations to the contrary. But that is to deal within the context of occurrences and happenings, not history. To make the claim that Jesus is the Christ, the Son of the Living

God, takes us beyond occurrence into history. The point to be remembered, however, is that this *history* within the Church, or this *history*
claimed publicly by a believer, is, in itself, only an occurrence to the
outsider, the listener, or observer. How many times we hear people say,
"Sure, Jesus must have lived; but I don't go along with this divinity claim.
He was just a good man with powerful and relevant ideas." For such
individuals, the "divinity claim" of the Church is simply a mistaken claim.
Until my spiritual identity makes such a claim an event, the claims of the
Church will fall on deaf ears. In fact, many Church leaders postpone
arduous doctrinal teachings to children simply because they are aware
that the children are not ready for such an eventful commitment. Most
often in cases when a young person of ten or twelve makes his "commitment to Christ," he is making his commitment to the minister or priest
who has established an *I-Thou* relation with him. We know from long and
extended experience that such commitments to the Christ which are, in
effect, secondhand, do not last, even though the original commitment to
the person may continue.

What can we mean, then, when we state that Christianity is a historical faith? Perhaps we can say that Christianity, like all other religious
expressions and claims, can be observed as a pattern of activity, organization, and stated beliefs which may or may not be eventful or meaningful
to the outsider. From the outside, Christianity is only an occurrence
whose origins, development, and expression can be objectively verified.
From the inside, Christianity is history. It is eventful, meaningful, and
part of the life-style adopted to express a spiritual identity. It is an
acknowledgment of my *Thou* relationship with God. From the outside,
the faith claims of Christianity—that God reveals himself to man, that
God was in Christ reconciling the world to Himself, that God was Christ,
that Christ was crucified, died, and was buried, then rose from the
dead—are existentially meaningless. They are not even occurrences in
any publicly verifiable way. Therefore, if someone outside Christianity
does find the religion eventful, it is because the organized expression of
the faith, the Church, in some way has an effect on his identity or
life-style. At this point, Christianity becomes history, even though it has
not yet become a faith. I do not believe that it is an exaggeration to say
that Christianity, understood in this way, has become history for almost
all the peoples and cultures of Western civilization. Christianity as an
organization, as a public philosophy, and as a dominant morality has so
marked Western culture that it is virtually impossible not to think of it as
history. This is a point which H. Richard Niebuhr makes in the prologue
to his book *The Responsible Self:*

> I call myself a Christian because my relation to God has been, so
> far as I can see, deeply conditioned by this presence of Jesus
> Christ in my history and in our history. In one sense I must call

myself a Christian in the same way that I call myself a twentieth-century man. To be a Christian is simply part of my fate, as it is the fate of another to be a Muslim or a Jew. In this sense a very large part of mankind is today Christian; it has come under the influence of Jesus Christ so that even its Judaism and Mohammedanism bears witness to the fact that Jesus Christ has been among us.[10]

It is also possible for Christianity to become historical for me because of my relations to another who professes this as his faith, even though I do not. Because of my respect, love, or maybe even hatred for this person, those experiences and contexts which have been influential in his life and in the shaping of his identity, become important for me. It would be almost impossible to number the lives which have been touched in an important, meaningful way by such men of faith as Kagawa, Schweitzer, James S. Stewart, Reinhold Niebuhr, Martin Luther King, Jr.—men who have reached out to humanity, but always in the name of the Christ so that no one could finally disassociate the two.

This is partially what it means to say that Christianity is a historical faith. On this point, both those inside as well as those outside could agree. However, the Christian himself means more than just this. He means that when history becomes the entree to faith, to the revelation of God, then he can see, in terms of his own identity, his own self-consciousness, that the historical event and the divine event are one. At that point, he can make the affirmation of faith: "Jesus is the Christ." At once, in that statement, the act of faith ("Thou art the Christ") and the assertion of history (Jesus was a great man) are brought together in what the Christian believes to be his historical faith. Put in another way, Christianity can be seen as the authentic expression of the *(I)Me* context. The intimate act of faith, of encounter, prayer, and adoration is *I-Thou;* the public act of historical analysis, of observation, power, and interrelations is *I-It;* the life of the Christian which incorporates both expressions of *being* must be *(I)Me.* This means that his life is, as I have already indicated in the discussion of *(I)Me,* both time-full and timeful. It is responsive in terms of identity and change, *now* and the present. Christian faith is always *now* and a matter of presence; Christian organizational structure and power are always present. The life of the Christian in the world is always both.

However, it is just because Christianity claims to be a historical faith, in the ambiguous way I just indicated, that it takes the form or expression it does in the world. Because of the experience of faith which can identify itself in and through the historical event and therefore be one with it, the Christian believes that God will so express himself to all men in a similar way. It is not as though God could not speak to man directly in terms of a mystical *I-Thou* confrontation. If we are to believe the histories of all religions, not simply that of Christianity, then we must accept the witness of countless numbers that such a revelation has indeed occurred. But the limitations of *being* human, our fragility of mind and body, our susceptibility to fantasy, imagination, and neuroses, always produce doubts and questions about the authenticity of the experience—let alone its nature; the variety of religions attests to that. The revelation of God is not the only experience characterized as self-authenticating; any *I-Thou* relation is such. It is a *now* experience which simply precludes final objective confirmation. Yet it is here, and specifically in the historical person of Jesus, that Christianity claims to bring some objectivity to bear. Of course, the immediate experience of faith, the confrontation, remains subject-to-subject and does defy objectification; but in the task of *being* a Christian, in expressing my faith through my identity and in my choice of life-styles, the historical correlation with the New Testament figure of Jesus is necessary if my *being* is to be comprehensively expressed. The historical Jesus is that point of correlation, whom I acknowledge to be the Christ of faith. In Him, I judge my self-conscious and my historical responses. The nature of the Christ-event will be discussed in the last chapter of the book.

Convinced that such a correlation does exist, it is the obligation of Christianity, more specifically the Church, to witness *now* and in the present the reality of the eventfulness of its own occurrence. The Church, through its preaching, teaching, social action, regard for tradition, and study of Scriptures, must make itself available to anyone searching for identity and meaning, so that what may to some be mere occurrence can become the historical ground of revelation and faith. It is worthy of note that the Bible itself is grounded in such a correlation. Much of Scripture is a historical account of the life of the Jews and the early Christians; it is written in the context of clock time and can be verified in an objective way by cross-reference of *histories,* archeological finds, etc. However, a good portion of Scripture is written in the context of *now*—wisdom literature, devotional literature, poetry, homiletics. In these, chronology is of no importance, for the writers concerned themselves with the *I-Thou* relationship of man with God and /or with man. In yet other portions of Scripture, the correlation is not simply implied by common inclusion but by explicit statement. In this category would fall most of the prophetic literature, many of the sayings of Jesus, and the letters of Paul. Admittedly these are generalizations, but they hold true, as generalizations.

Because history changes as identity develops, the nature and meaning of Christianity as a historical faith, of the Church as an institution, and of Scripture as a mediator for the Word of God all change and develop. The relevance and meaning of these expressions is present and *now*. Consequently, man cannot have an enshrinement of the historical past as though it were finally fixed and sacrosanct; that would be idolatry. Faith, as the expression of the encounter between man and God, can only *be;* history, as an expression of the past, can only respond to my identity *now*. Outside of that, there are only occurrences which are potentially meaningful but can make no claim on their own.

4

Reason and Revelation

Any attempt at making a theological statement has, eventually, to come to grips with man's power to reason; for theology, by definition, is the reasoned expression of man's religious life. What is reason? What is reason's relationship to *being*? What is reason's relationship to truth? Is reason truth? Can reason know or understand God? Can reason perceive God? Is God himself reasonable? Is God the ground of reason? Along with these questions and a host of others just like them are the problems of the relationship between reason and revelation. Does God reveal Himself to me through reason? Are reason and revelation one and the same thing? Is revelation an irrational presence or sense which reason must symbolically structure into ideas, laws, and order? Can reason lead to faith? Are faith and reason identical? Are they mutually exclusive? Is reason my response to perception while faith is my response to revelation? Can we agree with St. Augustine that reason presupposes faith, that reason cannot validate or justify itself? Can we agree with Thomas Aquinas that faith and reason are autonomous; that each can lead us to God; that each tells us something different about God? Can we agree with Karl Barth that there can be no knowledge of God outside of God's self-revelation; that there can be no natural theology; that reason, unaided, can only mislead us? All of these questions and positions have been important in the development of Christian theology. All are worthy of study, and all have merited volumes of scholarly analysis and argumentation. However, in keeping with the attempt to present a theology of encounter consistent with the new ontological stance, what we must do is attempt to redefine reason in terms of that stance. If reality is *being*, what is the nature and function of reason, and what implications are there for the nature and function of revelation?

In keeping with the twofold nature of the expression of *being*, *I-Thou* and *I-It*, a distinction must be made in the activities which have generally been included under the label of reasoning. Before going any further, it should be noted that reason is not some *thing*, nor is it some absolute order or structure which we can designate (if not define) by using a capital *R;* such claims reflect the classical metaphysics we have rejected. Reason is an activity in which the self participates with another and as such is an expression of the encounter of *beings.* Consequently, it must reflect those aspects and contours of *being* which we have already discussed. Most properly, then, we should discuss reasoning, reason being the abstract result—good, bad, or indifferent—of that particular process. For purposes of denotation and distinction, I should like to reserve the word *reasoning* for that activity of self which we share with another. In other words, *reasoning is corporate.* This specific idea will be developed later in the chapter. However, if we use *reasoning* to refer to a corporate activity, then we must use another word for that mental activity which I perform by myself. For this, I shall use the word *thinking* and, for the sake of clarity, we shall begin our analysis with this word.

Thinking is the mental activity in which I engage by myself when I purposefully consider my world and my place in it. But *thinking* itself is not a simple term, for not only do there seem to be a variety of kinds of thinking, but there also is a form of thinking which does not seem purposeful at all. Therefore, we must make yet another distinction in our analysis. I shall call this nonpurposeful activity of the brain "consciousness."

The brain is a physical structure of the body whose apparent function is to express appropriately man's awareness of the world. By *appropriately,* we can mean only that different forms of perception seem to produce different symbols, images, sensations, and reactions with a certain consistency, i.e., we don't often confuse sight with smell, though because the brain is an interrelated thing it is possible for an odor or a sight to activate the memory of an associated sense experience. (A certain rubber eraser smell can bring back or make present a whole childhood school context for us which may have happened thirty or forty years ago.) The brain, functioning on this level of awareness and association, is engaged in the activity of being conscious. This is not a willed activity; it is simply one natural activity of the brain, just as the natural activity of the eye is to see. I do not mean to belittle the complexity of this activity of the brain nor to claim to understand how consciousness occurs or sensations interrelate. These are matters about which the physiologists and psychologists can best instruct us. All that is necessary for us to understand at this point is the general function of the brain which we commonly call "consciousness"—that which we lose when we go to sleep or are hit over the head. Such a working definition also excludes what is often referred to as the subconscious. The role and relationship of the subconscious or the unconscious vis-à-vis the conscious mind is by definition mysterious and vague. However, because of what we have surmised indirectly, it seems proper to assume that the subconscious is likewise an expression of *being*—perhaps even the opera-tion of the mind on the neuro-mechanical level of *being*, i.e., neuro-physically controlled response, association, and reaction.

Consciousness is that awareness of mind with which I uncritically respond to the world which sensuously imposes itself upon me. Such awareness is truly to be understood as other-directed. My mind wanders wherever the stimuli and resulting associations take it. It is that "state" of mind I am in when I perform daily routines, habits, functions which take no concentration and which I do "automatically." It is the world of daydreams and fantasies. It is an activity of mind which can be produc-tive, but only accidentally so. However, because consciousness is such an undifferentiated experience does not mean that it is not compelling or pleasurable. It is effortless; it can be highly entertaining, delightfully irresponsible. It is sometimes startling to note how long we have been sitting "just gazing out the window"—certainly a euphemism for wander-ing consciousness. How often we are reading, only to find that our minds had wandered off some pages before, or that we had been staring at the same page for "how long?" but with no comprehension. Consciousness is an expression of being present, but it is not a self-conscious awareness of the present; sheer consciousness is not reflexive.

But consciousness, even though we spend a large, perhaps the largest, portion of clock time there, is not all entertaining and delightful. To be conscious is to be open to the world where many occurrences are hurtful, tragic, distasteful, or are threatening, challenging, and /or de-manding. Such exposure jars us into thought, a purposeful concentra-tion which enables us to ignore or to eliminate the now peripheral impo-sitions on our consciousness. *Purposeful* is an important word here, for it differentiates thinking from states of neuroses and psychoses in which the same concentration takes place but the experience is uncontrolled, disorienting rather than orienting. Thinking is a function of self-consciousness; it is a directed activity of the self which is expressive of my identity. Thinking is an arbitrary focus of my awareness in order to delineate my relation to the world and in the world. The form of think-ing results from the nature of the focus: it can be judgment, considera-tion, evaluation, determination, recollection, memorization, or ratiocina-tion. Thinking is always productive, even if it is not productive in terms of desired results. It is a potential source of knowledge about one's self and the world, or it may be simply a source of pleasure—the solving of a puzzle, doing recreational mathematics, or reading detective stories.

Because thinking is a willful activity of my self-consciousness, the probability of my thinking in any given context is directly related to the involvement of my identity. If the issue or context is relatively unimpor-tant, then my focus or concentration will be correspondingly weak or irresolute. You may be reading this book simply because someone thought you should, but if it has proved to be of little interest to you, then you will have wandered off into sheer consciousness many times, as I suggested earlier. However, if you are passionately interested in something because it does involve you in its scope, then your thought concentration is such that it shuts everything else out. When a book excites us, it is possible, at least temporarily, to forget meals or to ignore the need for sleep. Thought, as purposeful concentration, can be at any level between these extremes. When people enjoin us to "stop and think," what they are saying to us is "focus your undivided attention on this," which does have the effect of stopping all peripheral conscious activity.

If we can say that thinking is a willful concentration of mind, what can we say about those situations in which I claim that "I just can't stop thinking about it"? Under these circumstances, what we are usually referring to is an emotionally charged experience which keeps imposing itself on our consciousness. There are at least two ways of coping with this pseudo-thought: one is to think about the experience—analyze it, examine it, subject it to the discipline of psychoanalysis; the other way is determinedly to focus on some other experience or interest. Under normal circumstances, i.e., when one is not neurotic or psychotic, the priority of activity is established by his self-consciousness. He can choose to think or not to think. For the most part, the movement in and out of thought is so frequent and so subtle that we are unaware of it. For the majority of us, we think when we "have to" and coast in consciousness when we can.

Thinking itself, therefore, is not merely the reception of percepts; it is the ordering of these percepts into meaningful sets which we call logic. Because thinking is a willful act, without which consciousness can only meander seemingly without the benefit of logical sets, it is fair to assume that the logic is in part an imposition of the mind, an imposition which can be described epistemologically in terms of the "laws of thought" or psychologically in terms of patterns of relations. But the very fact of imposition suggests (as it did in the dimension of time) that there is a correlation which exists between the world of identity and the world of It, that *I-It* is a basic category of *being,* a *given* or *thereness* within which thought is possible and relevant. The intricate and vast epistemological and psychological problems of thought-description need not concern us for the purposes of this study. It is enough for us to recognize that thinking is a self-willed function of the mind, an expression of our identity structured by an apparent natural consistency of *being.* The probability of such a natural consistency is enhanced by the fact that by honoring this consistency I can make my thoughts intelligible to others, others with whom I also share the intensely personal, self-authenticating experience of *I-Thou*. An identity achieved in *I-Thou* can subsequently be expressed, affirmed, and mutually acknowledged in symbolic terms of *I-It*. It is with this assurance, for example, that Elizabeth Barrett Browning confidently counts the ways of love for Robert Browning. In thought, the consistency of *being*'s twofold expression is symbolically expressed and communally verified.

Thinking is an act expressive of identity. To think clearly and "logically" is an art; we *learn* to think. One of the primary purposes of education is to teach a person to think; education is not just a matter of passing on information or acquiring large numbers of facts, formulas, or theories. Thus thinking is an art or skill which all men exercise with varying degrees of individual excellence which in turn seems to depend upon natural potential and personal discipline. However, such a thoughtful claim about thinking is tautological or it symbolically points beyond itself to some more inclusive condition of awareness. It is the contention of this study that thinking is directed toward such a "condition of awareness" which should be described as the corporate function: reason.

The results of thinking are ideas, attitudes, judgments, actions, and decisions. Such results have an objective character about them in that they can be shared, written down, compared, contrasted, adopted, or abandoned. The results, once formulated, have become a part of the *It* world. But the question arises, What is the ontological status of an idea? Three conditions implied by the word *idea* need to be considered. First, in terms of the *fact* (i.e., *being*) of the idea, it has no ontological status other than one of dependence on the thinker. It is the abstract product of the interaction of his mind and the world. Second, in terms of the objective symbols for that abstract product—its public expression as language, music, art, etc.—it has the objective status of the *It* world and remains present so long as the specific medium persists, e.g., we can still study the recorded ideas of a Jeremiah or a Plato by reading texts attributed to them. Third, in terms of the content of ideas, more seems to be implied, e.g., Bach wrote great music; or Beauty is Truth. In each of these thoughts, a universal claim seems to be made which transcends the individual's or the symbol's particular ontological status. Does this mean that some ideas (generalizations, universals) have special ontological status and others not? I believe not. The difficulty is the result of an inadequate understanding of what is being said. Because ideas are the products of human thought, the statement "Bach wrote great music" is, in fact, incomplete. What is being said (in part by implication) is: "*I think* Bach wrote great music," or " *I* think Beauty is Truth." In each case, the words *I think* add the ontologically qualifying context of the statement. What appears to have independent status or universal validity in reality has neither.

One of the things besides syntax which misleads us is the apparent timelessness of such statements; they seem untouched by clock time: what is true for Keats is true for me concerning beauty. But again we are in danger of confusing reality with a symbol status for that reality. Three critical observations are relevant here. One, such generalizations, once removed from any particular instance, are thought-abstracts, thoughts about thoughts. But as such, their *being* is only of a derivative nature. Because *being* alone has to do with "time," these derivative claims are seemingly timeless. The ontological participation of such ideas in *being* is only in terms of their form, their symbolicity, not in terms of their content: thus the illusion of timelessness. Therefore, the seeming timelessness of such a claim as "Beauty is Truth" rests with the fact that the statement is reflective of *my* identity (I believe . . .) and therefore participates in *my now* which is beyond clock time, or it is an objective thought of convenience, a universal—a symbol for several symbols— whose only reality is that of an epistemological function. Consequently, its *content* or *meaning* appears timeless. But, again, that should warn us immediately of its unreality, i.e., there *is* no metaphysical Reality (immutable and eternal) which is *Beauty* or *Truth*. All *being* (including that of God) has to do with "time," and what does not must be the imaginative function or result of knowing, having ontological form but not content. Two, because an idea objectively persists is no guarantee that its original meaning can readily be grasped (What is the nature of Keats' aesthetic judgment?) or that its validity is thereby enhanced. Persistence is not a sufficient truth-claim: there are still people who believe that the earth is flat or that the sun moves around the earth. Three, ideas, for all their seeming timelessness, do go out of date, do change, or are forgotten. Independent metaphysical Reality could not tolerate such abuse.

Just as the results of thinking belong to the *It* world, so thinking itself is expressive of the *I-It* nature of *being* and represents a spectrum of contexts from *(I)Me-You(Thou)* to the qualified *Me-You(It)*. Thinking, in terms of *(I)Me*, is critical and imaginative thought which is expressive of my life-style and my sense of identity. As such it is personal, responsible, creative, and evaluative. It is the considered expression of the educator, the politician, the writer. Thinking, in terms of *Me-You*, is nonreflexive logical thought. It is an expression of technique in which the self as a self is only nominally involved. As such it is impersonal, utilitarian, and objectively productive. The distinction is one that we could make between the man who, as a concerned citizen of his town or city, voluntarily involves himself in responsible civic study and action in the problems of urban pollution; and that same man who, as an expert in insurance adjusting, is called upon to provide only a commercial function. However, both of these emphases in thought have to do with competence, excellence, and integrity. These qualities are general characteristics of thought which apply to both *(I)Me* and *Me-You* contexts.

Despite these uses and functions of thinking, all of which we find involved in our own lives and some of which dominate our lives, there is a coldness, an incompleteness, a sterility about life lived in terms of these functions only. In the first place, thinking is an intensely individual operation. While I may receive help in terms of ideas or techniques from others or may intensify this experience in a "think-tank," and while I am dependent upon the world about me which provides the substance for my thinking, the process is privately, particularly, and peculiarly mine. When I am thinking I cease to deal with the world as it is and consider it symbolically; in deep thought the focus of my attention is such that I virtually become unaware of everything but the particular symbols about which I am deliberating. The intricate process of dialectic by which thought proceeds need not concern us here except to note that I alone am involved in that dialectic no matter how much I attribute the presence of my mental images to another to whom I am intimately related, the process remains isolated within me. My concern for my wife's or my son's self-fulfillment is simply *that—my* concern. Of course, any statement or action on my part objectifies and makes public such a concern, but at that point I am engaged in something more than sheer thinking.

While such thinking is natural for me and necessary for the expression of my identity, it still excludes by its nature those *I-Thou* experiences which are creatively effective for my life; it separates me from others by focusing on the world, by objectifying my relationship to another in terms of some "third" point of reference. Thinking at best can be only creatively expressive of *my* life. Such an observation does not dispute the need or excellence of thinking; it only indicates one of its major limitations. It is only when thinking presumes to be more than it is that it becomes distorting, destructive, and (theologically speaking) evil. When I assume that my thoughts alone are infallible and worthy of implementation, then I have denied the corporate nature of truth-claims (the authenticity of my thought) in which *being*-as-encounter involves me and have arrogantly abused the identity context to which my thinking is responsible and of which it is expressive.

A second limitation of thinking which has already been implied is the objective nature of its process and product. In thinking, my self-awareness is involved in a reflexive and expressive way but not in an identity-creative way, so that my relationship to the world and others is from a position of central fixity. This orientation can be maintained only so long as any potential *I-Thou* relationship remains potential rather than becoming actual. When my relationships are so ordered, they are, by definition, relationships which are objectively structured. This is most appropriate for all interactions within the *It* world, for all cultural relationships, but is inadequate to cope with any *Thou* demands upon my life. The world which is objective to me is satisfied with the objectivity of my thought—in fact demands it; but the meaningful world of identity-relation finds such objectivity ontologically inappropriate. The language, ideas, and movement of argumentation in this book are appropriate to the context of theology, but they are hardly sufficient or appropriate expressions of love, faith, or worship. The distinction holds true in our relationships to other people. To meet another in terms of thought is to meet him on "neutral" ground. We are kept apart as people by the inherent limitations of thought. Thus, for example, my thought concentration in making an important purchase for my house should have nothing to do with the nature of my personal relationship to the salesman. When such neutral lines are trespassed, we are often angered or annoyed—as when a salesman, who does not know me, calls me "Charlie" or "Chuck" or gives me a friendly slap on the back in order to enhance his possibility for a sale by engendering some vague sense of personal responsiveness rather than the conviction of product excellence. Another way of understanding this limitation of objectivity is to note that because ideas, actions, and relationships are objective they participate in clock time, in the present, past, and future but not in the *now*. The *now* implications of thought have to do with my identity, not the content of my thought itself, as we observed earlier. To meet another in clock time is to meet in the objective relation of *I-It*.

There are still other limitations of thinking, which ought to be noted. I am limited by my competence, by my native abilities. There are some people who, through no accomplishment or fault of their own, have superior minds capable of more complex or intricate thinking. But such a distinction is a relative measure, i.e., the relationship between the superior and the ordinary mind is one of degree, not kind: I cannot comprehend Einstein's mathematics, but I am certain that he could comprehend mine. Thus all minds are limited to their natural endowment in *being;* none is omniscient. This observation alerts us to a related limitation: my thinking is limited by the nature and extent of my experience, my exposure to the world. It is not its excellence or keenness that is called into question here, but its scope. The aphorism is true—He knows not England who only England knows. My thinking is limited, as well, by the possibility of rationalization, of justifying a desire, an emotion, or a belief by thought in such a way that it appears, even to me, as the product of that thought rather than its motivation. Since Freud, no man has consciously been able to exempt himself from such a limitation. Civil Rights, war, poverty, and pollution are problem areas where the rationalizations of prejudice and greed often pass themselves off as thinking. It is not that thinking cannot consider areas of emotion or belief; it is just that when thinking does consider them, it must attempt to do so objectively. This brings us to one further limitation of thinking. The emotional, the irrational, the intuitive are all forces which powerfully affect men in the living out of their lives. Thinking purposefully tries to eliminate any excessive influence of these forces from their own function except as they become objective content for thought. However, their impact is existential, i.e., immediate and personal, and thinking can only compete, not cope, with this.

What becomes apparent is that thinking per se, invaluable and necessary as it is, is not able to express adequately the full nature of *being* human. Thinking must ignore the *now* which is the context of my self-consciousness, and it cannot effectively deal with its own limitations. Therefore, it seems as though we need a larger, more comprehensive term to express the full nature of *being* human. For this task I would propose the word *Reason*. Until now the term has been scrupulously avoided because of its traditional use, and because it is desired that a redefinition of reason can be established. During the eighteenth century, Rationalism arrogantly assumed the supremacy of reason in the quest for knowledge and truth; but the psychological and philosophical insights of the nineteenth and twentieth centuries have challenged all that. Psychology, as we have noted, has demonstrated to us that much of our thinking is rationalization, the justification of an idea or position for which or to which there has already been an emotional commitment. Such an insight does not eliminate thinking as one of man's most important functions, it simply acknowledges the ambiguity of thought and the bias of its results. The process of redefinition is also furthered by the insights of existentialist philosophy which remind man that he cannot understand himself by objective analysis, for he is first and foremost a subjective *being*. This means that man, in terms of his own reality, must take into account his moods, his feelings, his intuitions, his imaginings, as well as his thinking. Man is not only rational, he is irrational as well. What existentialism has demonstrated to us is that if we hold to the definition of reason as the ratiocinative functioning of the mind, then we must see that human understanding is a greater, more complex experience than the "logical" functioning of the brain. A third tradition which has contributed to the redefinition of reason is traditional British empiricism. Empiricism was not content to let reason be self-sufficient as the source of knowledge but insisted upon the primacy of experience, experimentation, and even feeling. Under such strictures, it is the function of reason to organize, coordinate, and interpret the data provided by such experience and experimentation. This is, in part, the function which we have already defined as "thinking" earlier in this chapter.

How, then, shall we define reason? Initially let us say that reason is my self-expression, my identity, within the *Thou* world context, in which the context takes precedence over the self. Reason, in other words, is a corporate affair; it is not aloof and atomistic as thinking is. Reason depends upon my willingness to enter into an *I-Thou* or potential *I-Thou* with another in such a way that my self-expression is involved with (not simply engaged by) the self-expression of another, and from this encounter the identity of both or either one may change. Because my identity is involved, so is my thinking, but only as *one* of the constituents of the encounter, not as the sole one. What reason seeks with another is rapport, not facts or information. Facts and information alone can only be part of the *It* world and can only be secondarily involved in the *Thou* world as part of its milieu. The rapport which reason seeks is personal, social, and intellectual, so that in reason *now* and the present are brought together in one coordinate stance. Thinking belongs in the present, and only its context is set by the implied *now.* The ecstatic *I-Thou* experience belongs to the *now,* and only its context is fixed by the implied present. In reason the two are brought together as men encounter each other in terms of their identity and their physical presence. Reason is therefore the expression and substance of the *(I)Me-You-(Thou)* relation as it moves toward *I-Thou.*

What is the nature of this *Thou* context within which reason takes place? It is a community stance to which the "price of admission" is not I.Q. or technical competence, but the willingness to meet with another in terms of respect, tolerance, sensitivity, humility, and responsibility. What reason is searching for is maturity, not power, meaning, not information; in the expression of *being,* reason takes priority over thought because it includes both natural expressions—*Thou* and *It.* While thought is the mark and means of man's cultural achievements, reason is the mark and means of his significance and community without which such achievements turn to dust. Our age is one in which we are very close to learning this the hard way. Refusal to reason together can only be destructive—for individuals or for those who represent us as nations. In a world where The Bomb has made total war obsolete, i.e., suicidal, confrontation in reason is the only hope for survival. The ancient but explosive hatreds and jealousies which mark the conflicts on almost every continent all involve identity, human rights, and dignity—perhaps even more than land, wealth, or power. Only a reasonable solution, one which acknowledges and accepts the dignity of all men, can possibly prevent our self-destruction.

The quality of reason cannot be measured or judged by any external standards but can only be reflected in the integrity and authenticity of the encounter. If the encounter is one which encourages the continued expression of respect, sensitivity, tolerance, responsibility, and humility, and at the same time encourages the continuation of the free exchange of thought, then one is self-assured that the encounter is a valid and meaningful one. By implication we are admitting that it is possible for me to impose thinking upon a community situation and to deny the function of reason. This, of course, does take place, but the denial of reason, of meaningful rapport, becomes a denial of authentic *being* and genuine community. The degrading results of welfare paternalism is a case in point. Important and as destructive as that is, man often follows such a course of denial out of the more immediate motives of fear—fear of the unknown or fear of betrayal by another—or out of motives of greed immediately realizable in terms of goods, power, position. The individual action of thought suggests itself to such people because it seems safe, controllable, and predictable. The penalty of such shortsightedness is self-destruction or alienation. Anyone, for example, entering into marriage who says to himself: "I'll stay with her until I am tired of her" is acknowledging that the *I-Thou* relation does not exist. Such a marriage courts emotional disaster for both parties. Or, in a more objective and corporate sense, one of the most dramatic international examples of greed is our destruction of the natural resources of our planet for quick profit. In our wastefulness we are in fact destroying ourselves. Such selfish action also suggests itself because thought alone, as we have seen, can give the impression that "I am central," "I am the authority in command." Such claims, which ignore the ambiguity of thought, its variety of limitations, and most of all its dependence upon the fundamental expression of *being* in *I-Thou,* may insensitively or unwittingly lead to social destruction. Political communities and nations which insist upon such an approach to world problems—an appeal to some abstract, absolute, sovereign principle of "Our Right"—can only exist in terms of armed hostility toward one another, which may now mean mutual annihilation.

Only reason can save us from ourselves, because reason is a humanism which acknowledges as its ground the primacy of life. Primacy does not mean longevity, but that mystery or holiness which is *given* in terms of our self-consciousness. I have used mystery as an alternative to holiness, for there are those like Albert Camus for whom the fact of religious humanism is inexplicable; i.e., for him the religious rationale is unacceptable or unknown. For the Christian, such humanism is both mysterious and holy. The Christian, too, finds the fact of humanism inexplicable, but he also finds in its expression a revelation of God.

Before turning our attention to revelation, however, let us look at the nature of consciousness, thinking, and reason within the context of *being* and time. Consciousness, which is functional and involuntary, takes place in the context of *I-It.* Because of its nondiscriminatory nature and lack of personal involvement, it is in the most objective of categories which concerns me, the "Me-It." As such, consciousness is in the present although it is unaware of the present per se. The normal response of anyone in the state of sheer consciousness to the question "What are you thinking about?" is usually "Nothing." What is implied here is not vacuity but lack of intentionality or discipline. If this person is challenged to give an account of his consciousness, it very often proves to be impossible for him to do. He doesn't know *where* he has been; he simply *is* and has been.

Thinking, although it does differ from consciousness by its form and intentionality, still belongs to the world of *I-It.* Because it involves discipline and direction, and involves my life-style in public life, thinking belongs in the subcategories of "Me-You" as well as "Me-It." And since thinking involves my personal life, it is also an expression of (or presupposes) my identity, the *(I)Me-You(Thou)* category. Thinking does not effect my self-consciousness, but it can affect my *expression* of identity. Thus, while thinking does belong to the world of *I-It,* it presupposes the world of *I-Thou.* Like consciousness, thinking is in the present, but unlike sheer consciousness, it is aware of its context. This means that thinking presupposes the *now* of identity in thinking-in-and-about-the-present. It is in thinking that the past and the future become usable and recognizable references to the present. Because of this versatility, an objective discipline of science and the more interpretive discipline of history are expressions of thinking.

Reason belongs to the world of *I-It* and of *I-Thou.* However, reason does not participate in the extremes of either of these categories. Reason is not involved with sheer consciousness, nor is it completely identified with the ecstasy of exclusive *I-Thou.* Reason primarily functions in the category "(I)Me-You(Thou)" along with thinking, but its reference to the *I-Thou* or potential *I-Thou* is active rather than merely presupposed. Reason involves the total person and is consequently actively expressing the *now* of identity. Because reason is an active participant in *I-Thou,* self-awareness itself may be affected. As with thinking, reason, in terms of its encounter, is a participant in the present, but the emphasis is upon the *now* rather than the present, upon qualities of expression rather than quantities of action, upon categories of meaning rather than categories of calculation.

Revelation has been generally understood in Christian thought to mean God's self-disclosure. It is, as the etymology indicates, a drawing back of the veil, a disclosure of that which is ordinarily hidden or secret—namely, the "person" or "will" of God. But just for this reason, revelation has always been difficult for Christianity, for it implies something extraordinary, something disruptive of the normal scheme of things, something which transcends all the ordinary "rules" of cognition, something which seems to be available only to the "chosen" or "called," something which is private and not public. For those who claim to have received the revelation of God, who "know" and are known by God, such strictures pose no problems. To the uninitiated, however, to the skeptic, these same strictures become barriers to belief which are seemingly insurmountable. But the situation is altered when reality is considered in terms of *being*.

For the new ontology, the phenomenon of revelation is not an extraordinary or exclusively divine event. Revelation in terms of *being* must be understood as the activity of *being;* as such, revelation is the disclosure, not enclosure, of *being*, the exposure, not imposition, of *being*, the expression, not impression, of *being*. It is, in short, the self-presentation of *being*—all *being*. Consequently, we must consider revelation as occurring in the *It* world as well as in the *Thou* world. This self-presentation of *being* does not necessarily imply personal intentionality, that is, presentation meant for me alone. Revelation is simply part of the natural expression of *being;* it is the projection of *is*ness, although by saying that one is guilty of redundancy, for *is*ness is projection, revelation. Thus my dog Fricka reveals herself, her particular "dogginess," to me simply by *being*. The fact that I attribute great personal significance to this and complex personal qualities to her is perhaps more the product of my responsiveness and imagination than the reception of sheer revelation (though I admit that this situation becomes more complicated when I consider the relationship one of *I-Thou* rather than *I-It*). What is revealed, what is disclosed or exposed to me, is the mystery of her *being* as this particular dog. To make the revelational claim about another human *being* is, of course, more readily understood. The context of *I-Thou* encounter is one of mutual and uninhibited revelation, the disclosure in *being* "with" another.

Such revelation is as evident and valid for the agnostic as it is for the Christian. No one can simply choose to ignore the mystery of his or another's *being*. For men such as Heidegger or Sartre, one cannot get beyond the mystery to an explanation; one accepts the mystery as a first principle, a *given*. I am, to cite Heidegger, *Dasein*, "being-there"; my truth *is*. For the Christian, the situation is a bit more complicated. In the Christian's acceptance of the new ontological expression-as-reality, the revelation of *being* occurs in the context of the *I-It* and *I-Thou* relations. By implication, then, I cannot "know myself" in isolation, atomistically. I am aware of the mystery of *being* only in terms of those things and others whom I encounter, thus the mystery of *being* is the mystery of *being-in-relation* and only derivatively one of sheer *being*. It is a mystery of thingness but also of personhood; it is a mystery of objectivity but also of subjectivity; it is a mystery of distinction but also of mutuality; it is a mystery of order but also of chaos. All this involves revelation; all this is the disclosure and presentation of *being;* all this has to do with my meaning, my identity. Consequently, I identify such revelation with the revelation of God—acknowledging for the moment that the only thing I mean by the word *God* is *Being* of a personal order. However, because all reality is ontological, an analogy in terms of human revelation will be instructive.

Within the *I-Thou* relation, I become increasingly aware of not only myself but also the other whom I am meeting. But the process is not an immediate one. My first awareness of another is some physical form of perception—through vision, hearing, touching—as is his awareness of me. This revelation of my physical presence is uncontrolled (unless I am hiding from someone); I am "there" for others and the world. Through such mutual availability and recognition in the *It* world, I make myself available for the *I-Thou* encounter. In encounters less intimate than *I-Thou,* e.g., *(I)Me,* we actually self-regulate how much of our *selves,* i.e., our personal identity as opposed to our physical presence or activity, we will reveal to another. Sometimes we want to encourage an intimacy possibly productive of an *I-Thou* encounter; sometimes we want to deny another any access to our inner selves. However, if both of us are openly receptive as well as expressive, then we can leave the *(I)Me* contact and begin to know each other and ourselves in terms of the *I-Thou*. In the *I-Thou* relation, what I learn to know is the meaning of that other person for me and my meaning for him; I am sensitive to qualities of *being* in him and the presence or lack of such qualities in myself; I am aware of the growth, the maturing of my identity, in terms of this encounter; I experience the fact that revelation is two-way, an act of disclosure and reception for us both. The revelation of the objective self is, of course, immediate, but the revelation of the subjective self is gradual, a matter of will which is aware of the identity-risk involved in any *I-Thou* relation.

The religious mind finds this procedure to be analogous to man's relationship with God. The mystery of *being* is first made evident in the world about us, with the objects and others of this world in whose presence we first become aware of ourselves. The consistency and nature of these experiences encourage me to make myself available (to expose myself) to the mystery of *Being-Itself*. That is, I have the growing experience in and through all my particular encounters that I am being addressed in terms of my identity by the totality of reality; my life is concerned with all that is, and all that is is concerned with my life. This means not only my encounter with the mystery of the objective world but also my encounter with the mystery of the subjective world. This is not to resort to a form of panentheism, an appeal to a totally inclusive identity-in-*Being,* but is to recognize the basic and fundamental nature of my reality as contingent *being*-in-encounter. I recognize that the identity of my self-consciousness is called into question, and this is larger than simply my recognition of another. My recognition of another, my wife, for example, has a particularity about it which is no less real but yet other than my encounter with what I experience as the creative ground or reality. In the encounter with my creative ground, the contingency of my *being* is experienced in terms of personal responsibility, i.e., a moral responsibility for self for which acculturation cannot account but encounter can. I "know" that my identity, my self-consciousness, is engaged by that One who is Himself the ground of the mystery of *being* as *Being-Itself.* I use such pronouns as *One* and *Himself* because the experience has that same intense, personal quality that is characteristic of the particular *I-Thou* relation. The world is not impersonal, but intensely personal. If I attempt to treat the world as impersonal it is usually because of one of two reasons: I have defensively cut myself off from the world in such a way that I am not available for the *I-Thou* encounter, much as any paranoiac who mistrusts the intentions of others; or I have encountered the Other and find in "Him" only the promise of death, not life, and therefore "He" is to be rejected or ignored as long as possible. It is to this that H.R. Niebuhr points so eloquently:

> The natural mind is enmity to God; or to our natural mind the One intention in all intentions is animosity. In our wretchedness we see ourselves surrounded by animosity. We live and move and have our being in a realm that is not nothingness but that is ruled by destructive power, which brings us and all we love to nothing. The maker is the slayer; the affirmer is the denier; the creator is the destroyer; the life-giver is the death-dealer. There is indeed One intention in the light of which we interpret all the intentions of particular powers; there is One law of action that is present in all the specific laws of the systems that act upon us. We do respond to One action in all the many actions upon us, but that One in all the many is the *will* to destroy, or, if *will* be too anthropomorphic a term, the *law* of our destruction. It is not the law of our physical dying only or primarily, but the law in things, the ontological law as it were, by which the self and its communities and all that it prizes, all its labors, worthy and unworthy, its good deeds and its evil ones, must be relativized, be restricted and finally come to nothing. In a thousand variations our religions,

our poetry, our philosophies, our proverbial wisdom bring home
to us in this life from womb to grave, from war to war, the eschatological truth that "on us and all our race the slow, sure doom
falls pitiless and dark"; that "all lovely things must have an end-
ing, all lovely things must fade and die"; that "even this will pass
away"; that "in the midst of life we are in death"; that those are
happier who die young and those happiest who have never been
born; that our physic "but prolongs . . . sickly days."[1]

To understand the world in its ontological nature is to understand
reality as revelatory, to find *being* expressing itself in both the *It* and *Thou*
worlds in such a way that my identity is correspondingly engaged by each
world and ratified by each. "The self as one self among all the sys-
tematized reactions in which it engages seems to be the counterpart of a
unity that lies beyond, yet expresses itself in, all the manifold systems of
actions upon it. In religious language, the soul and God belong together
or otherwise stated, I am one within myself as I encounter the One in all
that acts upon me."[2]

It is this harmony of revelational encounter understood in terms of
the unity of my identity that provides the basic religious dimension to
man's life. Although it is expressed in a myriad of folktales, myths,
legends, and beliefs, it is this central mystery of identity-encounter in
which man's faith is grounded. Since it is so basic and fundamental to his
identity, it is easy to understand why primitive man and societies thought
of the gods as those who were individually concerned about each man or
about each tribe or nation. Israel did not think of Yahweh as anything
but a tribal god until about the time of Amos and Hosea. Yahweh was
Israel's god; other nations had their own. The early difference was one
of relative strength, never a question of personal encounter or legitimate
sovereignty. Yet even when the universality of Yahweh was suggested,
the nature of the revelation remained personal; identity remained central:

> Then I will make a covenant on behalf of Israel with the wild
> beasts, the birds of the air, and the things that creep on the earth,
> and I will break bow and sword and weapon of war and sweep
> them off the earth, so that all living creatures may lie down with-
> out fear. I will betroth you to myself for ever, betroth you in
> lawful wedlock with unfailing devotion and love; I will betroth
> you to myself to have and to hold, and you shall know the Lord.
> At that time I will give answer, says the Lord, I will answer for the
> heavens and they will answer for the earth. . . . (Hosea 2:18–21)

In the New Testament the witness is the same. Paul, too, wrote out of the
identity-context of this harmony of revelation:

For though everything belongs to you—Paul, Apollos, and Cephas, the world, life, and death, the present and the future, all of them belong to you—yet you belong to Christ, and Christ to God. (I Corinthians 3:21b–23)

Theologically considered, this harmony of revelation is discernible in the development of my personal response to *being* in terms of the *It* world and the *Thou* world. In my act of *being, being* involves me in not only the fact of my *is*ness but also the nature of my *am*ness, i.e., my physical presence and my identity. As I become sensitive to this inclusive revelation of *being* and respond to it, I soon discover that these two conditions of *being* are ontologically inseparable; I soon discover that my participation in *being* has become an encounter with *Being-Itself* at the deepest level of identity. However, I am immediately aware that the designation "Being-Itself " is descriptively inadequate. I am confronted not by *Being-Itself* but the Other who addresses me in terms of my self-consciousness. The human analogy is again instructive here. When I meet another, he becomes meaningful for me. As the relationship grows, I begin to recognize that he is meaningful for me but also to me, i.e., he no longer affects simply *what* I am but now *who* I am. As the relationship matures, I must acknowledge that he is meaningful *with* me—which is the relationship of *I-Thou*, the relationship of love.

In just such a way, my relationship with God develops. The mystery of *being*, the disclosure and presentation of *being* in and through the world, becomes meaningful for me. As I begin to recognize my own involvement in such *being*, to acknowledge my own contingency, I also recognize that the mystery of *being* has become the mystery of *Being-Itself* and as such is meaningful to me. Through this experience, I make myself available (receptive) to the revelation of *Being-Itself* and find myself confronted by the Other (God) *with* whom my life attains meaning in the active fulfilling of its potential expression. This does not mean a sense of achievement in the ordinary sense of that word; it means that my life is *being* lived in an open, free, authentic, and affirmative way. This claim does not imply that life is lived without problems, curtailments on activities, handicaps, or even tragedies. What it does imply is that my identity, my self-consciousness, is in no way finally impaired or crippled by any of these conditions, that my sense of *being* a person is as full and as fulfilling in tragedy as in joy, though, of course, one longs for a happy life rather than one of sadness. In the presence of the Other (God), my identity is creatively sustained.

In these terms instant "conversion," instant awareness of the Other, is about as authentic as instant love or blind love. As psychologists, sociologists, and theologians by the score have told us for some time, love is a long, delicate, involved, even arduous process despite (sometimes because of) its strong emotional nature. "Love," to quote Fromm, "is an art." The initial strong emotional attraction that we seem to have for another is an infatuation which may, indeed, become love. But infatuation is the initial stage of availability. The love itself takes time to mature, to trust, to risk, to expose, to give—actions which can only *be* through the appropriate existential confrontation. When these things occur, then one often looks back and says, "Yes, it was love at first sight," simply ignoring or forgetting all those other times under seemingly similar circumstances when the maturation did not take place. Such a process is familiar to us all in terms of human love; what we need to recognize is that it is likewise the nature of divine revelation. To "sense" the presence of God is not unlike the experience of infatuation in love. It is usually an emotionally charged experience when one first becomes aware of the mystery of *being*. At this point the response to God, like the response to another, is likely to be adulterated by sentimentality or magic. We so want something to be "there" for us that we partially create it in our imaginations. Such a reaction ignores the harsh realities through which such relationships are matured. This is one of the reasons why the superficial conversion experience under the direction of a traveling Evangelist in a place like Madison Square Garden or the Los Angeles Coliseum is of short duration. The convert does not get beyond the stage of infatuation with God. At best, such an experience can be an invitation to faith, though sometimes the unscrupulous Evangelist will encourage the sentimental or magical response because of its dramatic and immediate effect.

Genuine and full revelation must overcome the hurdles of my indifference, isolation, insensitivity, lack of response, distrust, egotism, and evil. It must assert and affirm itself in my life and be open to the confirmation of the community of faith. It is because of these obstacles that the Scottish churchman John Baillie states that we must "seek God 'carefully with tears.' "[3] The fact that faith requires such struggle and travail is not commentary on the nature of faith but on the condition of man who seeks and needs faith, just as the trials of love say more about the lover than the state. It should be evident that the spiritual legacy of genuine revelational encounter is humility and never the arrogance of the religious fanatic who claims religious infallibility and exclusive election or direction.

Let us now consider the revelation of God in terms of the other categories with which we have dealt: *I-Thou*, time and history, and reason. Revelation begins in the category of "I-It" through an awareness of *being* and even *Being-Itself*, but its true character is not understood until that revelation has been of the Other (God), *I-Eminent Thou*, who is *then* perceived in and through the category of "I-It," *Being-Itself.* In short, the revelation of God is *I-It* until it becomes *I-Thou,* after which time it is always *I-Thou* even through the *It* conditions. That is, I can perceive God in the birth of a child, the awesomeness of nature, the kindness of another, but only after an initial *Thou* encounter with God when the mystery of *being* has become identified with the mystery of the *Other.* To return to our analogy of love, the physical presence of the loved one points beyond itself by recalling or reaffirming the *I-Thou* relationship which lies beyond it. In each case, the *I-It* relationship is the initial mediator for the *I-Thou.* In revelation, we are led beyond the contingencies of *being* to *Being Itself,* who is God.

Revelation as God's self-disclosure is not an irresistible imposition upon me but requires my acceptance and personal response, so that I must understand revelation as an activity and not simply as a necessary state or bestowed information. Revelation in these terms is God's continuing presence to which I must be continually responsive and with which I must be continually involved; it is not something which happens to me once, after which I must constantly refer to the past. This assertion, however, involves us in the examination of revelation in terms of our definitions of time: clock time and identity time. Because the revelation of God is *I-Thou,* I experience the presence of God as *now* rather than of the present. And because the revelation of God is *I-It* in terms of the mystery of *being,* I experience the presence of God as continually present. God, as *Being-Itself,* contours the whole of my existence, subjective and objective, personal and impersonal, and consequently is perceived in both areas. Insofar as God reveals Himself to me in the mystery of the Other (*Thou* and *It*), I recognize that not only my identity but my very self-consciousness is at stake. I am because *He* is; *I* continue to be *I* because He continues me. As the ground of my *being,* He is the creator-ground of my timeful present; as the ground of my meaning, He is the creative encounter-possibility of my time-full presence. To the extent that God reveals Himself to me in the tragic mystery of *being,* that is, to the extent that He addresses me out of the "burning bush," out of sorrow, out of injustice, out of the ghetto, out of prejudice, out of any dehumanizing act, then I respond to Him in the present and acknowledge the importance of clock time in the expression of *being.* I am obliged by such revelation to respond economically, politically, socially, or physically as the case may be. I must recognize that what is granted to me *now* is demanded of me in the present, for which the past and future are preparation and anticipation. Insofar as God reveals Himself to me through the wonders of the world: out of creativity, out of rejuvenation, out of beauty, out of majesty, or out of faithfulness, I respond with gratitude, joy, responsibility, and trust which begin in the present but move beyond to the time-full awareness of His presence. The revelation of God is the ground for both my timeful and time-full existence, and He proves to *be* the rationale for the unity of life which I *am*.

Revelation is also the rationale for my historical stance. God, as the ground of my meaning, is the ground for my understanding of the continuity of history, i.e., the significance of occurrence. Because, as we noted earlier, history emerges out of the *now* to interpret the past, present, and future, it is a reflection of my revelatory experience. If I find no mystery of *being* evident in my life, no *I-Thou* encounter, then I find events chaotic, or at least a product of chance. Such a life-style would not recognize or acknowledge any process or continuity which could even be called "history." If my revelatory experience is one of the mystery of *being*, perhaps even *Being-Itself*, then my point of view out of the *now* is an objective one, reflecting the order which I experience in *Being-Itself*. The character of such order will reflect the creative encounter which I have had with *Being-Itself*, which has shaped my identity. We could not ask for a more pertinent expression of this than that from the French existentialist Albert Camus:

> I am not a philosopher, in fact I can only speak of what I have lived. I have lived nihilism, contradiction, violence, and the dizziness of destruction. But, at the same time, I have greeted the power to create and the honor of living. Nothing gives me the right to judge from above an epoch of which I am completely a part. I judge it from within, confusing myself with it. But I hold to the right of saying henceforth, what I know about myself and others, only on the condition that this may not add to the unbearable misery of the world, but rather will indicate, on the dark walls against which we grope, the yet invisible places where the gates may open. Yes, I hold to the right of saying what I know, and I shall say it. I am only interested in the renaissance.[4]

If my encounter is with God, my understanding of history will reflect that meeting. My identity is then such that I view all acts and occurrences as relative to the *Being* of God Himself. In older but ontologically altered vocabulary all history is *Heilsgeschichte*, holy history, for it reflects my identity as one who acknowledges God as the ground of all *being*. To say that history is "holy history" does not mean that events become sacrosanct, or that God spoke a particular word at this time and in this place, and for that reason it shall always be that holy time and that holy place in history. Such a decree would make an idol out of history, let alone to consign it to the past where history never truly *is*. To say that history is "holy history" is to claim that all events are interpreted and reinterpreted in terms of who I am *now* as I stand in the presence of God. Consequently, the same event can have different meanings for me

at different times. What I understand *now* about the ecumenical movement may not be what I understand ten years from now, but it is well to
remind ourselves at this point that we are referring to history as meaning, not occurrence. That is, the fact of the World Council of Churches is
the fact of the World Council of Churches—that does not change, but its
significance and meaning well may. Thus histories and historians differ
in their interpretations of events because they reflect their own revelatory experiences. This is a partial explanation of the dynamism of history.
Not only do events continue to occur, each historian views these occurrences from his own identity perspective.

That so many men agree about a meaning for history is witness to
the unity of the revelatory experience. The regularity and nature of our
encounter with *Being-Itself* appear so objectively and subjectively similar
that men assume that they can communicate with each other in a knowl-
edgeable way about these occurrences. Most historians, be they American, British, German, or Russian, could agree on the facticity of the
Treaty of Versailles, about the events which preceded it and those which
followed. To a large extent, they could agree on what the treaty *meant*
then and now if by *meant* we are indicating an apparent causal sequence.
To those whose revelatory experience is limited to *Being-Itself,* any difference of opinion should be resolvable by a further and more complete
study of the occurrences—both then and now. The fact that such
unanimity never occurs does not mean a lack of scholarship on the part
of our historians, but rather suggests that the creative process of identity
is always at work. It is likely that for the Germans the meaning of the
treaty will always be something different than for the Americans or
Russians, not because their history books are different but simply because they are different. For those who acknowledge that *Being-Itself* is
God, yet another dimension is added to the interpretation of the treaty. A
kind of universal humanism colors the apprehension of the occurrence,
so that judgment is now a human value judgment. Such an addition does
not simplify the process of history, but makes it more difficult, for the
subjective expression of identity now plays a more important part in the
interpretation. Those who claim to be historians out of such a context acknowledge such difficulties, but suggest that the reality of *being* leaves
them no choice. Of course, there are also historians who pay lip service to this level of revelatory history, but actually treat "holy history"
as though it were the objective result of *Being-Itself,* i.e., as the Church
all too often tries to treat the revelation of God to men as though it
were talking about the Treaty of Versailles. The only "religious" occurrence which can be treated in such a way is the public claim by an
individual or group that it has experienced or presently proclaims the
revelation of God. However, here one is talking about the *claim,* not the

revelation. The revelation is always present and *now*, so that if the earlier claim is valid, e.g., the claims of a St. Thomas or a Luther, they are validated *now*, to me, by God—not by St. Thomas or Luther. This is perhaps another way of saying that nothing is the authoritative herald of the sacred—tradition, apostolic succession, the saints, the clergy, the Church, or even Scriptures themselves—unless the revelation of God makes it so, *now*, to me, in terms of my own identity. Thus when the Jew celebrates Passover with his Seder feast, it is his present acknowledgment of his own (not just Moses') delivery out of "Egypt," an experience through which he understands the revelation of God to himself as a man and to himself as a Jew. His identity *now* is involved in both situations. The same thing is true of the Christian who celebrates Good Friday and Easter. His appropriation of these events does not come out of a book but out of the crucifixion and resurrection in his own life. In this revelatory experience, he is existentially engaged by the revelation of the Christ-event. His identity *now* is thus involved in both historical situations. The Exodus from Egypt and the Crucifixion are occurrences, but their religious meaning is only evident through the revelation of God.

In terms of consciousness, thinking, and reasoning, it is obvious by now that my reception of revelation, as an expression of *I-Thou*, is an activity of ecstasy and reason. Just as these are corporate actions involving my encounter with another, so revelation is corporate. Revelation addresses me in the totality of my *being*. Within the experience of revelation, I am confronted in a radical way by *Being-Itself*, God. Such a confrontation informs my self-consciousness and shapes my identity. This involves the process which we have called reason, though revelation obviously cannot be encompassed by reason. If I wish to critically examine this revelational experience, I may choose to think about it, to focus my conscious intellectual activity, but such an activity is an abstraction from the revelatory experience itself. What I am engaged in when I think about revelation is theology. It is for this reason that theological excellence bears little relevance to the depth and sincerity of a revelatory faith.

This is a point which is central to the theology of Emil Brunner, who, in terms of Buber's *I-Thou* orientation, did much to challenge the sterility of the traditional subject-object orientation of most classical and formal theologies:

> In His Word, God does not deliver to me a course of lectures in dogmatic theology, He does not submit to me or interpret for me the content of a confession of faith, but He makes Himself accessible to me. And likewise in faith I do not think, but God leads me to think; He does not communicate "something" to me, but "Himself." The counterpart is no longer as in thinking a something, a

something pondered and discussed which *I* infer through the energy of my thinking, but a Person who Himself speaks and discloses Himself, who Himself thus has the initiative and guidance and takes over the role (so to say) which in thinking I have myself. An exchange hence takes place here which is wholly without analogy in the sphere of thinking. The sole analogy is in the encounter between human beings, the meeting of person with person.[5]

While I have reservations about this restricted use of *thinking,* I am in agreement with the central point Brunner makes.

The profundities of faith speak in terms of reason; the profundities of theology are expressed in thought. For those who claim to be agnostics, philosophy rather than faith makes a similar distinction. The profundities of life, concern with *Being-Itself,* speak in terms of wisdom; the profundities of a philosophical system are expressed in thought. The idealist contention that these two modes are one and the same could be made only before the existential critiques were voiced. Reality moves through reason and revelation.

While it is true that reason directs thought, thinking can, in turn, be a preparation for critical reasoning. Thinking can make me "available" for the revelatory experience before it occurs by recognizing my need for encounter. This is the theory behind all educational process. We do not teach *life* in our schools, but we do try to prepare students for the experiences they are now having and those we anticipate they will have. In just such a way, the Church tries to prepare all its people for understanding the revelation of God, which they experience in part already and which in greater depth may yet follow. The Church cannot teach *faith* but it can so instruct an individual that he becomes available for the commitment of faith.

The two activities of the mind which stand at polar extremes for revelation are sheer consciousness and prayer. Consciousness per se is not in any way participation in the revelatory act. The undirected, uninstructed functioning of the brain is simply *that;* it does not affect or effect my identity and is therefore uninvolved in revelation. Prayer, however, is the ecstasy of reason expressing itself to God. Thus prayer can be a thoughtful articulation, i.e., presentation, of my deepest desires and needs, thanksgiving and joy, or it can simply be agonized prostration of myself in the presence of God—He who confronts me, who listens, who knows, and who cares. Prayer can be simply the inner acknowledgment of the presence of God, without specific direction or purpose; prayer is the language of love between man and God.

5

The Christ and the Church

Any theological attempt to understand, evaluate, or discuss Christianity must sooner or later focus on the figure of Jesus of Nazareth, who is called the Christ. It is from this man that the Church and its adherents derive their name. It has been the claim of the Church and of individual Christians that this man Jesus, the Christ, is the founder of their movement. But the claims are much more extravagant than that. The traditional claim of Christianity is that in Jesus, God was present in a unique way, that "God was in Christ reconciling the world to himself" (II Corinthians 5:19). God Himself has come to man as his redeemer, his savior, his mediator, his father and his brother—all in one, in Jesus. Thus Christianity calls Jesus: Holy One, Son of God, Son of Man, Savior, Messiah, Redeemer, Master, the Christ. It is an obvious deduction from such titles that mankind needed some help. Man found himself unable to cope with his fears, his anxieties, with death, even with himself, i.e., his identity; he was an alien in a promised land. However, good news counters despair: "God loved the world so much, that he gave his only Son, that everyone who has faith in him may not die but have eternal life" (John 3:16). Thus out of the context of salvation, the study of the man Jesus, about whom all these claims were made, came about. The study of Christology is the formalized assessment of the person of Jesus who is called the Christ.

The primitive Church, that is, the early Church reflected in the Book of Acts and in the letters of Paul, simply made the Gospel claim (the good news) that God was in Christ and that the world and all (at least responsive) men had been redeemed. This is an eschatological claim, a final claim about final things, which does not seem to need proof or justification. In fact, we would now say that the claim was existential. The members of that early movement fully expected the end of the world to occur within their lifetime, that God would act precipitously, even catastrophically, claiming his own at the same time. Under these conditions, there was no need to prove or support anything; the existential moment is its own verification. However, as Paul learned by the time he wrote his second letter to the Corinthians, *that* particular existential moment might be further away than first imagined. The delay of the eschatological claim at first proved disappointing and then embarrassing to the early Church. As the Parousia continued to be delayed, explanations were needed, not only for the delay itself, but also for the man Jesus about whom such divine claims were still being made. Both the Jewish and Hellenistic worlds began to demand some explanation for the Christian claim.

Consequently, Christology began to emerge in the second and third centuries, not as an affirmation of faith so much as a justification of belief. It was an effort to explain to the Jews and the Greco-Roman world *how* Jesus could be the Messiah or the Christ and what such a claim might mean in terms of their own reality-structure. For the Jews, this means a development of the prophetic-messianic motifs—Jesus must be both the promised Messiah and the Messiah of the Promise. For the Greco-Roman world, Jesus must be the Christ, the Form of God, the *Logos* incarnate in the man Jesus. These two claims, the personal Davidic Messiah and the personalized principle of rationality, were not only incompatible with each other, but they also seemed to be self-contradictory. For the Jews, the coming of the Messiah was the inauguration of the End; obviously that had not occurred; for the Gentiles, it seemed logically contradictory that the Church could claim that Jesus was God and man at the same time. The early Church made little headway with the Jews in its claim; tradition seemed too strong to be so radically altered. Hellenistic thought proved much more flexible and gave rise to a great number of ingenious attempts to solve the problem of how it could be possible for Jesus to be God and man at once.

The Church soon recognized the dangers in permitting the person of Jesus to become an intellectual puzzle for Hellenistic metaphysics—Jesus was the incarnate *Logos*, but the *Logos* was not coeternal and cosubstantial with God (fourth-century Arianism); because the holiness of God could not be entrusted to a sinful human being, the *Logos*, though He assumed human nature, was not a human person but a divine person, the Second Person of the Trinity (fourth-century Apollinarianism); Mary was not *Theotokos* ("the mother of God"), but *Christotokos* ("the mother of Christ"), effecting the union of the Divine *Logos* with impersonal humanity (fifth-century Nestorianism); Jesus the Christ was essentially divine, of two natures before the Incarnation but only of one after it (fifth-century Eutychianism). It was this central concern about the person of Jesus the Christ that led the Church into the first four great ecumenical councils. Here theologians tried to so define the person of Jesus that theological error could be detected and the existential truth of the Church's claim be protected. The two councils which are of most importance to us are Nicaea in 325 and Chalcedon in 451. In the Nicene Creed, the Church tried to prevent any docetic (e.g., Arian) diminution of the divinity of Jesus: "I believe . . . in one Lord Jesus Christ, the only-begotten Son of God, begotten of his Father before all worlds, God of God, Light of Light, very God of very God, begotten not made, being of one substance with the Father, by whom all things were made; who for us men and for our salvation came down from heaven, and was incarnate by the Holy Ghost of the Virgin Mary, and was made man. . . ." In the Chalcedonian formula, it is the humanity of Christ which was defended by the employment of the "Two-Nature" hypothesis:

> We confess one and the same Son, our Lord Jesus Christ, perfect in Godhead, perfect in Manhood, truly God and truly man, of a rational soul (anti-Apollinarian) and a body, of one substance with the Father with respect to the Godhead (anti-Arian), and of one substance with us in respect of the Manhood (anti-Eutychian), like us in everything except sin; begotten of the Father before the ages according to his Godhead (anti-Arian), but in these last days begotten of the Virgin Mary, the God-bearer (*Theotokos*) according to his Manhood (anti-Nestorian), for our sake and for the sake of our salvation; one and the same Christ, Son, Lord, only-begotten, confessed in two natures unconfusedly, unchangeably (anti-Eutychian), indivisibly, inseparably (anti-Nestorian); the distinction of the natures being in no way destroyed through their union (anti-Eutychian), but rather the peculiar quality of each nature being preserved and concurring in one Person and one Substance, not being parted and divided into two persons (anti-Nestorian), but one and the same Son and only-begotten God, the Word, the Lord Jesus Christ.[1]

The Christian Church has since lived within the confines of these two great definitions of Nicaea and Chalcedon, but the intellectual problems have remained. How can we do justice to the eternality of God and the transitory nature of Jesus in one and the same man? How can we understand the actuality and potentiality of God present in the man Jesus? How can we reconcile the limited freedom of Jesus with the limitless freedom of God; and, for that matter, how can we reconcile God's omnipotence, omniscience, and omnipresence with the obvious limitations of Jesus? Most puzzling of all: how could God die on the cross? It has been the response of the Church to say that there is and can be no answer to such questions. What we are dealing with here is the mystery of God which man cannot, by definition or nature, understand. To solve the mystery would be to claim the wisdom of God for man. Thus the best that the Church can do is to preserve that mystery as a mystery to protect man from his own intellectual arrogance. The insoluble theological dilemmas are symbolic of the imcomprehensible mystery of God's presence in Christ. Thus the Church can witness existentially to the fact that God was incarnate in Jesus, but it can only witness negatively in terms of essence by telling us what such an Incarnation *does not* mean rather than what it *does* mean. The early creeds of the Church are not "Affirmations of Faith," as so many books of worship like to call them. They are defensive statements designed to speak to speculative Hellenistic metaphysics in such a way as to protect the Gospel from becoming merely a truth-statement rather than the good news of God's personal salvation.

The Church's claim is that we have to do with a paradox and not a contradiction. It accepts the fact that in the divinity and manhood of the Christ we are witness to an apparent contradiction, one that the reasonable world finds hard to accept simply on the authority of the Church. For centuries, the Church has understood and accepted this logical rejection. It recognizes that final authority for the acceptance of such a claim must rest with the revelation of God in Christ. Anything less than that would be insufficient. It is this revelation which resolves the contradiction experientially so that what we affirm in faith is a paradox for reason rather than a contradiction. The only demonstrable claim which the Church can make to the world is one of consistency in terms of its own insights and faith-statements. For these reasons, as we saw earlier, Karl Barth states that there is no revelation except the one revelation of God in Jesus Christ. All that preceded the life of Jesus and has followed is a part of that central revelation of God of Himself. There is no mechanical or "natural" way in which I can gain such knowledge and faith—not through the Church, Scriptures, or tradition, though any one of these may be the way in which God will reach out to me in the Christ.

In this twentieth century, however, traditional Greek metaphysics has been called into question and with it comes all the intellectual witness of the Church concerning the dual nature of Jesus the Christ. It may be that the meaning of the Gospel and the nature of faith can be more authentically represented if it does not have to be sifted through the seine of Platonic metaphysics. By making claims about the nature of ultimate reality—its oneness, its perfection, its sheer actuality, its eternality, freedom, and goodness—the Church has manufactured problems for itself and for those to whom it would reach out in the name of the Christ. In one sense, the traditional theological position of the Church may have inhibited faith rather than encourage it. Certainly as we look about at the state of the contemporary Church—its factionalism and theological idolatries—we are led to marvel what God has been able to do in spite of it. The most pertinent contribution which the Church seems to be making today is through its renewed sense of social responsibility rather than through its theological witness, but even here we must be careful to acknowledge the distinction between the sense of responsibility and the particular (and often divisive) stands on the issues themselves.

The theological situation is radically altered when we approach Christology from the insights of the new ontology which we have been exploring up to now. What does it mean for Christology when we think of God as *Being-Itself,* He who *is* in Himself and who sustains all that *is?* What does it now mean for Jesus to be called "the Christ"? What does this do to our understanding of our relationship to the Christ and our understanding of the Christ's relationship to God—if in fact we can use such terminology? What does the new ontology mean for the Church and its relationship to the Christ?

Perhaps the best way to approach this new orientation for Christology and the Church is to observe that no man has ever become a Christian without the Church. There simply has never been a public claim that some individual in a remote and inaccessible part of the world has emerged from his isolation to say, "Believe in the Lord Jesus Christ." This is not to say that people in isolation or who have not heard the good news from the Church are not religious; the claim here is that they are not Christians. We can even go so far as to observe that many such religious people seem to share insights about the nature of life, creation, and human relationship, with Christians. But they are not *Christians.* The word *Christian* is descriptively appropriate for anyone who acknowledges that Jesus who is called "the Christ" has a unique place in his religious understanding of life. The definition must be that broad just to cover the variety of expressions of Christianity which the world has known thus far. But to acknowledge Jesus in any such way has always been associated with the teaching and tradition of the Christian Church. This is not to imply that an individual must be a member of some particular Christian persuasion, that he must have made a public and organizational confession of faith; but it does mean that he is beholden to the Church at least to the extent that he has heard its teachings and proclamations.

What conclusions can we draw from this observation? The first general conclusion seems to be that Christianity is simply one form of particularized religious expression. We can say *that* much without reference to its relative excellence or even to its uniqueness. This is the implication of what Professor H. Richard Niebuhr writes: "There is no such being, or source of being, surely, as a Christian God (though there may be Christian idols), but there is a Christian relation to God and I cannot abstract from that, as no Jew or Mohammedan can abstract from a Jewish or Muslim relation."[2] Niebuhr makes this further observation about what it means to call oneself a "Christian":

> I call myself a Christian simply because I also am a follower of Jesus Christ, though I travel at a great distance from him not only in time but in the spirit of my traveling; because I believe that my

way of thinking about life, myself, my human companions and our destiny has been so modified by his presence in our history that I cannot get away from his influence; and also because I do not want to get away from it; above all, I call myself a Christian because my relation to God has been, so far as I can see, deeply conditioned by this presence of Jesus Christ in my history and in our history. In one sense I must call myself a Christian in the same way that I call myself a twentieth-century man. To be a Christian is simply part of my fate, as it is the fate of another to be a Muslim or a Jew.[3]

The second conclusion we can draw from our initial observation about Christianity is that the occurrence of the life of Jesus, in and of itself, is not enough to convert the world. There is nothing coercive about the fact that Jesus lived twenty centuries ago, even though there is something persuasive about the fact that his influence is still so strongly with us after so many centuries. It is impossible to associate necessity in terms of faith with the life of Jesus. We may be surrounded by marks of his life and thought and not be persuaded to call ourselves Christians— as any survey of contemporary Western culture will bear out. As a matter of fact, with many of the world's younger generation, there is almost a hostility associated with the witness of the Church (though the hostility is more likely the result of a lack of true witness by the Church rather than its faithful expression). More telling evidence against an objective crite- rion of faith is the fact that even during Jesus' lifetime, during his actual ministry, which culminates in his death and ("witnessed") Resurrection, most do not follow, and only a few believe that this man is surely the "Son of God."

Perhaps the shortest explanation of why traditional factual evidence is not sufficient for commitment is that Christian faith is characterized by the spiritual gestalt of the *I-Thou* encounter. The word *faith,* as used here, is not something which I can possess or arbitrarily acquire; it is a relational act. This is not to claim a special Christian definition for the word *faith,* but it does suggest that a distinction in usage should be observed. Since we understand the *It* world as well as the *Thou* world to be revelational in *being,* it is correct to assume that my "faithful" *being* in the world, i.e., my trustful response, may be evidenced in both *It* and *Thou* contexts. Faith in terms of another, or God, is personally (subjec- tively) responsive; faith in terms of the world, or sheer *is*ness, of even *Being-Itself,* is impersonally (objectively) responsive. Faith becomes *Chris- tian* when my responsiveness is to God who encounters me in the Christ-event.

The lack of awareness of such a distinction between faith as *I-It* and as *I-Thou* has caused much misunderstanding among men over the span of time marked by the Christian witness. This fact was never truer than it is today in a world dominated by scientific methodology. There are many men, brilliant scientists and laymen, who have been accused of having no faith at all—and under the exclusivism of the current popular definition of the term *faith* ("I believe in God The Father Almighty") believe themselves to be faithless—simply because they have never made the step between *I-It* and *I-Thou*. But that these men are faithless is hardly the case; some are truly men of profound faith—faith in the ability of the human mind to cope with and respond to objective reality, faith in the consistency of physical expression and identity, faith in the timeful-expression of their own being and *Being-Itself.* It is my belief that most profound faith moves from this orientation through a spiritual development to an acknowledgment of God: my awareness of being, *Being-Itself,* and finallyGod who addresses me personally in terms of my own *being.* This progression is often obscured somewhat by the exposure which some of us received as children growing up within a pedantic and essentialist Christian tradition. We were told right from the beginning that all creatures and all creation really belong to God; that God knows, sees, and orders all things; and that we should not be afraid because this all-powerful God is love. Proof of this is in the fact that God loved us so much He sent us Jesus, and our parents and Church told us so. As a child growing up through all the intricacies of human relationships—family, peer, and other—it is difficult to sort out fact, faith, and fantasy. What usually happens is that one day, because of some experience or series of experiences, we are startled to discover that we no longer believe that God and Jesus love us just because the Bible tells us so. Our relationship with God has got to be more profound than that. It must be something which I don't just learn or accept on the authority of another, but a relationship in which I must be an active participant. Faith in God and belief in the Christ are personal acts in which I must risk involvement. Faith is an acknowledgment that my very identity is at stake. Faith is, as Blaise Pascal assures us, an existential wager.

What we have learned through such a venture is that there are limitations to the "truth" of tradition, that tradition is not its own justification. When we look about us we see many places of worship, not all of them Christian, which have existed for centuries. What such places tell us is not about God, but about man who seems to acknowledge—and, so far as we can discover, has always acknowledged—that there is a religious dimension which is the focus of human life. Places of worship signify that man believes his life to be a meaningful quest. We also learn through our study of literature, art, music, architecture, and government that religion—the search for a meaningful existence—has had a profound effect on all aspects of human life, not just on formal ceremonial expression. No man can study the development of Western culture without being impressed by the part which Christianity has played in that development. Yet such an impression does not make us Christians, though it does make us acknowledge that our lives have been profoundly conditioned by Christian thought and tradition. To come full circle, what an individual learns by his agnostic experience is that even the exposure to Scripture itself does not necessarily make him a Christian, a follower of the Christ. Scripture may be a special source of or medium for God's revelation, but it is not *necessarily* persuasive.

This last point needs further explication. What startles me as I read and study Scripture is that I do not even have a clear option about whether to follow Jesus or not, for there is in Scripture no place that I can get a detailed and accurate picture of the historical Jesus. New Testament scholarship has made us aware of the fact that what has been preserved for me in Scripture is not the life of the man Jesus but rather the faithful and confessional declaration of the early Church. In terms of our earlier vocabulary, the occurrence of Jesus' life is not available to me for independent judgment. All that is available is the historical image given through the eyes of faith. The only Jesus whom I am permitted to see is Jesus the Messiah or the Christ; this is true whether I am reading the synoptic Gospels or the Fourth Gospel, John, for each is interpretive in its own way. Even the question as to whether Jesus ever lived at all cannot be existentially answered. Scholars can only document that fact the way any occurrence in the past is documented: by the corroboration of a variety of witnesses and the probability of such an occurrence within the coherent scheme of things as one now perceives it to be. Under these conditions and contingencies, there are few if any scholars who would doubt the physical existence of Jesus in the early years of the first century.

One interesting thing to note here, however, is that even should there be universal acceptance of the physical existence of Jesus, that would not alter the point that concerns us. That is, the factual and impersonal details of Jesus' life are quite useless to the quest of faith. Even his teachings, with few exceptions, seem to be traditional within the Jewish religious heritage—wisdom literature, prophecy, priestly admonishments, or law. The unique claim is about the man himself, and any uniqueness concerning his teachings and actions has come from this personal orientation and not from some new knowledge or information. What concerns us is the disciples' and apostles' startling claim that in this man Jesus, God is addressing us *now,* that in Jesus the *Being* of God is made personally and publicly accessible for the first time, that because of the Resurrection God continues actively to address us in this man who *is.* That which was *present* has become *now.* "It is about his Son: on the human level he was born of David's stock, but on the level of the spirit—

the Holy Spirit—he was declared Son of God by a mighty act in that he rose from the dead: it is about Jesus Christ our Lord" (Romans 1:3–4).

It has been the experience and belief of those who call themselves Christians that the presence of the *Eminent Thou* which I experience within the mystery of the *I-Thou* encounter with God is one with the presence of Jesus the Christ, which may be revealed to me through the Scriptures. This experience of identical presence becomes a confirmation of the witness of the disciples. The actual verification of such an association comes through an identity confirmation which I experience with reference to my self. That is, I recognize that each *I-Thou* experience I have has its own character and its own creative effect upon my identity. An individual never confuses the identities of those whom he loves; each relationship is distinct. In the case of God and Jesus the Christ, the identity context which is affirmed for me by each is one and the same. While the relationship with God or God in Christ may deepen, its fundamental character, its effectiveness, does not alter. The single basic confirmation of my *I* remains. Any ambiguity in such a claim is only the limitation of any self-authenticating experience and is not peculiar to faith.

Thus the act of faith in which I acknowledge Jesus as the Christ begins with the act of faith in which I acknowledge the mystery of *being* to be involved with *Being-Itself,* whom I address as God. It is the reality of that encounter—mysterious as it may be—which affects and effects my identity and makes me "available" for the witness of the Church. The tradition of the Church, which is past and present, has potentially become *my history.* My history, as an expression of my identity, moves that tradition out of the past and into the present. Therefore, the community of scholars and saints, i.e., the historical Church, becomes that to which I belong and in which I participate. Barth, Wesley, Calvin, Luther, Thomas, Francis, Augustine—all address me in terms of the continuity and development of my own identity. The lives of these men and their thoughts have to do directly and presently with my development. This is so because all of us have to do *now* with Him whom we call the Christ; we are meaningfully contemporaneous with each other in the presence of the Christ.

In my historical focus on the man Jesus the Christ, I am conscious of being confronted by One who has to do with my self-awareness, not simply my expressed life-style. It is this fact which makes the Christian claim unique. History, we have determined earlier, is the meaning which I bring to occurrences, out of my own identity. History moves within the *now* and from the present toward the past, making that past presently meaningful. In the case of the Christ-event, through the revelational encounter, the past event is not only understood in terms of the present and the *now;* it actively reconfirms the *now* out of the past. The effect is actually that of an ontological tautology; the affirmation from within the historical stance is one with the affirmation out of which the historical stance originated. The effect of such an ontological tautology is to confirm the continuity of the creative expression of *Being-Itself,* as well as the continuity of my self-awareness; it is a confirmation, not a proof, that the subjective and objective orders of *being* are together singly expressive of the creativity of God. I am confronted not simply by the mystery of the presence of God but by that mystery as it is "known" to me in the person of Jesus the Christ.

To claim this is to acknowledge that my confrontation with God in the Christ-event is not one of sheer mystical communion. God is revealed to us in Jesus through the witness of the disciples; my relationship is not directly with the man Jesus. But this is actually a necessary condition of the physical, objective witness of God. If God chooses to reveal Himself within the world, then the conditions of the world order must be maintained or the claim becomes self-destructive. Within the conditions and contingencies of finite human existence, it is impossible for any man to witness to himself. It is impossible for finite man to become totally self-transcendent. That is, his attempt to witness to himself would be part of the self-image which the world would see and from which the man himself could never detach himself to see. This is the reason that most great statesmen have said most candidly: "Only history can judge what contributions I (or we) have made." The point is clear: Jesus could not witness to himself, and if God has chosen to reveal Himself through Jesus, this limitation must be part of that picture. This is another way of saying that the witness of the disciples is a necessary part of the revelation in the Christ-event. The witness of the disciples does not remove Jesus from me but actually makes him available. The revelation of God is not simply that "Here is a divine man," but rather "Here am I." That affirmation, through the *humanity* of Jesus, necessitates the human affirmation of the disciples who were with the man. Anything more or less than this would violate the natural historical revelation of God.

The response of an individual who has become "available" for the revelation in Scripture is not an affirmation of the disciples or even of the validity of the disciples' witness—though both of these may follow indirectly the experience of revelation. The response is the experience or claim that the One who is proclaimed in Scripture is the One who now confronts me. This confrontation with Jesus whom I now acknowledge to be the Christ has to do with *who* I am, more than *what* I am or even *how* I act. The confrontation is an *I-Thou* experience, not an *I-It.* As indicated earlier, this confrontation has to do with my self-conscious awareness prior to any alteration of my life-style. For this reason, the disciples and the Church have always clung to the idea of *conversion* despite the fact that word has been so misused and abused. In the experience of confrontation, my total orientation toward the world has changed because I have changed. It is a creative confrontation as all *I-Thou* experiences are. Paul Tillich talks of this experience in Jesus and in ourselves as being the expression of the "New Being"—the expression of a new relationship to God, a reestablishment of the original relationship to God. In any case, the Christian claim is that the confrontation is basic to my consciousness of self and of God. The risk of ambiguity, the risk of encounter, is now willingly assumed.

The following are evident to us in this revelation: the person of Jesus and *Being* of God, but this is an intellectual distinction, not an ontological one. The revelatory experience is not of Jesus *and* God, but of Jesus in whom God addresses me, i.e., Jesus who is the Christ. The fact that the revelation is singular is the reason for the title bestowed on Jesus. However, for purposes of explication, the intellectual separation must be made, for it is in this fact that the unique claim for Christianity is made. In the encounter with the mystery of *Being-Itself,* whom I call God, my self-conscious awareness knows itself to be addressed by the presence of God. But such an address, as previously indicated, is highly ambiguous because of my human limitations and highly ephemeral because it is grounded in self-consciousness itself. Under these circumstances and subjective strictures, as the Jews have taught us, my response to God's presence must be a continuous process of responsible judgment, interpretation, and intuition—a process all too often filled with tragedy and error, rather than accomplishment and peace, because of my arrogance, insensitivity, and rebellion. Too many, as Job noted about his comforters, want to "argue the case for God" rather than listen and respond to Him. The revelation of God as a *Thou* encounter is conditioned by the maturity or immaturity of the responding *I.*

In the revelation of the *Being* of God through Jesus the Christ, there is an identity-context for the presence of God for the first time. In the Christ-event many of the insights of Old Testament humanism are vindicated, the continuity of the prophetic tradition becomes clear, and the nature of God's relationship to the world is made evident. In the Christ-event, the revelation takes on the character and nature of that event; I "know" and respond to God in terms of it. Part of God's revelation to me is the affirmation of Jesus' relation to Himself (God) and to the world. Thus in the revelation of God through the Christ-event, objective (life of Jesus) and subjective (sense of Presence) *Being* are united in an encounter which is timeful in my participation and time-full for my identity, so that my corresponding response must also be present and now, objective (acceptance of the world) and subjective (acknowledgment of God). The unity within the revelation informs and contours the unity of my response and affirms ontological continuity of *being*. Few passages in Scripture illustrate this intricate interrelationship better than Philippians 2:5–13. Although the *kenotic* metaphor of the hymn section of the following passage provides a very questionable Christology, this does not alter the revelational relations being discussed.

> Let your bearing towards one another arise out of your life in Christ Jesus. For the divine nature was his from the first; yet he did not think to snatch at equality with God, but made himself nothing, assuming the nature of a slave. Bearing the human likeness, revealed in human shape, he humbled himself, and in obedience accepted even death—death on a cross. Therefore God raised him to the heights and bestowed on him the name above all names, that at the name of Jesus every knee should bow—in heaven, on earth, and in the depths—and every tongue confess, "Jesus Christ is Lord," to the glory of God the Father.
>
> So you too, my friends, must be obedient, as always; . . . You must work out your own salvation in fear and trembling; for it is God who works in you, inspiring both the will and the deed, for his own chosen purpose.

Obviously, the affirmation of this encounter is other than the confirmation of some Absolute Principle of idealist metaphysics which in some mysterious way has solved all the riddles of the universe. I cannot go to the Bible or to Jesus to find out the solution of the Sino-Soviet-American dilemma, but in the Christ-event I am made aware of how I must live with every man; my ontological understanding must govern my political and social understanding, not vice versa. It is this which men like Mahatma Gandhi and Martin Luther King, Jr., have so effectively shown us. In fact, because of the Christ-event, love has been central to every expression of a Christian ethic. However, such an observation should not imply that Christian life and ethics are now self-evident. The Christ-event is still a revelational event necessitating response and interpretation. For this reason, Christian ethics is both one and many: one in origin and focus, many in interpretation and action. I still must, as Paul confirms, work out my salvation in fear and trembling.

Another important facet of this identity-context involving the presence of God is that identity is always the creative incorporation of *I* and *Thou*. In the revelation of God which I experience as *I-Thou*, He who is my *Thou* is the *Thou* who encounters me in Jesus the Christ. Because my encounter with Jesus who is the Christ is both *I-It* and *I-Thou*, my experience of God is both present and *now*. It is present because I am aware that the Jesus proclaimed by Scripture, who is authenticated in this revelation of God, is present in that proclamation and in this revelation, but not in the flesh. Although the physical Jesus "remains" in the past, his effect and symbols are present and his ontological *meaning* becomes present in the act of revelation. In terms of identity time, Jesus the Christ is *now,* and He shall always remain *now* in terms of my own identity. But the converse is likewise true, as He becomes *now* in my identity, so am I *now* in his identity. The *I-Thou* relation is always a reciprocal one with the identities resulting always in some measure interrelated. In short, the affirmation of *heaven* or *eternal life* (though I hesitate to use these terms because of their metaphysical freight) already exists in *I-Thou* revelation itself. What this means is almost impossible to describe other than to say that man is *now* with and of the *Being* of God, as Jesus the Christ is. That apparently does not mean continued physical existence as we have known it, but even this is a statement filled with ambiguities. Perhaps it is enough to say that the experience of the revelation of God in Jesus the Christ *is* the revelation of the Resurrection, Jesus' and ours; to know that I am *now* is to already have "eternal life," is to be *now* for the *Being* of God. When Jesus responds to the Sadducees about "eternal life," such an understanding seems to be implied: "But about the resurrection of the dead, have you never read what God himself said to you: 'I am the God of Abraham, the God of Isaac, and the God of Jacob'? He is not God of the dead but of the living" (Matthew 22:31–33a).

Because my relationship to God in Christ is *I-Thou,* this revelation, as all revelation in *I-Thou,* is to my reason; it is only indirectly and subsequently involved in my thinking. I am addressed in terms of my total self, an encounter which must then be thoughtfully considered in terms of my public and private life. Because the revelation is to my reason, my experience is one of wholeness but not completeness. My being is and, as timefully such, cannot be complete, but the realization of wholeness, i.e., meaningfulness, carries a sense of fullness which can only be described in terms of joy, wonder, or gratitude. Man's final orientation is not to the abyss or nothingness but rather to *Being-Itself,* to God. To be sure, man is not always in the existential context of encounter, yet he does have in his identity *now* the awareness of that encounter, which is part of his continuing self-awareness. Thus part of my identity is my perpetual "availability" for the existential presence of God.

The experience of the revelation of God "in" Christ is also the key to our understanding of the nature of the person of Jesus. By this I do not mean that man is able to penetrate into the inner mind of Jesus, to know his thoughts, to psychoanalyze his motivations. What revelation does is indicate the nature of the ontological reality implicit in the Christ-event. We have noted that the revelation of God in the Christ provides an identity-context for the presence of God and that identity is always the creative incorporation of *I* and *Thou*. We have also accepted the reality of the humanity of the man Jesus who suffered and died under the rule of Pontius Pilate. These two observations, God's presence "in" Jesus and Jesus' manhood (both substantiated in the witness of the Scriptures), argue for understanding Jesus' nature as the Christ in terms of his own *I-Thou* relation with God. Implicit in this statement is the claim that encounter rather than Incarnation is a more suitable symbol for the Christ-event.

Three contemporary philosophers, at least, have made suggestions for a christological development along this line—Martin Buber, Donald Baillie, and Karl Rahner—and it would be efficacious to begin our analysis with their thoughts. However, the absence of the prominent theologian Emil Brunner, who might be expected to appear in such a list, should be explained. Brunner was among the first to realize the contribution Buber was making to both Jewish and Christian theology. *I-Thou* and *I-It* had given us a new and startling way to talk about faith and man's relationship to God. The word *encounter* replaced the over-defined and, consequently, the virtually meaningless term *experience*. Encounter implies that an individual's relationship to God is personal, immediate, and existential and not objective, intellectual, and formal. Brunner likewise placed the blame for the banality of much traditional theology at the door of Greek metaphysics: "This Greek intellectualistic recasting of the understanding of revelation and faith has caused immeasurable damage in the Church to the present day."[4] Of course, the locus of primary concern is Scripture. Brunner is convinced that true biblical understanding could not be grasped through the subject-object antithesis so characteristic to Greek thinking. To objectify Scripture is to falsify it. This is a crucial point, for by means of Scripture, through its mediation, I encounter the living God, and uniquely so in the person of Jesus Christ. Even the language of the Bible should prepare us for this insight: "The decisive word-form in the language of the Bible is not the substantive, as in Greek, but the verb, the word of action. The thought of the Bible is not substantival, neuter, and abstract, but verbal, historical, and personal."[5]

For Brunner, it follows from the previous quotation that "what God wills to give us cannot really be given in words, but only in manifestation: Jesus Christ, God Himself *in persona* is the real gift."[6] But this assertion brings us to the pivotal point for this study. When Brunner comes to the central claim of the Incarnation, he abandons the ontological insight of Buber and remains (like his compatriot Karl Barth) true to the Reformation "Two Natures" Christology. As a result, all the contradictions of Chalcedon return, reintroducing the critical problems of time and eter-

nity, identity and essence, sovereign Will and history. In fact, Brunner
has a hard time avoiding the overtones of Docetism. In speaking of Jesus
as the God-Man, Brunner states:

> In His revealing, reconciling, redeeming, and royal work we feel
> compelled to express the mystery of His divine Person. Because
> He reveals God to us, as no human being could reveal Him, be-
> cause He reconciles us to God, as no human being could reconcile
> us to God, because He makes us trustful servants of God, as no
> human being could do, we know that we must confess Him to be
> the *God-Man,* we must confess Him as the One who is not only
> True Man, but at the same time—whether we understand it or
> not—True God.

Brunner's theological attempt to describe the incarnational act of God is
to employ the *kenotic* metaphor; yet the effect of this, were it successful,
would be to deny the force and theological advantages of the Two Natures theory.[7] Thus it is because of Brunner's traditional stance and his
abandonment of the ontological implications of God as *Being-Itself,* that,
despite the similarities of vocabulary, images, and terms, he does not
stand in the context of our present inquiry.

The first of the "new ontologists" for us to consider is Martin Buber.
Without specifying any uniqueness for Jesus, Martin Buber believes that
only the *I-Thou* relationship provides the context for unconditional relation which finally must characterize man's relationship to God:

> How powerful, even to being overpowering, and how legitimate,
> even to being self-evident, is the saying of *I* by Jesus! For it is the *I*
> of unconditional relation in which the man calls his *Thou* Father in
> such a way that he himself is simply Son, and nothing else but Son.
> Whenever he says *I* he can only mean the *I* of the holy primary
> word that has been raised for him into unconditional being. If
> separation ever touches him, his solidarity of relation is the
> greater; he speaks to others only out of this solidarity. It is useless
> to seek to limit this *I* to a power in itself or this *Thou* to something
> dwelling in ourselves, and once again to empty the real, the pres-
> ent relation, of reality. *I* and *Thou* abide; every man can say *Thou*
> and is then *I,* every man can say Father and is then Son: reality
> abides.[8]

For most Christians, this quotation will be a startling one coming as it
does from one who is a Jew of the Hasidic tradition.

A Christian theologian who makes his approach to Christology
through the experiential paradox of *I* and *Thou* is Donald Baillie. Citing
Martin Buber, Baillie writes:

> The reason why the element of paradox comes into all religious
> thought and statement is because God cannot be comprehended

in any human words or in any of the categories of our finite thought. God can be known only in a direct personal relationship, an "I-and-Thou" intercourse, in which He addresses us and we respond to Him. . . . We cannot know God by studying Him as an object, of which we can speak in the third person, in an "I-It" relationship, from a spectator-attitude. He eludes all our words and categories. We cannot objectify or conceptualize Him. When we try, we fall immediately into contradiction.[9]

For Baillie, the central paradox of Christian life is the paradox of Grace: "Its essence lies in the conviction which a Christian man possesses, that every good thing in him, every good thing he does, is somehow not wrought by himself but by God. This is a highly paradoxical conviction, for in ascribing all to God it does not abrogate human personality nor disclaim personal responsibility."[10] Baillie supports this paradox with a notable series of quotations from the history of Christian thought acknowledging the presence of the paradox. The most pertinent, perhaps, is a passage of Paul's first letter to the Corinthians: "By God's grace, I am what I am, nor has his grace been given to me in vain; on the contrary in my labors I have outdone them all—not I, indeed, but the grace of God working with me" (I Corinthians 15:10).

Baillie believes that this paradox is "virtually peculiar to Christianity. More than all the other paradoxes [e.g., freedom and determinism, law and gospel], it is a distinctive product of the religion of the Incarnation." Baillie's claim is that "this paradox of grace points the way more clearly and makes a better approach than anything else in our experience to the mystery of the Incarnation itself; that this paradox in its fragmentary form in our own Christian lives is a reflection of that perfect union of God and man in the Incarnation on which our whole Christian life depends. . . ."[11] Baillie justifies this analogy by citing those passages in Paul's letters, the Epistle to the Hebrews, and the Fourth Gospel which clearly indicate that both Jesus and the disciples considered Jesus' relationship to God as of a kind with all men. In fact, in the high Christology of the Fourth Gospel the claim is that all Christ's followers should have with Christ, and through Him with God the Father, the same kind of unity which Jesus had with the Father: "May they all be one: as thou, Father, art in me, and I in thee, so also may they be in us, that the world may believe that thou didst send me. The glory which thou gavest me I have given to them, that they may be one, as we are one; I in them and thou in me, may they be perfectly one. Then the world will learn that thou didst send me, that thou didst love them as thou didst me" (John 17:21–23).

Thus Baillie believes he is justified in stating that "if then Christ can be thus regarded as in some sense the prototype of the Christian life, may we not find a feeble analogue of the incarnate life in the experience of those who are His 'many brethren', and particularly in the central paradox of their experience: 'Not I, but the grace of God?'"[12] Baillie also believes that it is the maintenance of this paradox which keeps Christology from falling into the "Adoptionist" or "Ebionite" error which rewards Jesus for being a good man by elevating him to divinity or quasi divinity, or from falling into the error of the Docetists, Apollinarians, and Monophysites who simply denied that the human achievements had anything to do with the accomplishments of Jesus the Christ.

To briefly summarize these two positions, Martin Buber's suggestion, stimulating as it is, perhaps does not tell us enough. The suggestion seems to be that all men can stand in the position of sonship to God, may call God "Father" in the intimate way Jesus uses that word; but historically, at least, the Christian Chuch has meant more than just *that* potential when it points to the Christ. In general, the claim has been that there is something unique about the man called the Christ—more than just his priority in time or situation. Having said that, however, I must add that insights for an ontological Christology are in Buber's thought, and we shall return to his thinking later.

Donald Baillie, like Buber, does not seem to tell us enough, though one can never read Baillie without being impressed with the thoughtfulness of his writing. Baillie seems to make the error of psychologizing the Incarnation rather than "ontologizing" it. The result appears to be not a real hypostatic union but an apparent one, or a real hypostatic union which, however, denies a unity of self-consciousness, "I, yet not I. . . ." The problem seems to result from not distinguishing clearly between the claims of Incarnation and those of ontological encounter. Simultaneous claims are simply incompatible and therefore incomprehensible. However, as with Buber, we must not hold Baillie responsible for a developed Christology when all he has offered us is a suggestion for possible development.

A third and most stimulating philosopher for whom the new ontological insights of Martin Heidegger have proved most helpful is the Roman Catholic theologian Karl Rahner. In his christological deliberations, Rahner attempts to combine, and I believe unsuccessfully, the new ontology and scholastic metaphysics, but this should not prevent us from examining his thoughts on the Incarnation, which have been influenced by this new understanding of *being*. In fact, it is this ontological insight which provides Rahner with the descriptive vocabulary for the hypostatic unity of the Incarnation:

> But if what makes the human ek-sistent as something diverse
> from God, and what unites this nature with the Logos, are *strictly*
> the same, then we have a unity which (a) cannot, as a uniting unity

(*einende Einheit*), be confused with the united unity (*geeinte Einheit*) (this is not permissible); (b) which unites *precisely by* making existent, and *in this way* is grasped in a fullness of content without any relapse into the empty assertion of the united unity; and finally (c) which does not make the ἀσυγχύτως look like a sort of external counterbalance to the unity, always threatening to dissolve it again, but shows precisely how it enters into the *constitution* of the united unity as an intrinsic factor, in such a way that unity and distinction become mutually conditioning and intensifying characteristics, not competing ones.[13]

As it stands, this statement is ambiguous, for our interpretation will depend upon what values we can give words such as *uniting* and *making existent.* If by such terms Rahner means that *being* (in its new verbal interpretation) is the ground within which the *I-Thou* relation can occur, providing what he calls a "uniting unity" as opposed to a "united unity," then we can acknowledge that this truly is a new development in thinking about the hypostatic union. However, there is some evidence that Rahner, while appreciating this point, cannot bring himself to accept it. Further reading seems to indicate that what he has in mind is a more metaphysical interpretation of being rather than an ontological assertion of *being.* This becomes more clear when Rahner talks of the Incarnation and its relation to man:

> The incarnation of God is therefore the unique, *supreme,* case of the total actualization of human reality, which consists of the fact that man *is* [metaphysical, not ontological, claim] in so far as he gives up himself. For what does the *potentia oboedientialis* mean for the hypostatic union? What does it mean when we say that human nature has the possibility of being assumed by the person of the Word of God? Correctly understood, it means that this *potentia* is not one potentiality along with other possibilities in the constituent elements of human nature: it is objectively identical with the essence of man. . . .
>
> This effort does not mean, 1. that the possibility of the hypostatic union can be strictly perspicuous as such *a priori,* that is, independently of the revelation of its *de facto* existence. And it does not mean, 2. that such a possibility must be realized in every man who possesses this nature.[14]

Rahner goes on to suggest that the unfulfilled transcendence of human nature does not preclude meaning for our lives; rather, unfulfilled transcendence is a part of the mystery of life in which our freedom finds expression. At this point, we must recognize that, in the last analysis, with Rahner's Christology we have to do with scholastic metaphysics. For Rahner, God must remain immutable and perfect, outside of time. Man must remain incomplete and finite, within time. The Incarnation, however, demands that these two definitions come together—without violence to either one—in the person of Jesus the Christ. This puts Rahner in the classical problem of having to say that Jesus the Christ was a man like any man, and, at the same time, God and therefore unique and perfect.

Although I cannot begin within the small scope of this chapter to do justice to the complex theological system of Karl Rahner, it will be instructive to note how he thinks through the traditional christological dilemma previously mentioned. Rahner begins by identifying the Incarnation with the act of creation. After posing the question, In what sense does God not alter or change when He creates the world?, Rahner responds:

> Here it would be necessary to say that he does not in himself become other to himself when he himself becomes other to the world as what is other than he and derived from him, and *vice versa*. The same formula would have to be applied in Christology. In fact the whole of Christology could be seen as the unique and most radical realization of this basic relationship of God to what is other than himself, measured by which all else in creation would be only a deficient mode, fading away into indistinctness; it would be the sharpest realization of this basic relationship, which lies in the self-alienation of the God who remains with himself, and thereby radically unchanged.[15]

Rahner makes the claim that this is an argument of scholastic metaphysics and not Hegelian dialectic because what takes place in Christ is the history of God *himself*. He supports this claim with the following argument:

> The only way in which Christ's *concrete* humanity may be conceived of in itself as diverse from the Logos is by thinking of it *in so far as* it is united to the Logos. The unity with the Logos must constitute it in its diversity from him, that is, precisely as a human nature; the unity must itself be the ground of the diversity. In this way, the diverse term as such is the united reality of him who as prior unity (which can thus only be God) is the ground of the diverse term, and therefore, while remaining "immutable" "in himself," truly comes to be *in* what he constitutes *as* something united (geeinte) with him *and* diverse from him.[3] In other words, the ground by which the diverse term is constituted and the ground by which the unity with the diverse term is constituted must as such be strictly the same.

Footnote 3 continues:

> It follows from this statement that the assertion of God's "immutability," of the lack of any real relation between God and

the world, is in a true sense a dilectical statement. One may and indeed must say this, without for that reason being a Hegelian. For it is true, come what may, and a dogma, that the Logos himself has become man: thus that he himself has become something that he has not always been (formaliter); and therefore that what has so become is, as just itself and of itself, God's reality. Now if this is a truth of faith, ontology must allow itself to be guided by it (as in analogous instances in the doctrine of the Trinity), must seek enlightenment from it, and grant that while God remains immutable "in himself," he can come to be "in the other," and that *both* assertions must really and truly be made of the same God as God.[16]

The potentiality for such a radical relationship to God through creation is therefore extended to all men. "Whenever God—by his absolute self-communication—brings about man's self-transcendence into God, in such a way that both these factors form the irrevocable promise made to all men which has already reached its consummation in this man, there we have a hypostatic union." Rahner carries this thought to its logical conclusion in the following dramatic way: "And if God himself is man and remains so for ever, if all theology is therefore eternally an anthropology; if man is forbidden to belittle himself, because to do so would be to belittle God; and if this God remains the insoluble mystery, man is forever the articulate mystery of God." "Christology is the end and beginning of anthropology."[17] It must be noted at this point that this last statement by Rahner cannot be reversed; anthropology cannot be considered the end and beginning of Christology. The possibility and the uniqueness of the Christ-event must rest with the free act of God.[18]

This obviously means that Rahner must withdraw from a position which regards the person of Jesus the Christ as indistinguishable from mankind, unless he would support a kind of Adoptionist formula which, of course, he cannot do because of the claims he has just made. However, the danger of that appeal is real:

> We have constantly to remind ourselves that human-being is not some absolutely terminated quantity, which, while persisting as a quite self-contained whole indifferent to all else, is combined with some other thing (in this case the Logos) by a wholly external miracle. Human being is rather a reality absolutely open upwards; a reality which reaches its highest (though indeed "unexacted") perfection, the realization of the highest possibility of man's being, when in it the Logos himself becomes existent in the world. . . . The fact that an ("obediential") potency is only fulfilled by a free act from above is no argument against the view that this act is the pure fulfillment of just this potency for what it is in itself.[19]

Despite this appeal, Rahner cannot get beyond the classical christological statement with its classical problems: how can the *Logos* who is
infinite, impassible, and perfect become one with man who is finite,
changeable, and sinful? His answer moves away from the new ontological insights and retreats into the old ontological formulas of scholastic
(Greek) metaphysics:

> That there are other men who are not this self-utterance of God, not
> another way of being God himself, does not affect the issue. For
> "what" he is is the same in him and us: we call it human nature.
> But the unbridgeable difference is that in his case the "what" is
> uttered as his self-expression, which it is not in our case. And the
> fact that he pronounces as his reality precisely that which we are,
> also constitutes and redeems our very being and history.[20]

So long as one insists upon the context of classical metaphysics (in order
to avoid an obvious and incipient Docetism), the Incarnation must be
described in terms of contradiction, the dilemma of Nicaea and Chalcedon.

Even the posing of the radical question in the previous paragraph
takes the traditional form of the classical Two Natures theory:

> The Logos remains unchanged when it takes on something which,
> as a created reality, is subject to change, including the fact of its
> being assumed. Hence all changes and history, with all their trib-
> ulation, remain on this side of the absolute gulf which necessarily
> sunders the unchangeable God from the world of change and
> prevents them from mingling. But it still remains true that the
> Logos *became* man, that the changing history of this human reality
> is *his* own history: our time became the time of the eternal, our
> death the death of the immortal God himself. And no matter how
> we distribute the predicates which seem to contradict one another
> and some of which seem incompatible with God, dividing them up
> between two realities, the divine Word and created human na-
> ture, we still may not forget that one of these, the created reality,
> is that of the Logos of God himself. . . . It is the question of how to
> understand the truth that the immutability of God may not distort
> our view of the fact that what happened to Jesus on earth is
> precisely the history of the Word of God himself, and a process
> which *he* underwent.[21]

Rahner attempts to overcome some of these difficulties by employing the biblical notion of kenosis as the basis for the Incarnation.[22] "But
when the Word becomes man, his humanity is not prior. It is something
that comes to be and is constituted in essence and existence when and in
so far as the Logos empties himself. This man is, as such, the self-
utterance of God in its self-emptying, because God expresses himself
when he empties himself."[23]

In the incarnation, the Logos creates by taking on, and takes on by emptying himself. Hence we can verify here, in the most radical and specifically unique way the axiom of all relationship between God and creature, namely that the closeness and the distance, the submissiveness and the independence of the creature do not grow in inverse but in like proportion. Thus Christ is most radically man, and his humanity is the freest and most independent, not in spite of, but because of its being taken up, by being constituted as the self-utterance of God.[24]

Because this principle is obscure, Rahner's more detailed explanation of the Incarnation as Kenosis is as follows:

The Absolute, or more correctly, he who is the absolute, has, in the pure freedom of his infinite and abiding unrelatedness, the possibility of himself becoming that other thing, the finite; God, in and by the fact that he empties *himself* gives away *himself,* poses the other as his own reality. The basic element to begin with is not the concept of an assumption, which presupposes what is to be assumed as something obvious, and has nothing more to do than to assign it to the taker—a term, however, which it never really reaches, since it is rejected by his immutability and may never affect him, since he is unchangeable, when his immutability is considered undialectically and in isolation—in static concepts. On the contrary, the basic element according to our faith, is the *self*-emptying, the coming to be, the κ ἔνωσις and γένεσις of God himself, who can come to be by *becoming* another thing, derivative, in the act of constituting it, without having to change in his own proper reality which is the unoriginated origin. By the fact that he remains in his infinite fullness while he empties himself—because, being love, that is, the will to fill the void, he has that wherewith to fill all—the ensuing other is his own proper reality. He brings about that which is distinct from himself, in the act of retaining it as his own, and vice versa. . . .[25]

But such a position is filled with obstacles and difficulties. In the first place, it is hard to claim biblical authority for it. Almost all contemporary biblical scholarship believes that the portion of Paul's letter to the Philippians which contains the *kenotic* passage is part of an early hymn.[26] It is a lyrical outpouring of gratitude and joy for the condescension of God to man and an entreaty for a corresponding human humility. Such a passage is meant as poetry and not as a philosophical principle for scholastic metaphysics. Secondly, Rahner seems to be unaware of the Christologies and resulting criticism of the nineteenth- and twentieth-century *kenoticists*—German theologians such as Thomasius of Erlangen and Ebrard, or British theologians such as Fairbairn, Gore, Weston, and P.T. Forsythe.[27] Without dwelling in an inordinate way on criticism, some of the problems which these men faced, and Rahner faces, are the following: If God does remain immutable, then the *kenosis* is only apparent and not real, which means that the Incarnation did not take place. If it is the *Logos* of God who depotentiates himself, as Rahner seems to suggest, then does not the gap between God and man, the Christ and man, remain? To claim not is to divinize man, to make him of a kind with God even if not of equal power. This has not been the traditional claim of Christianity nor can it be Rahner's as we have already seen. Even greater problems result if a theologian insists upon limiting the *kenosis* to the *Logos,* for he is then in grave danger of abandoning the Trinity for some form of tritheism. Only tritheism can support exclusive *Logos* depotentiation. If the theologian responds that the *kenosis* is not a self-emptying, but rather a creative addition, then one wonders why the employment of the term *kenosis,* why the appeal to the "humiliation of the Christ"? The brutal fact seems to remain: if one maintains that God is immutable and perfect, then the Incarnation did not and cannot take place. If, however, the evidence of revelation is that the Incarnation did occur, then words like *immutable, impassible, unchangeable,* and *perfect actuality* become nonsense words when considering the *Being* of God. When Karl Rahner states that "ontology has to orientate itself according to the message of faith and not try to lecture it," he finds himself in this dilemma.[28] *Faith* in the previous statement refers to tradition and dogma, not the existential response to the presence of God. If Rahner had meant such a response, then I could have agreed with him, for *faith* is an ontological expression.

If Rahner's acknowledgment of the priority of tradition means a return to scholastic metaphysics, let us return to the theological insight with which we began this discussion of Rahner and see if an existential ontology will not permit a more meaningful and relevant Christology than metaphysical ontology does. Rahner's statement is this: "But if what makes the human ek-sistent as something diverse from God, and what unites this nature with the Logos, are *strictly* the same, then we have a unity which (a) cannot, as uniting unity (*einende Einheit*), be confused with the united unity (*geeinte Einheit*) (this is not permissible); (b) which unites *precisely by* making existent. . . ."[29] Taken existentially, what this statement could mean is that reality is fundamentally not *something* but rather a relationship, a *being* (an existing) which we experience as *I-Thou* and /or *I-It,* as contingent self-consciousness. Even as an agnostic, one recognizes his dependence upon and his independence from *Being-Itself* as correlative conditions because that is the nature of *being.* As a Christian or Jew, this contingent self-consciousness is my awareness of "uniting unity" with God. Such an awareness is, in both cases, what we have already termed "revelation." Revelation in terms of *being* seems to be natural and universal. Through such revelation, I gradually (because of my limitations) become aware of the *being,* and rhythm or consistency of *being,* in others and the world. The characteristics of such *being*—its fragility, its interrelatedness, its complexity, its dynamics, its beauty, and its meaning—have occupied religions for as long as we have records. Our tragic wars and the irresponsible waste of the earth simply indicate how slow we are to learn and how limited our vision is.

Christianity, however, claims that this revelation of God in and through *Being* has been particularized in Jesus the Christ. That in Jesus, the revelation, which up to His birth had been private in its subjectivity (to the prophets) as well as obscure in its objectivity (the prophetically interpreted relation between Covenant and sociopolitical events), has become public in its objectivity (the physical person of Jesus) and unlimited in its proffered subjectivity ("Whoever will acknowledge me before men. . . ."). That is, while man's confrontation by God in Christ is still limited in its timefulness and still noncoercive in its time-fullness, it nevertheless provides a point of common orientation about which I may meaningfully communicate with another. To say this, to witness to this, is to claim that Jesus was a man as well as being the Christ, the revelation of God. How is it possible to understand this paradox without retreating to the metaphysics of Scholasticism as Karl Rahner has done? In keeping with the nature of reality, we must say that the *being,* the self-conscious awareness, of Jesus is in fact a full and fulfilling awareness of the presence of God. To *be,* for Jesus, is to be aware of God in and through all that comprises his existence. Jesus' identity is an identity-in-awareness-of-Thou. Our very human experience of the ecstasy of love is analogous to this; one can only think of himself in terms of the other. Jesus could only think of himself in terms of the Father, as Buber has suggested.

At this stage, we cannot say more than that. Jesus epitomized to the disciples the man who is filled with the spirit of God. Such a witness was not totally strange to any devout Jew. The prophets were also such men, and many, therefore, thought Jesus was a prophet. The experience which radicalized the disciples is not Jesus' life, impressive as that may have been, nor his teachings, profound as they may have been. After all, it is common record that after the Crucifixion of Jesus, all of the disciples left or fled for their lives. What radically changed the disciples was the experience of the Resurrection. It is impossible to tell what happened at the time of the Resurrection; such a judgment is common knowledge. Not only are the Gospel records different, at points they tend to be contradictory. Having said that, however, we must go on to say that all the Gospel and New Testament accounts claim one thing in common: the experience of the presence of Jesus in such a way that he could no longer be thought of as departed, dead, and forever gone. In the Resurrection, the ontological tautology about which I have written became real for the disciples. The presence of God becomes indistinguishable from the presence of Jesus who is the Christ. For us who cannot in clock time stand in the presence of the Resurrection, the witness of the disciples becomes a necessary part of the Christ-event. Both his humanity and, "in" and "through" his humanity, the presence of God are acknowledged by those who were there, and in the mystery of this witness, the revelation is made to us. It would perhaps be wise to state again at this point that by *revelation* one does not mean knowledge or fact. By revelation we mean the sense of the presence of God addressing us in terms of our self-conscious awareness—it is that awareness of self only possible within the *I-Thou* experience; it is that reasonable awareness of the other only possible within the *I-Thou* encounter.

So in the Christ-event, Jesus'-life-and-Resurrection-as-witnessed-to-by-the-disciples, I am addressed by the presence of God in terms of my self-consciousness and, because of Jesus' humanity, in terms of my identity and life-style. To speak of his humanity does not mean that I am impressed by the fact that Jesus wore a beard and sandals, ate three meals a day, slept for eight hours a night, or employed effective homiletical devices. Rather, in the life of this man, through whom God addresses me, I am impressed by those ontological qualities of *being* which I share with him and in him toward God. Jesus' response to the presence of God is not simply an intellectual assent, a matter of thought; it is a matter of *being* in which the reasonable life is one of *being* faithful (not "having" faith like some possession), *being* obedient (not obeying the rules because "one has to") *being* humble (not subservient but rather open and accepting of all), *being* joyful (which is more than just gaiety), and *being* loving (not possessively but openly and freely acknowledging the interrelatedness of all creation). In Jesus, life in the presence of God is made manifest, and such a life is verified by the Resurrection and the witness of the disciples; in the experience of revelation, *that* life and witness addresses me, through the Church, in the present and is made meaningful *now*.

To say this, however, is still to avoid any real description of Jesus' relation to God. Therefore, let us see what we can say about that encounter. I think, considering what we have said about the ontological character of the Christ-event, that there has traditionally been too much emphasis on the person of Jesus in terms of the states of his being (as metaphysically understood)—his perfection, sinlessness, and self-conscious divinity. Such an emphasis has been the result of classical metaphysical thinking which insists upon such definitions. What is shown to us in Jesus is not the perfect man but a continuously consummating relationship to God. To try to describe Jesus in terms of perfection is to fall into a metaphysical trap, for human perfection must always be imperfection of the ideal if for no other reason than that it continues to change, to grow, and to develop. It is at this point that secular writers such as Camus are right in pointing out, in opposition to metaphysical perfection, Jesus' inevitable culpability in social evil, e.g., his feeling of regret and guilt because of the slaughter of the innocents; or his need for sleep and rest which prevented him from being with those who needed him and sought him out. Perfectionist thinking also makes us have to excuse Jesus' bursts of anger, his threats, his acts of physical violence. Simply to claim that in perfection there is a place for righteous indignation and action does not solve the problem but makes the metaphysics of perfection more difficult.

Perhaps this is another way of saying that tradition's word *Incarnation* is misleading. It is a word out of Greek metaphysical thinking—despite its Latin etymology. The *in-carnis,* the enfleshment of the *Logos,* the second person of the Trinity, all point to the dualism of the Platonic reality structure, to essence and existence, to infinite and finite. Metaphysically speaking, the Incarnation either becomes nonsense or it eliminates one side of the dualism—leaving us with God or man. To maintain this criticism of Incarnation is also to eliminate *kenosis* as a possible modus operandi of the Christ-event. *Kenosis,* in its poetic sense of humility and love, may be appropriate to describe what happened in the Christ-event, but only if it is understood as an ontological description and not a metaphysical one. In that case, any act of love in terms of *I-Thou* involves *kenosis* in the openness rather than the arrogance with which I meet another. The self-emptying of God in any metaphysical way is simply incomprehensible.

The new ontology has led us into a radically new way of understanding the Christ-event. If reality is a relational expression of *being* which we have characterized by the terms *I-Thou* and *I-It,* and if identity is therefore bound up with these relations rather than being understood atomistically, then we have a new way of understanding the truth which Paul wished to convey to the Corinthians when he wrote that "God was in Christ," or to the Galatians when he wrote: "The life I now live is not my life, but the life which Christ lives in me" (Galatians 2:20). I do not wish to imply that the thought-forms which I now suggest were in Paul's mind or in those of the disciples. What I am suggesting is that the reality of their experience may be more adequately understood and expressed in terms of the new ontology than the Greek metaphysics or Jewish mysticism of the time. That is, both the disciples and Paul were claiming that in some way God had chosen through the person of Jesus of Nazareth to reveal himself within the limited terms of human interrelationship, through the *I-Thou* confrontation. The uniqueness of the revelation is in its nature, not in its facticity. Ordinarily, my awareness of God is the result of a twofold process. I acknowledge the *Being* of God (maybe only originally the *being* of *Being-Itself*) in the mystery of my own direct confrontation with *Being*. I usually experience such a confrontation as the intense experience of being called to account for my life, for my authenticity as a free human *being,* for my affirmation of the power which I have been granted in terms of reason, creativity, endurance, evaluation, and control. The confrontation with God has to do, in short, with my identity. But my awareness of God also has to do with my community and its witness; my acknowledgment of God may be mediated to me through human *I-Thou* relationships in the nature of tradition and history. When my existential experience of the mystery of the presence of God tends to confirm what tradition has acknowledged or taught, I say (employing now a traditional, classical term) that the Holy Spirit confirms the reality of the tradition. Even when I have done this, however, I recognize that the ambiguity of subjective limitations is evident. My belief is always subject to modification and growth. This is the twofold process of my awareness of God: the mystery of God's presence confirmed by and confirming the tradition about His presence.

What we now suggest is that Jesus' experience of the presence of God is somewhat different from what I have just described. The confirmation of tradition is still there for the life of Jesus as is the mystery of God's presence, but it is the nature of Jesus' awareness of God that is of particular importance to us. For Jesus, the encounter with God is apparently total and full. That is, the experience of God is so vivid and so immediate that it takes priority over tradition. Perhaps this is what the story of Jesus' early confrontation with the Elders in the Temple was about. It was not that he contradicted authority or tradition; it was that his own personal authority seemed prior and more certain. His wisdom "astounded" them. But to say that the revelation of God to Jesus is full and inclusive does not mean that Jesus is the End Man, the culmination of the evolutionary process, which Teilhard and Rahner seem to suggest:

> The Incarnation means the renewal, the restoration, of all the energies and powers of the universe; Christ is the instrument, the Centre and the End of all creation, animate *and* material; through him everything is created, hallowed, quickened.[30]

> The finally decisive Event of history for all time to come has happened already: God's becoming man. To the stature of the Event all humanity can only asymptotically grow, in all its cosmic and moral dimensions, in the dimensions of grace and eschatology, whatever conceivable "evolution" it may undergo. It can never surpass this Event, because the summit of all "evolution,"

the irruption of God into the world and the radical opening of the world to the free infinity of God in Christ, has already been realized for the whole world, however true it may be that what has already taken place definitively in the Event must still reveal itself within the world in the reflexion and image of all history still to come, in an eschatological climax.[31]

Nor is Jesus the proleptic End Man which Pannenberg claims for the theology of history: "In the ministry of Jesus the futurity of the Reign of God became a power determining the present." "The finality of Jesus' ministry is based on its eschatological character, on the fact that through it the ultimate future of God's Reign becomes determinative of the present and therefore becomes present. Appearance and essential presence are here one."

> The arrival of what is future may be thought through to its conclusion only with the idea of repetition (which does not exclude the new), in the sense that in it the future *has* arrived in a *permanent* present.
>
> If we reflect once more upon our theological example, upon the *definitive meaning* of the appearance of God's future in Jesus of Nazareth, in which God's *love* is revealed, then perhaps this can be said: The future *wills* to become present; it tends toward its arrival in a permanent present.[32]

If reality is relational and ontological, then what we shall be or what creation may be in some other place in the universe is not yet determined or determinable. The only reality is *now* and present. What Jesus represents is the fullness of the ontological reality of *Being*. His identity, his authenticity is effected by and ratified by his *I-Thou* relation with God; his potentiality as man is being realized in his *being*. That he is the son of Mary and Joseph, that his procreation was normal, that he had brothers and sisters, that he got hungry, tired, and no doubt irritable is very much part of the reality of the man. In terms of this new ontological position, we can affirm this without having to justify it all in terms of human perfection.

We can also affirm Jesus' humanity without denying or disrupting the traditional affirmation of the Church that through the Christ-event God preeminently reveals Himself. The uniqueness of the event is grounded in the potentiality which is inherent in the event itself, i.e., its *I-Thou* nature. Just as any *I-Thou* encounter between any two people or between any person and God results in a reciprocity and identity which is unique to that encounter, so it would be for Jesus. Such an argument claims analogy, the witness of Scripture, and coherence for its validity. The a priori *Thou* for Jesus was preeminently God; the a priori *I* of Jesus was fully responsive to God. This does not exclude other *I-Thou* encounters for Jesus, but it suggests that from conception—before the *I* could be formed or uttered—the revelation of the presence of God was present. For Jesus to say "I" is to acknowledge implicitly and explicitly the *Thou* of God. The result of this encounter, made unique by the fullness with which God revealed Himself (Jesus calls God "Father"—a term of intimacy and awe) and also by the particularity and radiance with which that encounter revealed itself to others, is a life-style which induced his disciples to call him "Master." However, the nature of this divine encounter for Jesus had a fullness and a particularity of which even Jesus himself could not accurately judge or comprehend. It is only through hindsight made possible by the Resurrection that judgment about his life could be made and that the claim of revelation *could* become public and corporately affirmed: God was "in" Christ. It is in the life, death, and Resurrection of Christ that God reveals Himself; this is what is meant by the term *Christ-event*.

This understanding of the Christ-event avoids the obvious problems of Incarnation by not creating them in the first place. It avoids the "Adoptionist" heresy for there is no hint in such a position that Jesus in any way earned his unique relationship to God or merited the Resurrection; the relationship was there from the beginning as *I-Thou*. Jesus, in fact, is the identity-result of the relationship, not one of its originators. Reality is relation; it does not become relation. This understanding of the Christ-event also avoids the docetist error of denying the relevance of Jesus' humanity; in his encounter with God, he is always man. That which separates the Christ-event in its facticity from any other event is the Resurrection.

The specific witness of the Resurrection is that this event is like no other event simply insofar as God chooses continuously to use it as the revelation of Himself. Jesus is a man like any other man, but through the radiance of God's presence, Jesus continues to mediate God to us. In him, I find the ground for my authenticity as a man, for it is through him that God has chosen to reveal Himself through the fullness of human identity, i.e., *being*. For this reason I, like tradition, call him the Christ, the Anointed of God, the Chosen One, the Holy One, the Son of God.

Thus salvation, that is, my ability to cope with the existential anxieties of death, condemnation, and meaninglessness about which Paul Tillich instructs us, is accomplished in the Christ-*event*, not simply in the man Jesus of Nazareth. Through this man about whom I have heard from the disciples and my tradition, whose occurrence in time I do not doubt, God addresses me. My identity, my authenticity, and my potentiality are all effected by the *Thou* who addresses me in Jesus the Christ. Jesus is not God, yet it is through him that God encounters and confronts me. It is God who makes the event the historical center of reality by making it the ground for my identity. Through the act of revelation, the event has become *now* and present, though Jesus remains in the past. In this event, through whom my *I* is addressed by God, I have already transcended death and meaninglessness. Of course I shall die, but in terms of the affirmation of my life in the event, that is no longer of final importance. Eternal life begins with my identity in God.

The understanding of the Christ-event in ontological rather than metaphysical terms gains support from the evidence of Scripture itself. In some of the earliest traditions we have, Peter's sermons in Acts and the synoptic Gospels, there are no attempts to make any kind of "essential" metaphysical identification of Jesus as God: in Acts, Peter speaks of Jesus as "a man singled out by God" (2:22), "God worked . . . through him" (2:23), "God raised him to life again" (2:24), "The Jesus we speak of . . . received the Holy Spirit from the Father" (2:32–33), "God has made this Jesus . . . both Lord and Messiah" (2:36). In all of these references to Jesus, it is clear that Peter considers him distinct from God and his *being* contingent upon God, not coeternal with God. In the synoptic Gospels, the titles for Jesus and references to him all imply relation, and none necessarily imply Incarnation: "Son of God," "The Son of Man," "the son of man," "The Holy One of God," "Rabbi," "Prophet," and "Son of the Most High God."

The fact that the titles of Jesus signify what is intended becomes clear when we observe the interchangeability of these titles. This interchangeability is particularly striking when we turn our attention to that point in time at which the Gospel was accepted in extended compass by non-Jewish, hellenistic men, and therefore in areas outside of Palestine. In this world the Jewish titles, such as Messiah and Son of Man, which express the significance of Jesus' teaching and activity for salvation, are incomprehensible, or at the very least strange. For that reason either they are omitted—"Son of Man," for example, has disappeared from the Pauline churches—or they are transformed—"Messiah" becomes, in its Greek form "Christos," a personal name, and "Son of God" receives a new meaning. . . . Thus, in the place of Jewish titles, new titles now appear. . . . *First:* they are titles of divinity. Contrary to the practice in Judaism, where the Messiah, and even the pre-existent Son of Man of apocalyptic literature, belong within the realm of the creaturely, Jesus is now placed, in hellenistic circles, at the side of God by means of the attribution of these titles. His pre-existence, together with his participation in the creation of the world, his miraculous entry into the world, his ascension to the heavenly realm after his death, now achieve significance. . . .

Furthermore—and this is the *second* point—the titles mentioned above, which the hellenistic Christian applied to Jesus, like Jesus' Jewish titles, are by no means new creations. Rather, the religious milieu made them available. . . . This perceptible growth in dignity which occurs in the hellenistic sphere cannot be contested by pointing to the Jewish monotheism which accompanied developing Christianity on its way and which would forbid declaring a man to be divine, since even apart from the particularly complicated linguistic problem concerning the title κύριος, the tendency of the historical development is clear. In the hellenistic sphere Jesus is now described as the divine being whose death and resurrection, as in the case of Attis, Osiris, and Adonis, brings salvation to the devotee who sacramentally follows the way of his κύριος (see, for example, the oriental idea of participation in the fate of the God by sacramental means, which is presumed in Romans 6: 5ff). Or Jesus' way is regarded as descent and ascent after the manner of the gnostic redeemer figure (Phil. 2:6ff.; Eph. 4:8–10; John 3:13; 12:32ff.). That this myth likewise has non-Christian foundations needs no longer to be demonstrated in detail.[33]

A contingent relation is also implied in the three synoptic accounts of the Transfiguration (e.g., Luke 9:35, "This is my Son, my Chosen; listen to him."), or in Jesus' confrontation with the "Rich Young Ruler" (e.g., Mark 10:18, "Why do you call me good? No one is good but God alone."). The synoptic Gospels lend critical support to the ontological approach. The burden of proof rests with those who would turn such relational claims into incarnational ones. It is only in the explicit and Neo-Platonic references of John's Gospel ("The Word was God . . . the Word became flesh," John 1:1–14) and in the later epistolary literature which reflects a growing Hellenistic influence that the incarnational claim is made, and it is the contention of this study that the accounts in the synoptic Gospels more accurately represent the nature of the *being* of Jesus than the implied metaphysics of the Epistles or the Gospel of John.[34]

In all that we have had to say about the Christ-event, the Scriptures, the disciples, and the tradition have played a major part. This fact is one way of indicating that we cannot truly talk about the Christ-event without also going on to talk about the Church. The Church was probably first thought of in less than an organizational way. Early Christians were simply "followers of the Way," those who simply acknowledged a particular way of life within the structure of Jewish, Roman, or Greek culture. With the delay of the expected second coming of Christ, the Eschaton, it was obvious that a more formalized structure was necessary to preserve the Gospel, the "good news." The beginnings of the *ekklesia,* literally those who are "called out," appears as the fellowship of the saints. At this early juncture of the history of the Church, *saints* did not mean those carefully selected individuals singled out by the Church for their particular merit or devoutness, a tradition established around the tenth century. Anyone who acknowledged Jesus as the Christ was one of the saints and a part of the fellowship; thus Paul wrote "To all the saints in Christ Jesus who are at Philippi . . . (Philippians 1:1). The Church also picked up Pauline imagery and thought of the Church as the Body of Christ, of which He is the Head—a mystical reality whose physical-political expression may or may not accurately portray that reality. The Church has also been thought of as the Bride of Christ who is her Lord, a metaphor which indicates the most intimate possible human relationship, being symbolic of the union of man and God—a metaphor which, strikingly enough, is similar to that used to describe the relation between Yahweh and His chosen people, Israel: "You only have I *known* of all the families of the earth" (Amos 3:2). Another way of describing the Church, which also has Jewish origin, is "those who covenant with God in Christ," a reference which goes back to Abraham, perhaps even symbolically to Adam. This very short recitation of ideas about the nature of the Church is not meant to be historically exhaustive or even chronologically significant. What is significant, right from the beginning of Christianity, is that the understanding of the Church, its self-image, has always exhibited a strong ontological character. The Church has always been that congregation of people who believe that they have a living relationship—*now* and in the present—with God. The Church has not existed simply for the preservation of an ideal or some philosophical principle. It has always been a worshiping community expressing its adoration and devotion to God Who has and does address us in the Christ.

It is my contention that the theological shift indicated in this study of the Christ-event does not alter the ontological emphasis but in fact gives it an even more adequate theological description. The Church which is called into *being* by the Christ-event reflects the corporate nature of man: his own interrelatedness, and the contingency upon and interrelatedness of that nature with God. That is, the Church reflects man's orientation to God through the Christ-event, by acknowledging man's dependence upon others and upon God.

Specifically, the Church is comprised of those whose identities have been effected and affected through their encounter with God in the Christ-event. Consequently, in the Church, my commonality with others through that event is not only a matter of sheer *being*, but also a matter of creation by the grace of God. My commonality, therefore, is reflected in both *who* I am and *what* I am, in both *I-Thou* and *I-It* relationships. Thus in a real sense any man who is responsive to the Christ-event is not only a fellow human *being*, he is also my brother. He is one who shares with me the living of a life in faithfulness, hope, obedience, humility, love, and joy, as he finds that life dramatized and authenticated in the Christ-event. I not only accept him because he is a fellow human *being*, I must also accept responsibility for him because he is my brother—as I know that he must accept responsibility for me.

The Church is therefore the community of those whose unity is in the Christ-event, those whose identity has been and is being influenced by their encounter with God in this event. The Church is an ontological happening which recognizes both the objective and subjective structures of that happening (*I-It* and *I-Thou*) in its responsiveness to God and to the world both in clock time and identity time. But these points need to be made more explicit. The implication of calling the Church a community is not that the Church is some*thing* in any mystical or metaphysical sense of that term. The Church is never more than that group of people which has drawn together around the central revelation of the Christ-event. That is why it is a happening. It is both present and *now*. Of course, the Church has a socioeconomic and political structure; this is part of its *It* nature, its organizational thrust. The point, however, is that the Church in this organizational thrust must be responsive and responsible to God; that is, it must function in a way which is harmonious with the created order and is critically cooperative with the organizational orders of the community of mankind. What this means in terms of the mission of the Church we shall discuss later. The subjective structures of that happening which we call the Church have no collective identity; i.e., there is no single subjective entity called the Church. That there are subjective structures at all is due to the common faith which the members of the Church share in the Christ-event: "one-faith, one baptism, one Lord and Father of us all." The unique thing about the subjective structure of the Church is that it is a community-in-identity. The unifying force which binds us together is *Thou*, not *It;* the Church is therefore radically different from the Boy Scouts, the Red Cross, the Nation, or the United Nations, worthy as all these organizations are. In each of these cases, the unifying force is an ideal or a service, not a *Thou;* the result is an organization, not a community. As such a community, we can respond to God corporately (as we so often do in worship), and from our sense of corporate identity we can respond to the organizations of this world. The happening of the Church, we have stated, occurs in both clock time and identity time. This means that the Church, in its objective and subjective structures, can and must respond to the political, social, and spiritual issues of this world and must always respond to the people of the world by raising the question of identity. To confront the community of the Church is to be confronted by the question "Who am I?" and secondarily by the question "For what cause do I live?"

The unity of identity in the Christ-event is expressed first and foremost in the common act of worship. Here the focus is not on ourselves but on the awesomeness of God who has made Himself known to us in that event. Worship is primarily an expression of joy and gratitude for the gift of life; it is an acknowledgment of love, given and received; it is an awareness of beauty; it is the affirmation of meaning, often in the face of apparent absurdity; it is the reaffirmation of our commonality in spite of all the human issues which tend to disunite us; it is the acknowledgment of our failures and betrayals as well as our successes and accomplishments, all of which are understood in terms of the Christ-event. Worship is that activity of unity which can draw us together when all other attempts have failed. This is so because the ontology of confrontation can never be confused with theological, social, or political speculation. In worship, the limitations of human comprehension are overcome by the gracious presence of God.

Our unity in identity and in worship is also expressed in the unity of our historical perspective. Because reality is *now* and because we are one in the Christ-event, our orientation to the world has a common focal point; we see the world through common eyes. H. R. Niebuhr makes a similar point about the historical figure of the Christ.

> For the Jesus Christ of the New Testament is in our actual history, in history as we remember and live it, as it shapes our present faith and action. And this Jesus Christ is a definite person, one and the same whether he appears as man of flesh and blood or as risen Lord. He can never be confused with a Socrates, a Plato or an Aristotle, a Gautama, a Confucius, or a Mohammed, or even with an Amos or Isaiah. Interpreted by a monk, he may take on monastic characteristics; delineated by a socialist, he may show the features of a radical reformer; portrayed by a Hoffman, he may appear as a mild gentleman. But there always remain the original portraits with which all later pictures may be compared and by which all caricatures may be corrected.[35]

Our judgments about what is significant tend to coincide; our judgments about what is constructive or destructive are in general agreement; our assessment of the past and our anticipations for the future are predicated on the ontological reality of the Christ-event. In short, the Church could be the corporate expression of the unity of mankind which transcends the provincialisms of his political, economic, and social creeds which are oriented in the past, not the present, to a life-style, not an identity. It is only through such unity in the present that historical animosities can be breached, because the past is irrevocable. Our only escape from the causality of *I-It* is in the *now* of *I-Thou*.

What I have been describing thus far is not what the Church is presently but what the Church should be, what it could be were it to understand its ontological nature. There are many things which prevent the Church from fulfilling its role, and it would be well for us to examine some of these inhibitors, for some are remediable while others seem not. In this last category are two groups of people whose religious expressions tend to alter the above portrait of the Church.

The first group which does not experience the unity of the Church as we have previously described it is comprised of those who have not, or believe that they have not, experienced the revelation of God in the Christ-event, but are attracted to Christianity because of one or more of its cultural expressions—its social action, its art, music, literature, or worship forms. They may be those who find themselves, like Camus, attracted to the man Jesus but cannot admit to any spiritual uniqueness in or about the man. For such people, the Church is one among the many religious faiths seeking his allegiance, no one of which has yet become an identity-factor for him. From within the faith, we can surmise that what the seeker is searching for is the *Thou* which can finally give his life meaning and direction, though he may not realize that it is an ontological rather than metaphysical need which drives him. Such people, becoming disillusioned with the organizational Church, or believing that the Church requires some intellectually impossible metaphysical affirmation, often find a surrogate for faith in the love of another human being. We must admit that this is closer to the nature of reality than the belief that Christianity means the intellectual assent to the Apostles' Creed. Thus the Church has about it, but not as organically part of it, at least three groups: those who appreciate the cultural but not the spiritual character of the Church, those who would like to be spiritually a part of the Church but are looking for the wrong thing or have not yet "experienced" the right thing, and those who believe themselves to be a part of the Church but only because they think of it as an organization to join, an ecumenical Rotary Club. For all of these people, the unity of the Church as we have described it remains only a possibility or a promise, not a reality. The Church must always be open and available to such people, for no one can begin to predict when or in what way the Christ-event will become ontologically real. The fact that the Church is open to such people, that it seeks them out, gives the appearance of disunity and discord within the Church, but such an appearance causes concern (or gives pseudo-comfort) only to those who are not Christians. It is the very nature of Christian unity that it can never exclude, but it can be excluded. Such an openness is a mark of its affirmation of life rather than the arrogance of some truth-formula.

The second group who do not experience the unity of the Church as we have described it are those who are the dissemblers, the frauds. They knowingly use the Church or affirmations of Christianity to enhance their own position, needs, or power. The Scriptures call such people the hawkers of God's word (II Corinthians 2:17). Unfortunately, the past and present are filled with examples of such abuse. Those hungry for power within the Church, the politicians who cry "Lord, Lord!," the corporations and governments who colonialize whole nations in the name of the Christ, societies which keep whole races subservient by the promise of "eternal" justice or salvation. One needs only to read what Black writers in America such as Malcolm X, Eldridge Cleaver, or James Baldwin have to say about repression in the name of Christianity to understand the bitterness and hatred such bigotry has brought against the Church.

> In the realm of morals the role of Christianity has been, at best, ambivalent. Even leaving out of account the remarkable arrogance that assumed that the ways and morals of others were inferior to those of Christians, and that they therefore had every right, and could use any means, to change them, the collision between cultures—and the schizophrenia in the mind of Christendom—had rendered the domain of morals as chartless as the sea once was, and as treacherous as the sea still is. It is not too much to say that whoever wishes to become a truly moral human being ... must first divorce himself from all the prohibitions, crimes, and hypocrisies of the Christian church.[36]

The question is, can the Church recover from such misuse and abuse? We only dare to say yes because of the other side of the coin. While the Church has been abused by bigots, it has, in its own right, been the source of hope and help. It has led the fight for Civil Rights and continues to be active even to the paradoxical point of accepting and supporting a degree of Black separatism within the Church. For the Church, finally, it must always be "Black and White together." The Church has also been active in the demands for peace, the alleviation of poverty, and the conservation of natural resources. The claim of the Church, to unify mankind, can only be made with humility, penance, and love. If the Church survives, it will be because of these ontological virtues, not because of its past record or claims to superiority or effectiveness.

However, there are forces within the Church itself which tend to destroy the unity we seek, which are not necessary if we can understand the ontological nature of the Church, the Church as happening rather than the Church as Establishment. That is, the Church suffers when the past takes precedence over the present, the *now;* when tradition seeks to dominate the present by claiming to be the ground of historical understanding. This is not to say that wisdom of the past cannot authenticate itself in the present, but it is to say that the only reality there is for the Church is *in* the present. The past, recorded as primarily a series of disagreements, schisms, and metaphysical claims, can only divide us, as the record of our denominations and orthodox persuasions tragically illustrate. If the Church is responsive to the Christ-event which is *now, there* is our unity, *there* is our continuity, not in the past. It is only out of the *now,* my identity within the Christ-event, that I am able to historically see and understand the past, to deal with it constructively, to let it inform me of not only my heritage but also my potentiality for error. My sense of community *now* and in the present is the one thing which will permit me to overcome the past; it is the present and the *now* which, in fact, free us from the curse of causality. That the Church is truly beginning to understand this is one of the most exciting facts of this century; it may be "The Christian Century" yet, though not in the way that our nineteenth-century fathers thought it would be.

The dramatic and revolutionary ecumenism in the Roman Catholic Church, formally initiated by Vatican II but informally evident years earlier, is the most salient aspect contemporary Christian unity has to show. The parallel movement in Protestantism, the progress toward an ecumenical witness in "The Church of Christ, Uniting," may not be as dramatic because it lacks the classical forces of tradition and revolution at work; but it is nonetheless exciting. The fact that the word *Uniting* has been chosen rather than *United* is more than just an indication of continuous struggle and growth toward the ideal; it is a recognition of the inherent ontological nature of the Church itself, the continuous expression of *I* and *Thou,* the Church as *now.* It is not inconceivable that we shall be one Church uniting in the Christ-event by the end of this century; only our fear of our freedom, our fear of the responsibility of reality keeps us apart. Because we believe the past is set and secure and unchanging, we enshrine it, perhaps worship it. But life, reality, is not like that and to insist that it is is to court dissension, despair, and disaster. The meaning of the past is determined by our identity in the present, and refusal to accept responsibility for that is destructive; it can only lead to the kind of revolutionary ferment which we are experiencing now around the world. The past is *not* sacred; only the present can be sacred. The past can only be fixed. Denominations and orthodox factions have lost their relevance other than being part of the rich heritage out of which we have come and which now we must see in a new light, a new history.

A second area of divisiveness within the Church which prevents the realization of our unity as Christians is our insistence—because of our Greek metaphysical inheritance—on giving precedence to thought over reason and revelation. In more traditional language, it is because we have given precedence to creeds over faith that we have become divided into many factions and denominations. Theologies and creeds can be most helpful and useful, indeed they are necessary to the expression of the Church's position in the world. They are needed as the declaration of its own beliefs for its own edification as well as that of those who choose to remain outside the Church. But the priorities are wrong. Creeds and theologies are abstractions from the existential experience of faith, from the confrontation with God in the Christ-event. As such, they are partial, incomplete, and always ambiguous. To hold these as sacred or final is to misunderstand their role and to ask of them something which they cannot provide. What Roman Catholics, Orthodox, and Protestants are all discovering is that it is the Christ-event which unites us, and it is our creeds and intellectual formulas which divide us. Creeds must be seen as stimuli to faith, as a *part* of man's reasonable stance in the world, as a guard against gross errors or even minor stupidities, but not as a substitute for faith, *now.* What is most real about us is our encounter in love, in *I-Thou,* not our exercise in logic, in *I-It.* If logic were our only ground of faith, the ecumenical movement would have no chance at all. One of the most hopeful and humorous signs that we are beginning to understand this came at the Vatican II Council. During the council, the American presidential election campaign between Barry Goldwater and Lyndon Johnson was going on. One of Goldwater's campaign slogans was: "Deep in your heart you know he is right." It is reported that at Vatican II pictures of Luther were circulated by some delegates to the bishops and other delegates with Goldwater's slogan printed on the back! Even if the story is apocryphal, the spirit of the story conveys the point. If Roman Catholics and Protestants continue *unreasonably* to throw the Reformation and Counter-Reformation at each other, there will be no unity in the Christ-event; for both groups will have acknowledged, perhaps unwittingly, that the Christ-event *is* not central.

One further note about discord and the nature of the Church. Even though the Church talks in terms of potential universality—the Kingdom of God which involves all men or even the very unity in *being* which defines all men—we must still recognize that the Church, in fact, is a minority voice in the world. To say this is not to mitigate its importance in the development of Western culture or even to deny its minor role in the East; it is to recognize that when the Church "speaks" and "acts" it does so for a limited number. But in that very point is a source of tension for the Church. Because Christianity's sense of reality encompasses this world, the Church finds itself exerting social, political, and economic power in the world. These powers, by their very nature, are part of the coercive structure which governs any and every society. Therefore, the Church, which defines itself in terms of *I-Thou* primarily—in terms of its relation to the Christ-event—finds itself in an *I-It* relationship to a portion of the world. The *I-It* relation emphasizes distinction rather than identification. Thus the Church finds itself in the compromising situation of acting antithetically to its own avowed nature, a recognition of the universal oneness of mankind. Because the claims of Christianity involve my identity, as do the claims of any of the world's major religions—even if it is to finally deny all identity—there can be no happy religious hollandaise which will be an acceptable mixture of them all. Such eclecticism simply produces another claimant for reality, unrelated to any of its so-called progenitors. The hope which Christianity holds out under these circumstances is the admission of ambiguity, of human limitation. While Christianity makes its claim in terms of its faithful reason, it acknowledges such a claim as an affirmation of itself, not a negation of some other religious claim. Christianity does claim that it is relevant for all men; but *that* is not a denial of another's claim. The adjudication between such claims, or in the case of the world, among such claims, must—so far as Christianity is concerned—be left to the nature of our existential ontology.

The exertion of power outside the Church is divisive, but of equal concern is the divisiveness of the power exerted within it. Because the Church is *I-It*, because it must operate in a world of power responsibly and responsively, the power of authority must be exercised within the organization itself. Ideally we accept this as a necessary limitation on our personal freedom, because we recognize the limitations of men and our possible fallibility. We claim that revelation is reasonable, but that is not a claim that it is infallible. This is an insight long accepted by most Protestants and is the insight which motivates many contemporary Roman Catholic and Orthodox Churchmen to plea for collegiality rather than the absolute papal or patriarchal authority. But as we noticed earlier, theory or thought is at least one step removed from the reality of existential encounter. Again the *I-It* nature of the organizational Church threatens the *I-Thou* nature of the spiritual community. The answer, for Christianity, seems to lie in that aspect of the Christ-event which we call humility: humility in both the exercise and accession to power. Here our faith is put to the test, for it is only through *I-Thou* that the *I-It* can function. When the *I-It* takes precedence over the *I-Thou*, then the Church is in need of reform, for then the past has replaced the present, thought has replaced revelation, and tradition has replaced history. We are experiencing such a reformation, *now*.

The mission of the Church has traditionally been the preaching of the Word (the Christ or the Christ-event) and the proper administration of the sacraments. But such a statement is deceptively simple when we consider the symbolism and implications involved. The Church's mission, as the disciples' mission earlier, is to proclaim the Christ-event. Because of the identity factor involved and because identity is *now*, the Church actually becomes a part of the Christ-event for the rest of the world! We, if you like, assume the role of the witness, and it is our witness that becomes part of the event through which God addresses the world—as He continues to address us through the Word of the disciples and apostles. The Church is the primary time-datum, the historical evidence of the Christ-event through which God continues to reveal Himself. That He may reveal Himself in other ways through other media is not our concern. Our existential and ontological obligation is to proclaim *who* we are and *why*. What we are called upon to do is to present the Christ-event in a meaningful way to the rest of the world. After all, as I believe Harvey Cox reminds us: the main intention of God is not the renewal of the Church but the renewal of the world.

Because Christianity is a way of living, all aspects of that life are subject to Christian interpretation and involvement. The Church must not only be the innovator of community among men, it must also be the critic (but not rival) of all aspects of that community—social, political, and economic. What Christianity is claiming is that social attitudes and forms, political structures and forces, and economic forms and controls are all community skills to be employed for the benefit of the people of the community, not for their own establishment. Any action which tends to divinize a system, plan, or force—to make men subservient to it rather than it to men—is to run counter to the nature of ontological reality. I do not mean to imply by this that we should commit the errors of the 1920s and 1930s by establishing courses in our universities and colleges called "Christian Economics" or "Christian Physics." Academic disciplines such as economics and physics are abstracts from the ontological stance of reality and must be treated as such; they have a logical integrity of their own. What Christianity is concerned about is the nature of that integrity, i.e., the rightful place of physics, economics, or art, within the total scheme of an interrelating reality. Intellectual skills are descriptive and objective; faith is existential and ontological. Intellectual skills are tools and forms through which man's identity-in-*being* objectively expresses itself. Christianity has nothing to say about the structure of atomic fission, but it feels compelled to cry out against its use as a weapon of destruction. Christianity has nothing to say about the construction of housing, but it believes itself compelled to object to any housing which provides a basis for racial discrimination. The preaching of the Word is for Christianity the proclamation of the Christ-event; it is the reasonable expression of man's encounter with his God and of his community with his fellow man.

In the sacraments, and at this juncture it is unimportant whether one accepts the seven sacraments of the Roman Church or the two of most Protestant Churches, the Church is symbolically making its commitment to God and to His creation. It acknowledges the creation as meaningful and commits itself to that creation as servant. Now it is true that the understanding of the traditional sacrament as that "outward and visible sign of an inward and spiritual grace" has a classical metaphysical interpretation in terms of essence and accident, appearance and reality. But there is no reason why the symbolism of the sacrament cannot adapt itself to the ontological-reality about which we have been speaking. In the sacrament, we do symbolize that *being* which by definition can have no set form because it is the ground of form itself. In the sacrament, I not only acknowledge the authenticity of my relation to God, I also make a willful commitment to Him and to His creation. I must participate in the suffering and conflict of this world, not out of superiority of insight but because of an integrity of dedication. My role as a Christian, which is an acknowledgment that all life is sacramental, may take many different forms and life-styles; my action may even at times seem contradictory to thought, but at no time will it be contradictory to reason. The mission of the Church is to achieve community, a oneness through the Christ-event, so that every man may affirm with freedom his authentic *being* with God and with his fellowmen.

Notes

Chapter 1

1. For a more adequate survey of the period, from three different points of view, see Basil Willey, *19th Century Studies* (New York: Columbia University Press, 1950); Karl Barth, *Protestant Thought from Rousseau to Ritschl* (New York: Harper & Row, 1959); Charles Ketcham, *The Search for Meaningful Existence* (New York: Weybright and Talley, 1968).

2. Ontology in its classical definition refers to *being* as a noun denoting existence, as in the phrase *human being*. The more current definition of ontology, assumed in this book, refers to *being* in the verbal sense of *am*ness or *is*ness rather than substantially as *thing*ness. This distinction will be elaborated later in this chapter and in chapter 3.

3. See Tillich's discussion in chapters 1 and 5 of *The Courage To Be* (New Haven: Yale University Press, 1952); see also *The Religious Situation* (Cleveland: World Publishing, 1956).

4. Søren Kierkegaard, *The Concluding Unscientific Postscript*, trans. David F. Swenson (Princeton: Princeton University Press, 1941), pp. 97-98.

5. See Alan Richardson, *Creeds in the Making* (New York: Macmillan, 1935), pp. 56-57.

6. Karl Barth, *Church Dogmatics, A Selection*, ed. G.W. Bromiley (New York: Harper Torchbooks, 1962), p. 113.

7. Friedrich Schleiermacher, *The Christian Faith*, ed. H.R. Mackintosh, J.S. Stewart, intro. R.R. Niebuhr (New York: Harper & Row, 1963), p. xvii.

8. Friedrich Schleiermacher, as quoted by R.R. Niebuhr, *Schleiermacher on Christ and Religion* (New York: Scribner, 1964), pp. 214-15.

9. Ibid., p. 226.

10. For a discussion of Pannenberg's historical approach, see *Revelation as History*, trans. David Granskou (London: Macmillan, 1968). See also "Theology as History," in *New Frontiers in Theology*, vol. 3, ed. J.M. Robinson and J.B. Cobb, Jr. (New York: Harper & Row, 1967).

11. H.R. Mackintosh, *Types of Modern Theology* (London: Nisbet, 1947), p. 190.

12. Ibid., p. 124.

13. Ludwig Feuerbach, *Lectures on the Essence of Religion*, trans. Ralph Manheim (New York: Harper & Row, 1967), p. 190.

14. See Altizer's essay "A Wager," in his edited book *Toward a New Christianity* (New York: Harcourt, Brace & World, 1967), pp. 303-21.

15. See Hamilton's essay "The Death of God Theologies Today," in *Radical Theology and the Death of God*, ed. Altizer and Hamilton (New York: Bobbs-Merrill, 1966).

16. Dietrich Bonhoeffer, *Letters and Papers from Prison,* ed. Eberhard Bethge, trans. R.H. Fuller (London: SCM Press, 1953).

17. Ernst Bloch, "Man As Possibility," in *The Future of Hope,* ed. Walter Capps (Philadelphia: Fortress Press, 1970), p. 66.

18. Ibid., p. 103.

19. Walter Capps, "Mapping the Hope Movement," in *The Future of Hope,* p. 29.

20. Ibid., p. 39.

21. Jürgen Moltmann, "Religion, Revolution, and the Future," in *The Future of Hope,* p. 117.

22. Jürgen Moltmann, *The Theology of Hope* (New York: Harper & Row, 1965), p. 16.

23. Moltmann, "Religion, Revolution, and the Future," p. 11.

24. Ibid., p. 121.

25. Moltmann, *The Theology of Hope,* p. 31.

26. In answer to two questions: Can faith resist the power of nonbeing in its most radical form? Can faith resist meaninglessness? Tillich writes: "The answer must accept, as its precondition, the state of meaninglessness. It is not an answer if it demands the removal of this state; for that is just what cannot be done. He who is in the grip of doubt and meaninglessness cannot liberate himself from this grip; but he asks for an answer which is valid within and not outside the situation of despair. He asks for the ultimate foundation of what we have called the 'courage of despair'. There is only one possible answer, if one does not try to escape the question: namely that the acceptance of despair is in itself faith. . . . " *The Courage to Be,* p. 175.

27. Moltmann, "Religion, Revolution, and the Future, pp. 1, 116.

28. Capps, *The Future of Hope,* p. 8.

29. Moltmann, *The Theology of Hope,* pp. 86 and 88. Italics added.

30. Søren Kierkegaard, *The Point of View for My Work as an Author,* trans. Walter Lowrie (New York: Harper & Brothers, 1962), p. 6.

31. Søren Kierkegaard, as quoted by Paul Sponheim, *Kierkegaard on Christ and Christian Coherence* (New York: Harper & Row, 1968), pp. 80, 176.

32. Martin Buber, *Between Man and Man,* trans. R.G. Smith (London: Routledge and Kegan Paul, 1947), p. 168.

33. Gerhard Ebeling, *The Nature of Faith,* trans. R.G. Smith (Philadelphia: Muhlenberg Press, 1961), p. 86.

34. Gerhard Ebeling, *God and Word,* trans. James W. Leitch (Philadelphia: Fortress Press, 1967), p. 44.

35. Ibid., p. 2.

36. Gerhard Ebeling, *Word and Faith,* trans. James W. Leitch (London: SCM Press, 1963), p. 325. See also the critique of Ebeling's thought in Philip Hefner's *Faith and the Vitalities of History* (New York: Harper & Row, 1966), pp. 156–67.

37. Gerhard Ebeling, *The Word of God and Tradition,* trans. S.H. Hooke (Philadelphia: Fortress Press, 1968), p. 202; see also *The Nature of Faith,* p. 92.

Chapter 2

1. Martin Buber, *I and Thou,* trans. R.G. Smith (Edinburgh: T. & T. Clark, 1937), pp. 11, 18; *Between Man and Man,* trans. R.G. Smith (London: Routledge

and Kegan Paul, 1947), p. 177. [Gabriel Marcel, whose thought was developing concurrently with Martin Buber, likewise believes that relation is in the beginning: *"Esse is Co-esse"* (*Creative Fidelity* [New York: Farrar, Straus, 1964], p. xvii). For Marcel, Being *is* intersubjectivity, an ontology of *we are* rather than *I am* or *I think.* "A complete and concrete knowledge of oneself cannot be heauto-centric; however paradoxical it may seem I should prefer to say that it must be heterocentric. The fact is that we can understand ourselves by starting from the other, or from others, and only by starting from them" (*The Mystery of Being* [Chicago: Regnery, 1951], 2:8).]

2. Buber has chosen the word *Thou* as the most intimate form of the second person *you.* Since most others have followed Buber in this, I, too, shall observe this custom.

3. Buber, *I and Thou,* pp. 100–101.

4. Ibid., pp. 25, 27.

5. Marcel, *The Mystery of Being,* 2:17.

6. Erich Fromm, *The Art of Loving* (New York: Harper & Row, Bantam Edition, 1965), pp. 8–9, 15–16.

7. Ibid., p. 32.

8. Buber, *I and Thou,* p. 24.

9. Ibid., p. 22.

10. Again there is support from Marcel's thought. For him the "intersubjective nexus" is an ontological affirmation. "The affirmation should possess a special character, that of being the root of every expressible affirmation. I should readily agree that it is the mysterious root of language" (*The Mystery of Being,* 2:11). See also Buber, *I and Thou,* p. 3. Italics added.

11. Buber, *I and Thou,* p. 3.

12. Ibid., pp. 14–15.

13. Ibid., p. 8.

14. Viktor E. Frankl, *Man's Search for Meaning* (New York: Washington Square Press, 1963), pp. 109–10.

15. Konrad Lorenz, *King Solomon's Ring* (London: Methuen, 1952).

16. Buber, *I and Thou,* pp. 6, 10.

17. Ibid., pp. 32–33.

18. Buber's point is not entirely clear here, for there seems to be a distinction between the genuine *I-Thou* with the mother and a projected or imagined *I-Thou* with the objective but (surely) unresponding world of bottles, diapers, and blankets.

19. Buber, *I and Thou,* p. 23.

20. T.S. Eliot, "East Coker," in *The Four Quartets* (New York: Harcourt, Brace and World, 1943), p. 12.

21. Buber, *I and Thou,* p. 34.

22. Ibid., pp. 31–32.

23. Ibid., pp. 62, 64. The sharp distinction between *I*'s, however, again raises the Kantian specter of dualism.

24. Ibid., pp. 62–63.

25. Ibid., p. 63.

26. Frankl, *Man's Search for Meaning,* pp. 58–59.

27. Buber, *I and Thou,* p. 75.

28. Ibid.

29. Buber, *I and Thou,* p. 76.

30. Ibid., p. 77.

31. *Creative Fidelity,* p. xxi.

32. Buber, *I and Thou,* p. 79.

33. Ibid., p. 82.

34. Ibid., pp. 60–61.

35. Ibid., p. 96. The phrase *compelled to take both to myself* seems to deny Buber's original claim that *I-Thou* and *I-It* are primary words. The action suggested here posits an independent, coordinating *I* that would expose Buber to the charge of atomism which he raises against Heidegger.

36. *Creative Fidelity,* p. 20.

37. I shall treat *Me* and *You* as generalized social equivalents within the *It* category, i.e., *me* is to *I* what *you* is to *Thou.*

38. H.R. Niebuhr, *The Responsible Self* (New York: Harper & Row, 1963), p. 114.

39. The Neo-Freudian analyst Karen Horney gives an excellent description of the possibilities of such self-analysis in chapter 4 of her book *Self-Analysis* (London: Routledge and Kegan Paul, 1962).

40. After this I shall use *(I)Me* as a sometime substitute symbol for the longer *(I)Me-You(Thou)* designation.

41. Buber, *I and Thou,* pp. 14–15.

42. Fromm, *The Art of Loving,* pp. 22–28.

43. Gabriel Marcel, *Homo Viator* (Chicago: Regnery, 1951), p. 21.

44. Throughout the rest of the text, I shall refer to the *Thou* encounter in terms of "subjective self-awareness" or, more simply, "self-consciousness." I shall refer to the *It* encounter as "objective self-awareness," or simply "self-awareness." It should be remembered that these terms *subjective* and *objective* so used are not to imply the classical, metaphysical distinctions between subject and object.

45. Marcel, *Creative Fidelity,* p. 36.

Chapter 3

1. Hereafter referred to as self-consciousness.

2. Hereafter referred to as self-awareness.

3. "Time-full" because of the very sense of totality involved. This form is also used to distinguish the subjective sense of "time" from the objective, i.e., "timeful."

4. Joseph Haroutunian, *Lust for Power* (New York: Scribner, 1949), p. 52.

5. All biblical quotes used in this study are from the *New English Bible.*

6. The acceleration of the natural process of subjective development through physical or objective means is an interesting, though offensive, affirmation of the interrelatedness of *being.* For a helpful account of the process of thought reform, see R.J. Lifton's *Thought Reform and the Psychology of Totalism* (New York: Norton, 1961).

7. This phrase is used to denote the impersonal, objective expression of *Being:* God in his creative relationship only, not in His "personal" relation. Paul Tillich makes a similar claim in his book *Love, Power, and Justice* (New York: Oxford University Press, 1960), when he distinguishes between the universal *Logos* and the divine *Logos.*

8. Albert Speer, as quoted by James P. O'Donnell, *New York Times Magazine,* 26 October 1969, p. 45.

9. Carl Michalson, *The Hinge of History* (New York: Scribner, 1959).

10. H.R. Niebuhr, *The Responsible Self*, p. 43.

Chapter 4

1. H.R. Niebuhr, *The Responsible Self*, p. 140.

2. Ibid., p. 122.

3. John Baillie, *Our Knowledge of God* (London: Oxford University Press, 1939), p. 56.

4. Albert Camus, as quoted by Thomas Hanna, *The Thought and Art of Albert Camus* (Chicago: Regnery, 1958), p. 188.

5. Emil Brunner, *The Divine-Human Encounter*, trans. Amandus Loos (Philadelphia: Westminster Press, 1943), p. 85.

Chapter 5

1. Richardson, *Creeds in the Making*, pp. 83–84.

2. H.R. Niebuhr, *The Responsible Self*, p. 45.

3. Ibid., p. 43.

4. Emil Brunner, *The Divine-Human Encounter*, p. 19.

5. Ibid., p. 47.

6. Ibid., p. 109.

7. Emil Brunner, *The Christian Doctrine of Creation and Redemption*, Dogmatics, vol. 2, trans. Olive Wyon (Philadelphia: Westminster Press, 1952), pp. 340, 357–65. A full discussion of Brunner's Christology is found in chapter 12, pp. 322–79. See also the essays of Georges Florovsky and Paul Tillich in *The Theology of Emil Brunner*, Library of Living Theology, vol. 3, ed. Charles W. Kegley (New York: Macmillan, 1962).

A discussion of the kenotic theory in relation to the Incarnation will be found later in this chapter in relation to the position of Karl Rahner.

8. Buber, *I and Thou*, pp. 66–67.

9. Donald Baillie, *God Was In Christ* (New York: Scribner, 1948), p. 108.

10. Ibid., p. 114.

11. Ibid., p. 117.

12. Ibid., p. 129.

13. Karl Rahner, S.J., *Theological Investigations*, trans. Cornelius Ernst, O.P. (Baltimore: Helicon Press, 1961), 1:182.

14. Rahner, *Theological Investigations*, 4:110.

15. Rahner, *Theological Investigations*, 1:176, n. 1.

16. Ibid., 181.

17. Rahner, *Theological Investigations*, 5:182, 4:116–17.

18. Rahner, *Theological Investigations*, 1:183–84.

19. Ibid.

20. Rahner, *Theological Investigations*, 4:116.

21. Ibid., p. 113.

22. The word *kenosis* comes from Paul's letter to the Philippians 2:5-7, "Have this mind among yourselves, which you have in Christ Jesus, who, though he was in the form of God, did not count equality with God a thing to be grasped, but emptied himself (èautòn èkénosen),taking the form of a servant, being born in the likeness of men" (Revised Standard Version).

23. Rahner, *Theological Investigations,* 4:116.

24. Ibid., p. 117.

25. Ibid., pp. 114-15.

26. See Ernst Käsemann's article "Kritische Analyse von Phil. 2, 5-11," now published in English in the *Journal for Theology and the Church,* "God and Christ, Existence and Province" (Harper Torchbooks, 1968), pp. 45-88.

27. For the best summary discussions of this position, see A.B. Bruce, *The Humiliation of Christ* (Edinburgh: T. & T. Clark, 1881), and D.G. Dawe, *The Form of a Servant* (Philadelphia: Westminster Press, 1963).

28. Rahner, *Theological Investigations,* 4:113-14, n. 4.

29. Rahner, *Theological Investigations,* 1:182.

30. Pierre Teilhard de Chardin, *The Hymn of the Universe* (New York: Harper & Row, 1965), p. 144.

31. Rahner, *Theological Investigations,* 1:198-99.

32. Wolfhart Pannenberg, "Appearance As the Arrival of the Future," in *New Theology No. 5,* ed. Martin E. Marty and Dean G. Peerman (New York: Macmillan, 1968), p. 129. See also pp. 119 and 121.

33. Herbert Braun, *Journal for Theology and the Church* (New York: Harper & Row, 1968), 5:97-100.

34. "The primitive community names Jesus the Son of Man[11] [Cullman, *Christology,* pp. 132-92] (e.g. Mt. 10:32f., against Lk. 12:8f). Perhaps the title 'Son of God'[12] [ibid., pp. 270-305] (baptism, temptation, transfiguration) is also Palestinian.[13] [P. Volz, *Die Eschatologie,* p. 174] Both terms, like the title 'Messiah,' point to the one who brings the final salvation, and do not intend a particular metaphysical pre-existence. When the primitive community took over the title 'Son of Man' from the apocalyptic literature, it did not take over the idea of pre-existence which had been connected with it.[14] [Ibid., p. 190.] The title 'Son of God' in the baptism of Jesus originally had an adoptionistic sense.[15] [H. Braun, "Entscheidende Motive" *ZthK,* 50, 1953, p. 41.] Both titles, including their eschatological content could only have meant, in the sense of the primitive community, that the paradox contained in Jesus' appearance, the paradox of radical seriousness and boundless openness, is valid. That is the way God deals with men, and such acts are eschatological acts." [Ibid., p. 96.]

35. H.R. Niebuhr, *Christ and Culture* (New York: Harper & Brothers, 1951), p. 13.

36. James Baldwin, "Letter from a Region in My Mind," *New Yorker,* 17 November 1962, p. 88.

Index